TO BUILD AS WELL AS DESTROY

TO BUILD AS WELL AS DESTROY

American Nation Building
in South Vietnam

Andrew J. Gawthorpe

CORNELL UNIVERSITY PRESS   ITHACA AND LONDON

First published 2018 by Cornell University Press

Printed in the United States of America

Library of Congress Cataloging-in-Publication Data

Names: Gawthorpe, Andrew J., author.
Title: To build as well as destroy : American nation building in South
    Vietnam / Andrew J. Gawthorpe.
Description: Ithaca [New York] : Cornell University Press, 2018. |
    Includes bibliographical references and index.
Identifiers: LCCN 2018022112 (print) | LCCN 2018022514 (ebook) | ISBN
    9781501709456 (pdf) | ISBN 9781501712098 (epub/mobi) | ISBN
    9781501712807 | ISBN 9781501712807 (cloth : alk. paper)
Subjects: LCSH: Nation-building—Vietnam (Republic) | Vietnam (Republic)—
    Foreign relations—United States. | United States—Foreign relations—Vietnam
    (Republic) | Vietnam (Republic)—Politics and government. | United States.
    Military Assistance Command, Vietnam. Office of Civil Operations and
    Revolutionary Development Support. | United States. Military Assistance
    Command, Vietnam. Civil Operations and Rural Development Support.
Classification: LCC DS556.9 (ebook) | LCC DS556.9 .G38 2018 (print) | DDC
    959.704/31—dc23
LC record available at https://lccn.loc.gov/2018022112

To my parents

Contents

Acknowledgments

A book, and especially one's first book, would not be possible without the assistance of countless individuals. Many individuals helped give shape to this work. I would like to thank Greg Kennedy, Geraint Hughes, Jeffrey Michaels, Anatol Lieven, and Patrick Porter at King's College London and Fredrik Logevall, Steven Miller, and Steve Walt for their input at the Harvard Kennedy School. Anne Miles, Brian Shaev, and Oliver Elliott read sections of the manuscript and provided valuable food for thought. I also wish to thank the staff of Cornell University Press, and especially Michael McGandy, for believing in this project and helping to see it to fruition. Several passages from chapters 1, 3, and 7 were previously published in the *Journal of Cold War Studies*.

The students and staff of the Joint Services Command and Staff College at Shrivenham shared with me their own experiences of nation building and counterinsurgency and pushed me to engage with the realities of these theoretical concepts. Quite against the intention of the British taxpayers who funded my time as a teaching fellow there, I think it was I who learned more from them.

I was fortunate enough to present this work at conferences and seminars, including those of the MIT Security Studies Program, the Society of Historians of American Foreign Relations, the Sir Michael Howard Seminar at King's College London, the Transatlantic Studies Association, the Canadian Historical Association, the Texas Tech Vietnam War Center and Archive, and the Harvard Belfer Center's International Security Program. On each occasion I received valuable feedback, and I would like to thank the organizers and convenors for making these presentations possible.

Grants from the Lyndon Johnson Foundation and from King's College London made research trips possible. Special thanks go to the staff of each of the archives I visited, especially those who had to wade through my hundreds of declassification requests. Outside the archive, Douglas C. Dacy provided me with a valuable trove of research materials, which considerably shaped the direction of my research.

Thanks are also due to my parents, who have supported me in ways that only they will ever know.

None of this would have been possible without the loving support of my wife, Janice, with whom I share this journey of discovery through life, along with, in the words of Arendt, an intense "wonder at what is as it is" in the world. I could truly ask for no better companion along the way. Credit for finding the images used in the book is also due to her.

Having received such abundant assistance, I can only conclude by noting that whatever errors or omissions remain could do so only through some fault of my own.

TO BUILD AS WELL AS DESTROY

THE NATION-BUILDING METAPHOR

Shortly before noon on April 30, 1975, North Vietnamese tanks crashed into the South Vietnamese Presidential Palace in Saigon. South Vietnam's last president, Duong Van "Big" Minh, had only just begun his fourth day on the job, and it now fell to him to greet the invaders. As the North Vietnamese attack intensified and long-serving strongman President Nguyen Van Thieu fled to Taiwan with suit-cases full of gold, Saigon's elite had turned to Minh in the hope that he might be able to negotiate a cease-fire with the Communists. But with complete military victory at hand, the North Vietnamese saw no need to parley.

Many of the top officials of the Saigon regime had already fled or committed sui-cide. Those who remained were now seated on two rows of chairs inside the palace, waiting for the inevitable. When the first North Vietnamese soldiers appeared, Minh announced that he was ready to hand over power. One of the Communist officers retorted that this was impossible. Minh's regime had already collapsed, and he could not hand over what he did not possess. In case there remained anyone in South Vietnam who was unclear on this point, the North Vietnamese conveyed Minh to the headquarters of Radio Saigon later that day to announce that the Government of Vietnam (GVN) had been formally dissolved at all levels.[1] Finally released by his president from the impossible task of further resistance, Nguyen Khoa Nam, com-manding general of GVN forces around Saigon, impassively shot himself dead in front of the North Vietnamese soldiers who arrived to take his surrender.[2]

As American forces were no longer engaged in fighting the war in Vietnam after the Paris Peace Accords of 1973, some have argued that the fall of Saigon was not technically a military defeat for the United States. But there is no mistaking the fact that it was a dramatic failure of U.S. nation building. The Saigon regime would never have lasted for so long if it were not for U.S. support and aid; in fact, it might never have existed at all, so reliant was it on its "American power source."[3] American currency, military hardware, and combat troops flowed into the country for over twenty years, sustaining the Saigon regime. But this flow was foreordained to one day stop. When it did, the GVN would need to be able to mobilize its own population and national resources to survive the continued battle with the Vietnamese Communist movement at a much-reduced level of American support. Successive generations of Americans and their counterparts in the South Vietnamese regime worked to address this problem of nation building even as their comrades prosecuted a brutal war. In the words of American president Lyndon B. Johnson, their goal was grandiose, even noble—it was "to build as well as to destroy."[4]

For good or ill, this is an impulse that has continued to animate the military ventures of the United States. The recent wars in Iraq and Afghanistan highlight both that the United States continues to involve itself in wars where nation building is necessary for victory and that success remains elusive. But for all the casual analogies to Vietnam that are drawn during debates over U.S. military intervention today, these discussions have been impoverished by the lack of any recent comprehensive analysis of the American experience of wartime nation building in South Vietnam.[5] Drawing on thousands of pages of previously untapped archival collections and new developments in our understanding of the war from the Vietnamese perspective, this book provides such an account.[6] It stands both as a contribution to the history of the Vietnam War and as a case study of nation building that ought to guide future strategists in how they analyze and think about the problem. Whether as historians attempting to understand a recurring pattern in the history of U.S. foreign relations, as officers in staff colleges around the world grappling with the issues raised by contemporary conflict, or simply as citizens concerned with the wars of our time, we have much to gain from a fresh look at wartime nation building in South Vietnam.

Wartime Nation Building in South Vietnam

Measured by the scale of its ambition or the quantity of resources expended, the Vietnam War saw the largest U.S. wartime nation-building effort in history. Its size was determined by the magnitude of the problem at hand. When South Vietnam came into existence in 1954, it was what modern theorists would refer to as a "weak state," one unable to exercise administrative control over much of its own territory. Like many other newly independent countries across Africa and Asia, South Vietnam contained central state institutions of limited power and reach. South Vietnam's first president, Ngo Dinh Diem, faced a dizzying array of problems even before the Vietnamese Communist insurgency got seriously off the ground. The GVN's very weakness created the conditions in which the Vietnamese Communist movement could flourish. It also made it difficult for the GVN to combat the movement once it began to claim control of large parts of South Vietnam for itself. When the insurgency did get seriously under way in the early 1960s, the challenges faced by the regime only multiplied.

Drawn into supporting Vietnam as part of the broader policy of Cold War containment of communism, the United States set about trying to help the GVN overcome this legacy of state weakness and enable it to remain an independent, non-Communist nation. Given that the governance of South Vietnam was the central issue in the conflict, viewing U.S. involvement in the Vietnam War as an exercise in nation building greatly aids our understanding of the war. The fact that the GVN was unable, because of its own weak institutions, to mobilize the domestic resources to battle the National Liberation Front (NLF, also often labeled "Viet Cong" by their Vietnamese opponents and later the Americans) and the North Vietnamese Army (NVA) had led directly to the Americanization of the war in 1965. From that point onward the United States faced not just a military challenge but also the task of aiding the GVN to develop its own domestic institutions and base of popular support in rural South Vietnam. These institutions not only had to be effective while the United States was expending significant quantities of its own resources to battle the GVN's enemies, but also had to be self-sustaining in the period after the U.S. withdrawal. Just as in later wars, nation building was the only U.S. exit strategy available.

The main scene of this struggle was South Vietnam's two-thousand-odd villages, divided into some twelve thousand hamlets and concentrated in the southern Mekong Delta and the coastal plain along the east side of the country. Although the population of South Vietnam living in urban areas rose sharply throughout the 1960s as many fled the ravages of war and sought new economic opportunities in the cities, over half of South Vietnam's population still lived in the countryside in 1971.[7] South Vietnam's predominantly agrarian economy meant that the countryside also contained the majority of the country's productive resources, whereas the urban economy was kept afloat largely by American largesse. Combined with the limited ability of the Vietnamese Communist movement to develop infrastructure and support in urban South Vietnam, this meant the battle for the control and allegiance of these rural citizens of South Vietnam was the cutting edge of the nation-building effort.

From 1967, the main weapon that the United States deployed in this effort was the Office of Civil Operations and Revolutionary Development Support (CORDS). CORDS was a part of the U.S. military mission under the Military Assistance Command, Vietnam (MACV), but incorporated staff from civilian agencies such as the State Department, the U.S. Agency for International Development (USAID), and the Central Intelligence Agency (CIA). CORDS had a presence all over the country, from the Presidential Palace in Saigon down to each of the rural provinces and districts of South Vietnam. In Saigon and regional capitals across the country, its officials worked with South Vietnamese officials to design policies and programs aimed at developing the GVN's institutions. In the villages and hamlets lower down the chain of command, CORDS personnel then tried to implement these policies and programs in unison with GVN province, district, and village chiefs. In sheer size and influence, CORDS was the largest and most comprehensive agency of its type in American history. From 1967, CORDS took charge of all U.S. efforts to bolster the GVN's position in the villages of South Vietnam, including the raising and development of local security forces, village economic development, the reform of village politics, and efforts to root out the NLF's guerrilla and political infrastructure at the grassroots level. CORDS did the work of trying to help the GVN extend its administrative reach and win the allegiance of its citizens—the key tasks of nation building as defined in this book.

Much of the literature on nation building in the Vietnam War has focused on the years 1954–1963, when Diem still ruled South Vietnam, or at most on the period before the Tet Offensive of 1968.[8] But the largest and most consequential U.S. nation-building effort in South Vietnam took place not before but after the commitment of American combat troops to the country in 1965. CORDS came into existence in 1967, and it was only after the Tet Offensive of 1968 that it was at its most influential and effective. There were two primary reasons for this: the Vietnamese Communist movement suffered a severe blow in the offensives of 1968, while President Lyndon Johnson's decision to begin the process of U.S. withdrawal from the war gave an immediate impetus to both Americans and South Vietnamese who worried about the future durability of the GVN.

Some revisionist authors claim that U.S. nation building in South Vietnam after 1968 was a success that was thrown away when the United States "abandoned" South Vietnam during the 1975 Communist offensives.[9] Such views have had an influence not only in academia but also in policy circles. Yet it is only the lack of a detailed archival study of nation building in the latter years of the war that has allowed this mistaken view to take root. The revisionist argument is based on claims that, as this book shows, are simply not backed up by the historical evidence.[10] While it is true that the period 1969–1972 was the GVN's high-water mark, this study demonstrates that the fundamental weaknesses of the Saigon regime were far from being addressed. Despite the eerie peace that settled over the South Vietnamese countryside during this period, true nation building was not achieved. There is little reason to suspect that the GVN's weaknesses would ever have been resolved, even had the United States given it another chance by intervening in 1975. With American patience in the Vietnam War always limited, the GVN had simply not been able to reform and strengthen itself fast enough to outrun the clock. This book shows why.

From the Halls of Montezuma

Although of recent vintage, the concept of nation building exists in the context of the broader stream of the history of U.S. foreign relations and Western imperial history. American soldiers and civilians have been using American power to shape foreign societies since the time of the frontier. During the foreign occupations the country carried out from the nineteenth century onward and in the colonies it acquired at the turn of the twentieth, the United States sought to influence local political, economic, and social structures in ways that furthered its ends.

Early American expansion across the frontier was based on the idea that the North American continent was a vast "unpeopled" area that could be settled without moral compunction. The U.S. Army sometimes imposed short-lived military rule in territories, such as Florida and Louisiana, that had previously been under the jurisdiction of European empires and contained culturally distinct populations. But as Anglo-Saxon settlement spread, these areas quickly became self-governing territories and, in time, equal states in the Union. A belief in the unique genius of the Anglo-Saxon people for self-government allowed Americans to reconcile the acquisition of a vast continental empire with their desire to maintain and extend republican forms of rule.[11] Insofar as they figured at all in this vision, the role of the existing inhabitants of the continent was to be submerged and eventually drowned in the Anglo-Saxon tide. Militarily overpowered and vastly outnumbered, Native Americans were subjected to brutal policies of relocation and concentration. U.S. policy swung toward assimilation in the latter half of the nineteenth century, but these efforts were focused not so much on the reordering of existing indigenous society as on its destruction and incorporation into the dominant Anglo-Saxon culture. It was simply the case, as one federal Indian commissioner noted in 1881, that "the few must yield to the many."[12] This was not nation building, but nation destroying.

When American armies of occupation traveled farther afield from the 1840s onward, it was they who became the few among the many. Surrounded by a foreign populace, they could not always expect to be greeted as liberators—a lesson that would have to be relearned again and again up to the present day. But nor could the American occupiers avoid involving themselves in the affairs and grievances of the local population, as Secretary of War William L. Marcy realized when he ordered Colonel Stephen Kearney to establish temporary governments in such parts of California and New Mexico as he might conquer during the Mexican-American War. "It is foreseen that what relates to civil government will be a difficult and unpleasant part of your duty," Marcy wrote, "and much must necessarily be left to your discretion."[13] His comments proved prescient. American proconsuls up to the present day have found their duties both "difficult and unpleasant," while their superiors in Washington have been frustrated by their inability to manage events from such a great distance.

During the Mexican-American War, U.S. forces under General Winfield Scott landed in the port city of Veracruz and struck overland to occupy Mexico City itself. The fabled "halls of Montezuma" that U.S. forces captured in the city are still celebrated in the United States Marines' Hymn as the scene of a foundational American military experience. But it was also from within these same halls that the U.S. administered its first extended foreign occupation. Scott held Mexico City, Veracruz, and points between for nearly ten months. Lacking the expansive goals of later American nation builders, he aimed only to maintain order and American control so as to bolster U.S. leverage in peace talks with the Mexican government. Although the United States was not aiming to transform Mexican institutions or society, American cultural influence was spread by the merchants, printers, and theater companies who followed in the wake of the occupying army. This roused in at least one American observer the belief that the war was "rapidly converting the people over to American notions"—the sort of cultural and societal conversion that would become a key ingredient of future nation-building efforts.[14]

In the possessions that America conquered in the Spanish-American War of 1898, the idea of spreading American notions became central rather than merely being regarded as a side-effect of the American presence. The U.S. victory in the war immediately raised the question of the political relationship between the United States and the Philippines, Cuba, and Puerto Rico. Would the "constitution follow the flag," as the contemporary phrase went, with the islands annexed as states in the Union and the inhabitants granted citizenship? This ultimately proved out of the question. Almost all American opinion regarded Filipinos, Cubans, and Puerto Ricans as racially inferior and "unfit for self-government." Just as American Indians had been denied membership of the national political community, thus it was for inhabitants of America's new insular empire. As historian Paul Kramer has noted, the Constitution ultimately followed only the race, not the flag.[15]

Yet U.S. policy makers still aspired to cling to their new possessions. The result was the country's first foray into overseas empire building. Like so many empire builders before it, the United States lacked the resources or the will to rule the islands entirely on its own without the help of cooperative local elites. American rule hence operated through colonial states, which relied on local collaborators. To have attempted to do otherwise would have undermined the ostensible purpose of the new U.S. empire, which was to educate these elites to one day take over from their American tutors. Meanwhile, the Americans and their local allies directed repressive violence against those who resisted the new colonial order, especially in the Philippines, where perhaps over 250,000 Filipinos perished in the initial years of the American presence alone.[16] In its focus on building administrative and coercive structures for local elites and in the "dialectic of violence and attraction" used to encourage acquiescence to them, U.S. colonial policy resembled future nation-building efforts.[17] But there were also crucial differences.

For one, although the United States technically promised future independence to its colonies, this was usually conceived as possible only after a generations-long work of education made them fit to govern themselves. Given that the international norms of the day legitimized colonies and that there were even times when Filipino elites themselves seemed to equivocate on the issue of independence, the United States was able to get away with usurping Filipino sovereignty seemingly indefinitely. But in the post-1945 world, with empires on the decline and nationalism in the ascendant, the United States could afford neither the reputational costs of usurping a country's sovereignty nor the material costs of doing so in the face of widespread armed resistance. This meant that even though many Americans might have thought the Vietnamese just as unfit for self-government in the 1960s and '70s as their forebears did the Filipinos in the early 1900s, they had to work within the established fact of South Vietnamese sovereignty.[18]

They also could not count on having generations in which to explore the dialectic of violence and attraction. American empire builders, like their European counterparts, often conceived of imperialism as a charitable act performed for the benefit of the "natives." Spreading the benefits of civilization to those less fortunate was seen as a way for the United States to claim its rightful place among the foremost nations of the world, but it did not respond to an urgent security need.[19] Considered alongside U.S. nation-building efforts in South Vietnam and later in Iraq and Afghanistan, where victory in important wars was dependent on a nation-building effort bearing fruit in a relatively short period of time, it was a comparatively leisurely business. "Whereas nineteenth-century imperial ventures were conceived as indefinite in duration," write two recent analysts, modern intervenors "want to rebuild self-supporting but politically and economically acceptable state structures and then leave as quickly as feasible."[20] And although violence simmered in most American colonies, it never matched the prolonged intensity of the Vietnam War, which produced levels of casualties that the American public would not tolerate for long. U.S. nation builders in South Vietnam hence faced a task not only much more difficult than that faced by their forebears, given the need to respect South Vietnamese sovereignty, but also one much more urgent.

The post–World War II occupations of Japan and Germany also presented only imperfect parallels with later U.S. nation-building efforts. In both cases, there were powerful—indeed, overly powerful—administrative and coercive state structures in existence with which the American occupation authorities cooperated. Rather than attempting to build the infrastructure of a state from the ground up as in South Vietnam, the U.S. task was to reform and reorient existing Japanese and German state structures into more democratic, peaceful forms. Both countries proved remarkably pliable in the face of military defeat. But even more significantly, as the 1940s rolled on and the Cold War began, the United States found it prudent to back off from trying to push dramatic change on the elites of these two countries and instead focused on winning them over to the global battle against communism. The precise ordering of their domestic politics and societies became a secondary issue.

American nation builders in South Vietnam could have profited from studying what their predecessors learned in Mexico and the Philippines. Some aspects of the mission overseas—the need to maintain good relations with the population and the inevitability of involvement in local politics—remain the same through the ages. But there is little evidence of Americans in Vietnam drawing extensively on studies of earlier U.S. interventions while designing their nation-building efforts in Vietnam; if anything, discussion of earlier conflicts is conspicuous by its absence. The same seems to be true of the Americans who went to Iraq or Afghanistan without a true understanding of the much stronger parallels between their own mission and that of their forebears in Vietnam. This was even more unfortunate, because in these cases the parallels are so strong and the potential for learning is so great. Even though acknowledging the similarities between contemporary and future wars and America's defeat in Vietnam may be unpopular, it is nevertheless necessary if we are to understand the place of nation building in modern conflict and the difficulties of achieving it.

The Nation-Building Metaphor

Despite enjoying widespread usage, the term "nation building" is the subject of competing definitions. Its very ubiquity, and the fact it is used to describe a wide range of activity, have contributed to watering down its meaning and making it highly context specific. As a consequence, "nation building" as a term has been used to describe activities as diverse as America's exit strategies from wars in Iraq and Afghanistan, United Nations peacekeeping missions in the aftermath of civil war, and the domestic policies of countries that seek to develop their national identity through educational programs.[21] Practices as diverse as educating children to forcibly herding their unfortunate parents into resettlement camps have fallen under the label.[22]

This lack of definitional clarity has been enabled by the fact that nation building is ultimately a metaphor rather than a description of a particular, concrete set of processes or actions. Any action that can plausibly be construed as developing either the institutions of a state or the sense of national identity and cohesion among its population can be classed as nation building. The term is malleable enough to refer to either wartime, peacetime, or a postwar period. As a metaphor, the idea of "building" implies a programmatic course of action that unfolds predictably according to a blueprint. It elides the fact that the shaping of state institutions and the molding of national identity are fundamentally political projects that unfold in messy and unpredictable ways, not according to a predetermined plan. The building of physical objects unfolds predictably because the material being worked with has no agency, whereas politics involves a multitude of unpredictable actors. The metaphor of nation building hence obscures the political nature of the actual processes and activities that it describes and gives a false impression of tractability and predictability.[23]

This is especially true when nation building involves an attempt by outsiders to shape the state institutions and national identity of a country. This understanding of the term is of Cold War vintage, and its widespread usage dates only from the Vietnam War. As Henry Kissinger has argued, U.S. involvement in the Vietnam War "spawn[ed] a new concept not previously found in the diplomatic vocabulary . . . the notion of 'nation-building.'"[24] The "notion" Kissinger was referring to was the idea that the United States could radically reshape the domestic politics, society, and economy of a foreign country as part of a military intervention.

The emergence of this understanding of nation building at this historical juncture served an important function. America's involvement in the Vietnam War occurred as European empires in the so-called Third World were disintegrating. As part of the broader Cold War, a struggle was beginning between the United States and the Soviet Union to shape the political development of the newly independent countries. The perceived necessity felt by American policy makers to control the political processes of the postimperial space made them highly receptive to the idea of nation building as something the United States could perform in the Third World.[25] This led to a shift in the term's usage. In the early years of decolonization, nation building was understood as a process that was occurring domestically within the new countries. Many postcolonial states possessed weak institutions and divided populations who did not share a sense of unified nationhood, and the attempts of their new rulers to overcome these legacies had been labeled "nation building." As late as 1962, a key reference work by leading political scientists on the topic of "nation-building" made no mention of the idea that it might be something accomplished by outside intervention.[26] Only with the Vietnam War did the concept as we understand it today take its place among the foreign policy tool kits of the United States and others, from where it has never subsequently been removed for long.

Understood as a metaphorical label for a broad range of foreign policy practices by the United States and others, the exact scope of activity defined as nation building requires careful definition in a historical study such as this. Three aspects of the term "nation building" as used in this book require clarification. The first is the extent to which nation building should be understood as a domestic or international process. The second is what the difference is, if any, between nation building and state building. The third is what activities fall under the definition of nation building as used in this book.

First, although nation building is now more routinely used to refer to international rather than domestic practices, this does not mean that it has lost meaning as a term used to refer to domestic policies aimed at strengthening state institutions and developing a unified national consciousness. In the case of South Vietnam, the GVN's colonial inheritance left it with understaffed, illegitimate, and ineffective state institutions and the absence of a South Vietnamese national identity except among some of the educated and urban classes of the population. Although they addressed these problems with varying degrees of wisdom and urgency from the time of President Ngo Dinh Diem onward, the GVN's ruling class had to constantly struggle to strengthen state institutions and establish the legitimacy of their rule. Attempts to inculcate a specifically "South Vietnamese" national identity often formed part of their efforts. Thus, alongside American attempts to reshape South Vietnam through nation building, the country's own rulers were engaged in nation building of their own.

Throughout this work, the term "nation building" is thus used to refer both to certain U.S. policies in South Vietnam *and also* the domestic program of the

South Vietnamese government toward the same ends. This is justified because the use of a single term to refer to the policies and actions of both Americans and Vietnamese focuses attention on the fact that they shared the same goal of creating a viable and sustainable GVN that would eventually be able to survive at a much-reduced level of American support. It also highlights the fact that there was so much disagreement between—and also within—these two sets of actors on *how* to bring about this result. This disagreement about what historian Edward Miller has called "the politics of nation-building" forms the central subject matter of this book.[27]

A second point requiring clarity is about the difference between nation building and state building. Whether to differentiate between the two at all is a point of contention. Where a differentiation is made, state building is generally taken to refer to the development of the state's administrative and coercive functions, allowing it to effectively control both its territory and population, and defeating rival entities that would seek to deny it the monopoly on the use of legitimate force. Nation building, on the other hand, refers to the formation of a sense of national identity among the population of a country. State institutions thereby come to be seen as legitimate across a country's territory and population groups because they represent the nation. In one representative definition, state building is said to refer to the creation of "a political entity or set of institutions," while nation building involves "the creation of a political community."[28] Other works combine both sets of activities—strengthening institutions and developing political community—under the sole rubric of either state building or nation building.[29]

This book makes sole use of the term "nation building" for two reasons. The first is that in practice, the distinction between the development of state institutions and attempts to ensure that these institutions are regarded as legitimate is an artificial one. Even the most repressive state cannot function for long if its institutions of rule—its police, courts, economic ministries, and local governors, among others—are not regarded as legitimate by a sufficient portion of the population. The GVN was attempting to impose and consolidate its rule in the face of a Communist movement that enjoyed widespread popularity and legitimacy among much of country's population. This made its own struggle to be recognized as legitimate even more crucial. Secondly, as a country that had only come into existence in 1954, the development of a specifically "South Vietnamese" political identity seemed like a prerequisite for the functioning of the South Vietnamese state. When the U.S. aid that had supported the Saigon regime for so long was withdrawn, the GVN would need to be able to draw on its own resources, both economic and human, to sustain itself. It would need not just the strong sinews of a coercive and administrative state, but also the support of a sizable section of its citizenry. The extent to which the development and use of the raw coercive power of the South Vietnamese state undermined its legitimacy was a key point of contention both within and between the separate camps of American and South Vietnamese nation builders. But only the use of the term "nation building" to encompass the development of both effective *and* legitimate state institutions fully captures the hubris of what they set out to accomplish.

A third issue that requires clarification is to define precisely what activities fall under the rubric of nation building. Rather than applying an abstract definition, this book takes a goal-oriented approach to defining nation building. Those activities that Americans or South Vietnamese undertook with the purpose of strengthening either the effectiveness or legitimacy of the GVN fall under the heading. It acknowledges, as thoughtful contemporary observers did also, that the basic problem for the Saigon regime was to establish mutual ties of obligation with its rural citizens that would allow the GVN to survive at a much-reduced level of American support. As Roger Hilsman, an adviser to President Kennedy, put it in 1962, the GVN needed to "tie the villages into the network of government administration and control" so that "information of the villagers' needs and problems can flow upward and government services can flow downward."[30] The desired outcome was a country in which a sufficient portion of the rural citizenry would align themselves with the GVN, providing the manpower, resources, and allegiance necessary to defeat the Communist movement. All U.S. and GVN programs that were oriented toward this result hence fall under the rubric of nation building. This way of defining what constituted nation building allows for the fact that the individuals working toward this end, both American and South Vietnamese, often had radically different and contradictory ideas about how to achieve it—and even what to call what they were doing.

Nations and Nation Building

Few Americans in Vietnam consistently used the term "nation building" themselves, preferring to talk about "pacification" or "the other war."[31] The usage of these terms was highly contested, not least because they reflected different perceptions of the best way to strengthen the effectiveness and legitimacy of the GVN. "The other war" seemed to relegate the political struggle in the villages to the sidelines of the primary war, the one fought with artillery, aircraft, and divisions of infantry. It defined rural nation building in the negative, without positive content of its own.[32]

Pacification, on the other hand, was a term with a well-established lineage. Inherited from French colonial vocabulary, *to pacify* implied the extension of the GVN's physical control into hamlets and villages formerly governed by the NLF. Soldiers of the Saigon regime would occupy a hamlet, arrest any Communist cadres they could find, and provide a security screen behind which GVN administrators, landlords, and police could return. In theory but not always in practice, pacification was combined with efforts to bring social or economic benefits to the rural population through small aid projects and the provision of services such as schools and clinics. Once local Communist cadre and guerrillas showed no further sign of resistance, the soldiers would then move on to another hamlet. This approach simply restored the old political and socioeconomic order in the hamlet while doing nothing to address the underlying drivers of support for the NLF; in fact, by returning landlords and abusive officials to the positions of power from which the revolution had driven them, it often only undermined the image of the GVN. While pacification aimed to strengthen the GVN by creating zones of security in which GVN administrators and police could govern effectively, it was often actively harmful to the regime's legitimacy. While the establishment of physical control by regime forces and the ejection of the armed elements of the Communist movement constituted nation building in its most limited form, such measures usually produced only ephemeral gains. One American critic described it as "like throwing a giant rock into the ocean. Big splash, then nothing."[33] And once Saigon's soldiers departed, the remaining administrators and police were left to face the wrath of the local Communist apparatus alone.

Many of the Americans and South Vietnamese whose story is told in this book rejected the concept of pacification and sought instead to actively build ties of mutual obligation between the GVN and the regime. Through thorough reform of the GVN, they hoped to create a solid reservoir of support for the regime that would outlast the presence of outside forces. To an extent that has been underappreciated by previous historians of the conflict, their attempts at nation building often drew on their understanding of the ways in which the Vietnamese Communist movement mobilized and motivated its own cadres and soldiers. A group of Americans including William Colby, John Paul Vann, Stuart Methven, and Frank Scotton worked with former Viet Minh like Tran Ngoc Chau and Nguyen Be to decentralize power over village affairs to the people themselves. Their ideas were most influential after Colby became head of CORDS in 1968 and implemented what was called the "village system." Aiming to create a participative experience of self-rule for villagers, much as the Communist movement did, the village system aimed to provide them with the authority and resources to implement the "three selfs"—self-government, self-defense, and self-development. An analysis

FIGURE 1.   Members of the 101st Airborne Division join children in a game of baseball north of Hue during pacification operations, 1970. Such short-term goodwill rarely translated into long-term support for the GVN.

National Archives identifier 531465, Photographs of American Military Activities, Record Group 111, National Archives II at College Park, Maryland.

of the village system allows us to move beyond the focus on development and modernization discourses that has marked much of our previous understanding of U.S. nation building in the Vietnam War.[34] Based as it was on Communist inspiration, the nation-building policy of CORDS in the later years of the war owed more to Lenin's ideas on political organization than Walt Rostow's vision of modernization.

The village system also sought to overcome one of the most significant problems for American nation builders in South Vietnam, which was the historical novelty of the idea of a "South Vietnamese" nation. Both the regimes in Hanoi and Saigon claimed to be the legitimate embodiment of the Vietnamese nation, which was generally recognized as encompassing the entire Vietnamese people who lived on the territory from the Gulf of Siam to the Chinese border. Yet from 1954, Vietnam was divided into two halves, north and south. While North

Vietnam shortly set about attempting to unify the country by force, the regime in Saigon was occupied with attempting to establish legitimate rule in the south. This proved difficult, for although regional rivalry was a strong part of Vietnamese politics, the country created south of the seventeenth parallel at the end of the French period had never been considered the object of a specifically "South Vietnamese" nationalism. On the other hand, from the 1930s onward, the Vietnamese Communist movement had been gradually carving out its place as the most significant embodiment of Vietnamese nationalism by leading the struggle against the French and sidelining, often brutally, its Vietnamese rivals. The Communist movement had always been weakest in the territory that became South Vietnam, but it still enjoyed substantial support. Even more important, leaders like Ho Chi Minh and rank-and-file fighters in the villagers were widely recognized as national heroes for their resistance to the French. Even if this perception was not universal, given the violence with which the Communists often dealt with their enemies, it was shared by a critical mass of rural citizens in South Vietnam. It is true that there were differences in the cultural, political, social, and economic legacies of North and South Vietnam, as there were within many decolonizing countries in this era. But the pull of unity, centered on both the historical basis of Vietnamese civilization in the Red River Delta of North Vietnam and the record of the resistance fighters against the French, was also strong—at least strong enough to cause the Saigon regime substantial problems in establishing its own claim to separateness, and probably strong enough to doom it from the beginning. A poem written by a North Vietnamese Army soldier in his notebook captured the essence of a Vietnamese nationalism that existed despite regional differences: "But I am here on foreign soil," two lines read. "And yet the South too is still our country."[35]

The Saigon regime could never pose a direct threat to this nationalist appeal or offer a unified vision of the future to the entire national space. Many of the generals, police, and officials of the Saigon regime had collaborated with the French colonists, and after 1965 they stayed in power only with the assistance of hundreds of thousands of foreign troops.[36] Most Americans were unreflective about this problem, and seemed to work on the assumption that the creation of state institutions would over time lead inexorably to the creation of national sentiment attached to those institutions. This accorded with then-current theories of development and "modernization," which held that nationalism was an inevitable product of the shift from traditional to modern, impersonal forms of governance as represented by modern state bureaucracies.[37] But these theories held an excessively materialistic view of what a nation is. As Benedict Anderson explained in his own famous theory of nationalism, a nation is not the product of purely material forces but is more accurately seen as a cultural construct based on a shared belief of membership in the same "imagined community."[38] Such a shared imagined community was sorely lacking in South Vietnam.

This book explores attempts by American and South Vietnamese nation builders to overcome this problem by drawing on the lessons of the Communist movement's success. In its own efforts to organize and inspire South Vietnam's rural citizens, the Communist movement drew on the imagined community of the Vietnamese nation without solely relying on it. In fact, in its appeals to the rural population in the South, it usually focused on the population's concrete interests within their village communities. This principle—which historian Jeffrey Race calls "communalism"—accorded with the fact that in a fragmented society such as rural South Vietnam, politics was overwhelmingly local.[39] Especially later in the war, American and South Vietnamese nation builders took the same approach to building support for the GVN. Rather than attempting to appeal to a South Vietnamese nationalism that had no meaning in most rural communities, Colby and his allies tried to address the concrete political and socioeconomic grievances of rural villagers so that they identified their self-interest with the continuation of GVN rule.

Yet the Americans and South Vietnamese who worked to try to tie the GVN's citizens into bonds of mutual obligation with their government were always struggling against the tide. They faced an entrenched system of patronage and corruption that was extremely difficult to undo, not least because it served the interests of so many GVN officials and officers even while being detrimental to the interests of the peasantry. High officials in the Saigon regime personally profited from this structure and also relied on it to ensure their own rule over the longer term. They frequently worked to sideline the influence of those South Vietnamese who were most focused on empowering the country's rural citizens. The influence of those working to establish a sense of identification and trust between those citizens and their government hence always ran up against sharp limits, and their goal remained unachieved at the time of American withdrawal in 1973.

Structure of the Book

This book is divided into seven chapters. Its narrative stretches from the corridors of power in which the framework of nation-building policy was formulated in Washington and Saigon down to the individual villages of South Vietnamese in which it was implemented. This provides a comprehensive overview of how the challenge of nation building appeared to policy makers and practitioners at all levels.

Chapter 1 examines the legacies of French colonialism for South Vietnam and the role of these legacies in shaping both the GVN and the Vietnamese Communist movement. It then examines attempts by Americans and South Vietnamese to strengthen the Diem regime through nation building both in Saigon and out in the countryside, exploring the different approaches they took to nation building. The chapter brings the narrative to Diem's overthrow in 1963.

Chapter 2 examines the evolution of President Lyndon Johnson's relationship to the problem of nation building in South Vietnam. It argues that Johnson entered office with little interest in the problem, but soon came to realize both how important it was for the war effort and how it allowed him to portray the war as a constructive rather than a destructive activity. Although his initial interest was in large-scale development projects, Johnson eventually came to recognize that a bottom-up approach based on the provision of local security was most appropriate at this stage in the war. As a result, he decided to create CORDS and sent his aide Robert Komer to lead it in May 1967.

Chapter 3 returns the narrative to South Vietnam itself, considering the impact of Johnson's two most consequential decisions for nation building: the dispatch of American combat troops in 1965 and the establishment of CORDS in 1967. It explores the initial functioning of CORDS and the problems that arose in Komer's approach to leveraging change from the GVN. By the end of 1967, CORDS seemed to have achieved little, and the fundamental weaknesses of the GVN and drivers of support for the Communist movement remained unaddressed.

Chapter 4 considers the impact of the series of offensives that wracked South Vietnam in 1968, beginning with the Tet Offensive. It demonstrates how President Nguyen Van Thieu used the offensive as an opportunity to consolidate his authority, a process in which CORDS was instrumental. By allying himself with the Americans, Thieu not only eclipsed his rivals but also created the conditions for CORDS to finally have greater influence over the GVN.

In chapter 5, the narrative switches back to Washington to explore the Nixon administration's outlook on nation building in South Vietnam. Nixon and his key national security aide Henry Kissinger were skeptical of the possibility of bolstering the legitimacy of the GVN but had a keen interest in its ability to exercise control over its territory and population. Such control, they believed, would strengthen their hands in the peace talks that had been opened in the aftermath of the Tet Offensive. Kissinger also established a sophisticated system for assessing the progress of nation building in South Vietnam, one that far surpassed anything the Johnson administration had constructed. The results of its assessments suggested the GVN would struggle to maintain its position after U.S. withdrawal.

Chapter 6 explores the evolution of the village system in the period 1969–1972. It investigates the lineage of the ideas that came to animate CORDS under Colby, and the Thieu regime's attitude toward them. While the Nixon administration was not as interested as its predecessor in the reform of the GVN, this period of the war saw the most effective and comprehensive attempt by the United States to develop an effective and legitimate GVN.

Finally, chapter 7 explores how the village system unfolded in practice. It starts with a consideration of the general problems faced by CORDS advisers in understanding and influencing rural South Vietnam. It then examines the effects that CORDS was able to have across each of the "three selfs"—self-government, self-defense, and self-development. In each case it concludes that the impact of CORDS was ephemeral and did not amount to the genuine establishment of ties of mutual obligation between the GVN and its rural citizens. As a result, the Saigon regime would not be strong enough to stand up to the challenge of the Vietnamese Communist movement in the future.

THE DIEM YEARS

The territory that eventually constituted the country of South Vietnam had a rich and complex history, but one scarcely known to most Americans who went there as nation builders. Most of the Americans who served as nation builders in South Vietnam did so after the downfall of Ngo Dinh Diem's regime, which lasted from 1954 until his overthrow and murder in 1963. The challenges these nation builders faced were influenced not just by the events of Diem's rule but also by South Vietnam's colonial inheritance. The socioeconomic problems that afflicted rural peasants, the attitudes and foibles of South Vietnam's rulers, and the Communist challenge the country faced were all shaped by the legacy of French colonialism. Diem's inability to overcome these legacies stimulated the first American attempts at nation building in South Vietnam. Although unsuccessful in their goal of overseeing the emergence of an effective and legitimate GVN before Diem's overthrow in 1963, these attempts showcased a variety of American approaches to the problem of nation building that would influence the more comprehensive and organized efforts of CORDS later in the decade.

The French Inheritance

Upon its independence, South Vietnam inherited largely intact the governing apparatus that had collaborated with the French in their rule over Cochinchina and southern Annam. As a tool for nation building, this apparatus had grave deficiencies. The

French had always paid lip service to their *mission civilisatrice*, the quest to transform Vietnam into a modern nation-state. But the main aim of colonial governance had been to protect the interests of French exporters and investors.[1] One consequence of running Indochina as a business was that it created an incentive to keep costs down, meaning that the French did not develop colonial government beyond the level necessary to maintain order, levy taxes, and secure major towns and communication routes. French administration had its grip weakened further by the Japanese occupation of Indochina during World War II and the subsequent war against the Viet Minh. The GVN hence inherited a colonial governmental bureaucracy with little experience or tradition of involvement in the South Vietnamese countryside, precisely the area that was the source of the Vietnamese Communist movement's strength.

Recent events aside, the story of Vietnamese history writ large suggested that the Saigon regime would struggle to exert its authority over South Vietnam. The historic center of Vietnamese civilization was the Red River Delta in North Vietnam, and the Vietnamese people had spread south only gradually. The Mekong Delta, the heartland of South Vietnam, had held a sizable Vietnamese population only from the late eighteenth century. The new settlers in the south developed what historian Li Tana calls "a new way of being Vietnamese," one in which society was more fluid and less amenable to central control.[2] The Nguyen family who ruled southern Vietnam first as princes and then as a dynasty after Vietnam was unified under Emperor Gia Long in 1802 did so only through loosely controlled intermediaries. An attempt by the emperor Minh Mang—himself a southerner—to impose direct rule in 1833 led to a bloody insurrection that was quelled only after two years, underscoring how lightly the emperors had to tread in ruling the fractious southern populace. The confusing and shifting landscape of the delta, where even "the boundaries between water and land are often indistinct," had hence rarely known the firm hand of state authority.[3]

As concerned Americans realized, the GVN's success or failure at a task that had eluded the emperors would depend on the effectiveness and outlook of its administrators.[4] French colonization had interrupted Vietnam's long tradition of mandarin governance, which dated back to the time the country was a Chinese dependency. This system had been based on the cultivation of a scholar-gentry steeped in Confucian learning, ultimately serving the emperor but responsive to the needs of the population in the province or district that they governed. Poor communication routes meant that the emperors were perpetually "starved of information" about events in their dominion, and the mandarinate provided a means to mediate between the imperial state and the tens of thousands of villages across Vietnam.[5] The French transformed this system out of both necessity and desire. When the colonialists arrived in Cochinchina, most local mandarins refused to collaborate with them, forcing them to rely on parvenus with little knowledge of how precolonial governance had functioned.[6] This new class of officials owed its position not to the honor and prestige associated with passing the traditional mandarin examinations, but instead on its willingness to collaborate. One member of the traditional scholar-gentry who refused to follow suit derided them as acting like "merchant[s] chancing on a pearl," a particularly damning indictment, given that merchants were typically considered to lie at the bottom of the Confucian social order.[7] Eventually the French abolished the mandarin examinations altogether and adopted a system of training for civil servants fashioned on the European model.

Nevertheless, the French were never able to find enough capable and willing local candidates to enter the civil service, and had difficulty trusting them even when they did. The result was a disproportionately large corps of French civil servants in residence. By 1925 Indochina had five thousand European officials, the same number that watched over a population ten times its size in India. Ho Chi Minh later complained that they spread "like tropical vegetation."[8] In consequence, there was a severe lack of experienced Vietnamese administrators to staff the GVN after independence. Vietnamese had not been permitted to occupy the highest rungs of the civil service until 1949, and even after that only 120 were given this distinction.[9] When French officials were repatriated en masse following South Vietnam's independence, mass promotions of the unqualified were necessary to fill the gaps in the bureaucracy. In turn, these newly empowered officials also had to be replaced from below. President Diem himself branded his civil servants "incompetent," and most Americans agreed.[10]

In the lower ranks of the civil service, French colonialism had produced a governing class drawn from a narrow social stratum and whose cultural outlook differed from that of the rural population. Almost all the civil servants recruited in the years before and after 1954 hailed from the urban middle class and had been educated in schools following French, or later American, curricula. The recruiting center and main institutions of higher education were in Saigon, meaning that the well-connected children of the Saigon elite predominated.[11] Catholics were also present in disproportionate numbers. South Vietnam's administrative class was hence drawn from the part of society most associated with French colonialism, and whose outlook and values had shifted much more rapidly than those of the rural population.

The GVN's bureaucracy also inherited a pervasive centralism and formalism that discouraged local initiative. This legacy was hard to shake off. In a colonial civil service, it had been natural that French proconsuls wanted to make sure that their Vietnamese subordinates were not exceeding their authority. But the practice approached absurdity, with district chiefs not even able to officially commend a subordinate for a job well done without French approval.[12] After independence, many GVN civil servants continued to pass every small decision upward. This was not just because they had difficulty assuming responsibility but also because the French bureaucratic tradition in which they had been trained prized centralization as a virtue. Writing in the 1850s, just before the French colonization of Cochinchina gathered steam, Alexis de Tocqueville had complained that French ministers "were seized with a mania for seeing with their own eyes the details of every thing, and managing every thing at Paris," a trait he said dated back to the late Bourbon era.[13] The GVN still showed the heavy imprint of this tendency a century later, which made it all the more challenging to confront a Communist movement that was skilled at adapting itself to local conditions.

The French inheritance left the GVN without a substantial connection to many of its rural citizens. This was due not only to the cultural outlook of its administrators but also to their physical presence, which was overwhelmingly concentrated in Hanoi, Hue, Saigon, and provincial towns. As the security situation worsened toward the end of French rule, this problem was only exacerbated. During the independence war, French forces occupied major towns and communication routes while mostly declining to contest control of the countryside on a sustained basis.[14] Officials from the French collaborationist regime withdrew from many rural areas in the face of Viet Minh assassination campaigns, leaving the GVN with what future President Nguyen Van Thieu once referred to as a "huge head and small buttocks problem." Over 80 percent of the regime's personnel were stationed in the Saigon area, with the remainder mostly clinging to the safety of provincial capitals.[15]

Despite its relatively small size, the French colonial regime confronted Vietnamese peasants with an oppressive state of unprecedented efficiency, which historian David Marr writes "had capacities to control and to coerce never dreamed of by previous rulers."[16] Whereas the emperors had shown significant deference to local interests, the colonial state was powerful enough to enforce its will without the need to do so. Above all else this meant maximizing rice exports to generate profits while enforcing the maintenance of the socioeconomic order that made this possible. Those who collaborated with the French were rewarded with large tracts of land, while poorer peasants increasingly found themselves working as tenant farmers or sharecroppers. By 1930, 57 percent of the rural population in Cochinchina did not own any land, transforming tenancy into what one Vietnamese historian calls "a ubiquitous fact of life."[17] After the 1954 partition of the country, 2 percent of the population controlled 45 percent of the land, while 72 percent held only 15 percent.[18] Village authorities, who had once performed the function of representatives of their commune's interest, were increasingly placemen who defended this unequal socioeconomic order on behalf of landowners and the French. Village heads often had to pay for their positions, and in turn they squeezed villagers through myriad petty forms of corruption to generate the cash needed to maintain them.[19] The introduction of new legal codes and French notions of private property meant that those poor and uneducated Vietnamese who were slowest to adapt and had the least access to power were often dispossessed of their land.[20] The result was the breakdown within several generations of the inherited social order in the villages, and increased polarization between different classes of villagers. In turn, this did much to fuel the rise of the Viet Minh and later the NLF as the vehicle for the aspirations of poorer peasants.[21]

The grip of the French colonial state remained strong until the outset of World War II. A rebellion in the province of Quang Nam in 1908 and a larger uprising in the provinces of Nghe An and Ha Tinh in 1930–1931 had been brutally suppressed by the colonial state. These local rebellions never coalesced into national movements able to challenge French power. It would take a national movement with the ability to sustain its effectiveness and legitimacy over a long period to undermine and eventually overthrow this regime. This challenge to French imperialism eventually arrived in the form of the Vietnamese Communist movement.

The Rise of the Vietnamese Communist Movement

Sometime in the mid-1940s, two Vietnamese sisters from Saigon were on a trip with their father when he became embroiled in a road rage incident with a French driver. Nguyen Thi Thu-Lam and Nguyen Thi Tuyet Mai watched in horror as their father remonstrated with the Frenchman and then slapped him across the cheek. As they sped away from the scene, both girls understood that their father had violated one of the central taboos of the colonial state. The concept of a Vietnamese laying his hands on a Frenchman was so scandalous that it generated outraged coverage in colonial newspapers. The authorities tried to force the girls' father into apologizing, something he refused to do. Looking back on the incident in their memoirs over forty years later, both women remembered experiencing the mixture of pride and foreboding that filled many Vietnamese when they challenged French authority in those years.[22] But decades later, they were also in a position to see that this incident came at a pivotal moment for French rule in Vietnam. A colonial state whose grip seemed so absolute that it could trouble itself with minor incidents of road rage would soon be unable to maintain its position even with nearly a half a million troops at its disposal.

The rise of the Vietnamese Communist movement was instrumental in bringing about this change. The movement's success lay in its ability to attract an effective base of rural support and then build an enduring administrative and military machine on top of that base. Previous uprisings against the emperors and the French had mostly been limited in their scope and aims, directed more at addressing specific grievances in the context of existing Vietnamese society. By contrast, the Communist movement aimed to overthrow that society entirely in a revolution. "Thus, a rebellion reacts to facts," wrote the Vietnamese historian Huynh Kim Khanh, "whereas a revolution involves principles."[23] The national, as opposed to local, orientation of the movement also made its leaders aware of the need to marshal their resources for a long struggle. From their humble beginnings in the 1920s the Communists eventually built a nationwide movement that could reconstitute itself after waves of repression and mobilize the resources to defeat the French colonial state in battle. The Communist leadership made many missteps along the way, but their movement's remarkable regenerative properties allowed it to eventually achieve victory. Along the way, the Vietnamese Communist movement's leaders successfully transformed themselves from nationalists into nation builders.

The Indochinese Communist Party (ICP) was founded in 1930 under the guiding hand of veteran revolutionary Ho Chi Minh. After playing a role in the Nghe-Tinh uprising that began that same year, the party suffered the first of many waves of repression that nearly drove it into oblivion. The party's leaders learned from these early experiences that if they were to avoid the fate of previous anti-French movements, they needed to learn to carefully marshal their resources and avoid premature rebellion until victory was assured. Ho and other leaders eyed their chance when the Japanese occupied French Indochina in 1940 as part of their war effort in the wider Pacific. At an ICP meeting in May 1941, the party founded the League for the Independence of Vietnam, commonly referred to as the Viet Minh. While key anti-Communist Vietnamese nationalists such as Vu Hong Khanh and Nguyen Hai Than bided their time in southern China waiting for the moment when Chiang Kai-shek's Guomindang could sweep them into power, the Communists began the hard work of building their organization in Vietnam itself. As a front organization, the Viet Minh was designed to mobilize nationalist sentiment across all of Vietnamese society while eliding the role of the Communists, whose social and economic agenda risked alienating key groups. Despite this front, the Communists occupied all leadership roles in the Viet Minh and dictated its strategy. This was the model of a broad-based movement directed by an ideological hard core that would impress many Americans and South Vietnamese and inspire their attempts at emulation.

The ICP planned to launch their revolution when the Pacific War came to an end, judging that this would be the moment of the colonial authority's maximum weakness. Conditions developed even further in their favor owing to a devastating famine that struck northern Vietnam in 1944–1945. Both the Japanese and the French stood by as millions died; in fact, the Japanese continued to requisition rice for their war effort, spreading outrage and revolutionary fervor in the wake of death.[24] With perhaps 10 percent of the population of Tonkin and upper Annam perishing, peasant anger was directed not just at the two foreign occupiers but also the network of native provincial and district officials and notables whose circumstances shielded them from the worst effects of the famine. The situation became even more fragile in May 1945, when an uneasy coexistence between the French colonial authorities and the Japanese occupation forces came to an end as the latter launched a coup d'état, dismantling the French administration in Vietnam altogether. Seeing their erstwhile masters swept aside by fellow Asians had a profound psychological impact on many Vietnamese, for whom the myth of white superiority had formed a powerful bar in the cage of colonial rule. Amid the chaotic summer that followed, the Viet Minh seized Hanoi and many other urban centers in what came to be known as the August Revolution.

Yet as the leaders of the Saigon regime would later discover, ruling a country was much more difficult than merely occupying its capital. By the time of the August Revolution, the Viet Minh had established a presence in every province of Vietnam, but it was in a far from dominant position throughout most of the country. The movement was strongest in Tonkin and northern Annam, whereas in Cochinchina—the future heartland of South Vietnam—it was only one political actor among many. When France attempted to regain control of its colony by force from 1946 onward, the movement was driven out of the urban centers it had seized during the August Revolution and fell back onto a strategy of rural mobilization. From remote base areas beyond the reach of French power, the leaders of the movement directed a nationwide infrastructure that prevented the French from ever reestablishing a firm grip on rural Vietnam. The degree to which the Communists were able to organize and mobilize the rural population continued to vary throughout the country, but with Chinese Communist aid from 1950 onward, they were able to build a formidable politico-military machine that defeated France at the battle of Dien Bien Phu and finally forced Paris to sue for terms in 1954.

While other Vietnamese rulers such as the emperors, the French, and the Diem regime attempted to impose their state from the top down, the Vietnamese Communists built theirs from the bottom up. They were able to accomplish the essential tasks of nation building—constructing a state apparatus with administrative, coercive, and extractive functions while ensuring it enjoyed enough popular legitimacy to run smoothly—because their effort was organic to rural society in a way that the French or Diem regimes never were. The Viet Minh did not enjoy the support of all classes of rural peasants or all regions of the country, and it used violence as well as persuasion to enforce its will. Especially after the initial patriotic wave of the August Revolution passed and French repression returned, it came increasingly to rely on the support of poorer peasants.[25] But even though the movement was directed by distant leaders, and the weapons its members carried were often manufactured in foreign lands, its animating force was the ability to motivate and organize a sufficient portion of rural society to struggle and suffer in the name of the Viet Minh. After using this system to beat the French, the Vietnamese Communist movement later reconstituted it in the battle against the Saigon regime and its American allies.

The basic unit of Viet Minh administration was the village. In this respect, the Viet Minh were no different from every other Vietnamese regime stretching back into time immemorial. A village was a collection of hamlets with several thousand inhabitants that enjoyed substantial autonomy and performed all-encompassing governmental functions for its inhabitants. The competence of the village authorities extended "beyond insurance or welfare to include law and order, property rights, courts, and self-defense."[26] Although peasant mobility was increasing in the twentieth century, it remained the case that "for the overwhelming majority of the Vietnamese population, 'government' has always meant simply the village council—the peasant has little experience of any other."[27] An old adage on communal autonomy holds that "the emperor's authority stops at the village gate," although this reflected an idealized form of a more complex reality. During the colonial period, the French had increasingly transformed village authorities into placemen whose function was to collect taxes and defend the interests of a colonial socioeconomic system that marginalized the majority of peasants. The Communist movement was so successful at mobilization because it did not attempt to turn all these peasants into true believers in the national revolution, but rather to address concrete grievances against the existing structure of village government. Jeffrey Race called this the principle of "communalism."[28]

The advent of Viet Minh village rule was announced by the overthrow of the traditional governing council, which the Viet Minh decried as a "French puppet administration," and the establishment of a new council.[29] After the new body convened, members would mete out revolutionary justice to members of the previous regime, form village committees to deal with various issues, and organize a militia.[30] The Viet Minh's front strategy meant that all social and economic classes were initially welcomed as part of the new regime, and in parts of the south where the ICP was weak it appears that local landlords and notables often simply reconstituted themselves as the new council. While this allowed the Viet Minh to claim nominal control of much of the area that would later become South Vietnam, many of these landlords and rich peasants were happy to transfer their allegiance back to the French when the colonial authorities reoccupied their areas. A similar trend occurred when forces aligned with the Diem regime reoccupied the South Vietnamese countryside after the Geneva Accords, and the upper strata of rural society flocked back to the banner of a regime that would protect their interests. The inherent unreliability of members of the front meant that over time the Communist movement came to rest on a much narrower but more reliable socioeconomic base of landless, poor, and middle peasants. Socioeconomic conflict within the village, and the differing bases of support for the GVN and the NLF, would prove key factors in the course of U.S. and GVN nation-building efforts.

The Viet Minh village administration, like its NLF successor, had two main functions. The first was to win support for the movement within the village and to inoculate the population against government appeals. This was achieved through a mixture of propaganda, socioeconomic reforms, and targeted coercion. As a Communist publication from the early 1960s explained, cadres should "choose the right moment to act . . . when the people's rights have been endangered" by actions such as "corruption, high taxation, forced money donations, land robbing, military draft." The cadres could then organize the people to agitate for their rights and ultimately seize power, focusing their appeals on precisely those individuals the regime had oppressed.[31] Show trials were sometimes held to condemn landlords and regime officials to harsh punishments, and cadres would make sure that the villagers participated in these events to dramatize their break with the old regime and to serve *pour encourager les autres*. By taking these concrete actions that affected peasants within their own sphere of interests in the villages, the party and its fronts were able to establish a reservoir of supporters and accomplices. Even if government forces briefly reoccupied the area, all those who had benefited from the Communist seizure of power would have little reason to give the authorities their active support.[32]

The second function of the Communist village administration was to use this base of durable support to mobilize resources for the war effort. Rather than staffing its political and military apparatus with outsiders who then attempted to impose their authority on the village, the Communist movement built its structures of authority from the village upward. Its system of military recruitment had three levels. The first was the village militia, a group that in theory included every able-bodied adult member of a village, although only some were armed. After gaining experience in the armed militia, some members would graduate upward into the regional forces, full-time guerrillas who fought primarily in their own district. In turn, the regional forces served as the recruiting pool for main force regiments, which were both more heavily armed and more mobile. At each level the military and ideological elite was favored for promotion into the higher echelons, with the village militia serving as the start of the conveyor belt. Likewise on the political side, the Communist hierarchy consisted of six echelons, of which the village council was the bottom. Each layer drew some of its members from the secretaries of the layers below and had the primary task of adapting directives received from above to local conditions. A large degree of autonomy was built into the system, with a Communist village secretary having more power over matters like land reform than a province chief had in the highly central- ized GVN.[33] The autonomy, power, and opportunities for advancement that this system afforded to previously marginalized members of the village gave them a strong interest in providing the taxes and manpower needed to maintain the new order. "It can be explained very simply to the peasants," a veteran Communist told a Western observer in the late 1960s, recalling this earlier time. "If you want to keep your land, you must fight the imperialists, and if you want to fight the imperialists, your son must go into the army and you must pay taxes. That is the strategic line of the Party."[34] In this way, the movement stitched together thou- sands of disparate village rebellions to make its revolution.

During the Franco–Viet Minh War, Tonkin remained the hub of Viet Minh power and recruitment. It was also the scene of most of the fight- ing. In Tonkin and Annam the movement ultimately deployed six combat divisions, whereas in Cochinchina it was never able to field forces larger than battalions.[35] The south was also beyond the reach of the Chinese sup- plies that eventually made Viet Minh divisions in the north equal or even superior to their French rivals in firepower.[36] The Communists also faced a more complicated political situation in Cochinchina, where two popular grassroots religious groups—the Cao Dai and Hoa Hao—held sway over a considerable part of the rural population, and were deeply distrustful of the Viet Minh. The latter's murder of the Hoa Hao's spiritual leader, Huynh Phu So, turned distrust into hate. Given these problems, the Viet Minh effort in Cochinchina during the war against the French had focused on protecting its core infrastructure, collecting taxes, and carrying out low-level harass- ment of the colonists. The division of Vietnam into two halves at the Geneva Conference reflected this balance of power, with the Communist movement strongest in what eventually became North Vietnam and weakest in the south. In line with the accords, Hanoi ordered the majority of its political and military cadres in South Vietnam to relocate north in the years imme- diately after 1954. Most of those who relocated came from southern Annam, reflecting the party's greater presence in that region. While it is unclear how many cadres remained undercover in South Vietnam, estimates settle on about ten thousand.[37] Doubting that the GVN would hold the national uni- fication elections scheduled for 1956, the Communist leadership in Hanoi wanted to focus on domestic affairs in North Vietnam.[38] But given the Communist movement's demonstrated strengths at mobilization and expansion, the skeletal party infrastructure remaining in the south could also serve as the basis of an anti-GVN uprising if circumstances required it.

The Diem Regime

Ngo Dinh Diem arrived in South Vietnam in June 1954 to become prime minister of the State of Vietnam (SVN). The SVN was a French colonial creation that claimed sovereignty over all of Vietnam but whose authority was circumscribed both by the de facto control of much of its territory by the Viet Minh and by French restrictions on its power and autonomy. Just weeks before Diem arrived, the guns had fallen silent at Dien Bien Phu. When the Geneva Conference concluded in July, Vietnam was split into two countries, with the Vietnamese Communist movement setting up the government of North Vietnam in Hanoi, and Diem's SVN limited to the territory south of the seventeenth parallel.

Diem's primary challenge became consolidating his government's authority over this attenuated territory, which after a 1955 referendum came to be known as the Republic of Vietnam (RVN), widely referred to as South Vietnam. Diem faced challenges not just from non-state politico-religious groups who held a third of South Vietnam's population and territory in their grasp, but also from the remnants of French influence and, later in the decade, a resurgent Communist movement. But Diem also had formidable assets on his side. Despite missteps that would eventually bring about his downfall, he proved he could be a wily and capable political operator who had a vision for how to build and consolidate the power of the GVN. For most of his tenure he could draw on the support of the world's most powerful country, the United States, which funneled over $2 billion in military and economic aid to his regime between 1955 and 1961.[39] Diem could also rely on the support of a succession of U.S. presidents, who dispatched aid workers, military advisers, and covert political operatives to assist him in the consolidation of his rule.

Until recently, many historians portrayed Diem as either an unthinking American puppet or a hopeless reactionary who lacked a vision for South Vietnam. Recent scholarship has demonstrated that neither of these views is true.[40] Diem served in a series of positions in the French colonial regime in the 1920s and '30s, reaching the position of interior minister in the imperial court of Hue in 1933. But he resigned soon after when France rejected his proposals to grant more political power to the Vietnamese, a move that burnished his nationalist credentials. At the same time, Diem was developing his ideas for the future of Vietnam. Violently opposed to the Communist movement that began to gather strength in the 1920s, Diem instead based his vision on an idiosyncratic blend of Catholicism and Confucianism. Rather than a reactionary retreat into tradition, as it has often been understood, Diem's governing philosophy was based on an activist and even revolutionary understanding of both his Catholic faith and his country's Confucian tradition. Diem sought to fashion a "third force" out of these two belief systems, one that could offer a vision of the Vietnamese future that was both anticolonial and anti-Communist. In particular, he was influenced by Vietnamese nationalist Phan Boi Chau, a thinker at the forefront of early nationalist meditations on how Vietnam's traditions could become the basis for the country's path into modernity. In the early twentieth century, Chau had been one of the writers leading the way in introducing terms such as "revolution," "nation," and "citizen" into Vietnamese political discourse, displacing an earlier discourse based on the link between the emperor and his subjects rather than the people and their nation.[41] Chau, a long-term mentor of Diem, had come to believe that "only a sweeping reorganization of Vietnamese society would guarantee the true liberation of the Vietnamese people" from both French colonialism and inherited tradition.[42] A flexible, modern Confucianism would nevertheless be a key part of this postcolonial Vietnamese renewal, which Diem himself often described as a "revolution."[43]

In keeping with his search for a "third force," Diem refused to take a side in the Franco–Viet Minh War, rejecting both the French and the Communists. Eventually fearing his life was at risk in the polarized climate of the war, he left the country in 1950 to enter self-imposed exile, much of which was spent in the United States. When he returned in 1954 to take over the reins of the SVN on the invitation of the aging emperor Bao Dai, he finally had the chance to put his ideas for a "third force" into action as he sought to consolidate the Saigon regime's power. In this effort he was joined by his brother and counselor Ngo Dinh Nhu. Nearly a decade younger than Diem, Nhu had spent the 1930s in France, where he developed an interest in the teachings of the Catholic philosopher Emmanuel Mounier. Mounier advocated a belief system known as Personalism, which rejected both liberal capitalism and communism as overly materialist and neglectful of the social and spiritual needs of individuals.[44] As Diem's closest confidant and a powerful figure in the GVN in his own right, Nhu would also be influential in the development of the regime's nation-building vision.

Yet both Diem's "third force" and Nhu's Personalism proved vague and opaque in practice. The GVN under Diem never managed to articulate a vision of the Vietnamese future that resonated with enough of its citizens to allow the regime to spread legitimate power across South Vietnam. All too often, the high-minded promises of social, political, and economic reform that Diem and the Nhu made turned into coercive and regressive policies when implemented on the ground.

Diem and Nhu's erratic personalities, their authoritarian and intolerant natures, and both the instruments of rule that they inherited from the French and those they developed themselves undermined their attempt at anti-Communist nation building in South Vietnam. By the early 1960s their rule had sparked peasant uprisings across the country, and when they were ousted in a 1963 coup, they left behind a regime that had little to show for nearly a decade of attempts at rural nation building.

Faced with the diffusion of power and loyalty across South Vietnam when they took power in Saigon in 1954, Diem and Nhu had stressed nationalism as a unifying force. The need for unity across regional and sectional groups had been a recurrent theme of Vietnamese nationalism under the French, and it now became a tool in the hands of the GVN. Local and sectional groups were commanded to subordinate their interests to that of the new South Vietnamese nation-state. "The interests of the nation at large must take precedence over the local interests," wrote Nghiem Dang, an influential thinker in Diem's regime, allowing that "the local population can always make itself heard, and indicate its wishes, demanding that measures be taken in the local interest, but only providing those measures do not hinder the putting into effect of the national policy."[45] The problem, according to one assessment by Diem's officials, was that because the GVN lacked a presence in most rural areas, the population delivered their loyalty to "whatever party, religious sect or local warlord . . . seemed to care for their welfare."[46] The long legacy of indirect rule practiced by both Vietnamese and French rulers in South Vietnam, combined with the territorial fragmentation caused by the war of independence, had done much to produce this situation. The forging of a South Vietnamese nation-state would mean centralizing governance in Saigon and displacing these groups, who might speak of pursuing the national interest but in reality looked after their sectional interests.[47]

Straightaway, this set the Diem regime on a collision course with the politico-religious groups the Cao Dai and Hoa Hao who held sway across large areas of South Vietnam, and also with countless peasant communities who were unprepared to take up the standard of South Vietnamese nationalism. It was this obstacle that would prove the most enduring. Diem succeeded in crushing the organized military power of the politico-religious groups in the first few years of his rule, earning him the title "America's Miracle Man in Asia." But he was now faced with the more difficult problem of stepping into the power vacuum left by their demise, and rallying the peasantry around the South Vietnamese flag.

This first meant creating a network of strong provincial and district governments who would owe their allegiance to the regime in Saigon rather than local political forces. Although the number of provinces in South Vietnam fluctuated as Diem combined and split them according to his whim, in 1962 it stood at forty-one. Each of these provinces was further subdivided into a number of districts. Aside from village heads, the district chief was the official who had the most contact with the local population, as had been the case since the Chinese first used a system of districts to rule Vietnam.[48] Diem appointed loyalists to these positions, and as the Communist insurgency grew he increasingly relied on officers from the Army of the Republic of Vietnam (ARVN) to fill them. In doing so he was following in the tradition of a long line of Vietnamese rulers who had tried to use military government to pacify the wild south.[49] By 1962, thirty-six out of forty-one province chiefs were from the military, as were the majority of district chiefs.[50]

This coercive and administrative apparatus now had to be used to establish bonds of mutual obligation with the peasantry across the country. Dang, who headed Saigon's National Institute of Administration (NIA) for much of its existence, believed that a key task for the GVN was "developing communication with the people" so that the latter could make demands on the former and see the benefit of submitting to GVN rule.[51] At the NIA, Dang attempted to develop a new generation of GVN administrators who would throw off the colonial inheritance and concern themselves with the well-being of the rural population. He believed that the French colonial regime's reliance on administrators from a narrow, urban social class had caused a profound rupture between the government and the population. Like Diem, he saw the answer in a new governing philosophy that would draw on certain aspects of Vietnam's Confucian inheritance while reinterpreting them in a modern context. In Dang's view, Confucian administrators had been tasked not so much with executing central policy as with resolving local problems and achieving consensus within a broad purview. The fact they received a humanist education tended to enlarge their field of vision. By contrast, French-educated Vietnamese administrators were trained in the law. They limited their scope of action to enforcing colonial law, abandoning the paternalistic concern for the people's general welfare that had been part of the mandarin ideology. The fact that this law dealt mainly with extracting labor and taxes, combined with the lack of cultural identification between the rulers and the ruled, produced what Dang described as "a breach between the new attitude of the civil servant who withdraws more and more behind the passivity of legal texts and rules and the traditional behavior of the people who persist in seeing in him the proxy of the Son of Heaven." In Dang's view, this explained "the relative effectiveness of the colonial administrative machine in that it tended to exploit the country to the profit of the colonial power and, on the other hand, the complete failure of that same machine in promoting the well-being of the population."[52]

The solution, according to Dang, was to inculcate graduates of the NIA academy with a philosophy inspired by his understanding of the old mandarinate.

These graduates were encouraged to see government as a two-way process in which local administrators had a responsibility to communicate the wishes of the population up to the central government, as well as imposing the whims of Saigon. As Dang explained, using the example of the district level of government: "The district chief is responsible for presenting to the people the policies of the government and for communicating to the central government the wishes of the population."[53] "Anh" (a pseudonym), an NIA graduate who worked in a number of local government positions, explained how he saw his position: "I am appointed, and as an appointee I am responsible to the central government. Yet, I am a Vietnamese administrator who has an obligation to serve the people. But suppose there is a conflict of interest between the government and the people. What position should I take? I serve my people. Sometimes the government is too far from the people, and I'm close to them and know their aspirations."[54]

Yet the overall influence of the NIA was limited. While the NIA produced a corps of administrators who had a socially conscious and expansive view of their role, the absolute number of graduates of the academy was small. In the early 1960s it was training about one hundred administrators a year at a time when the GVN civil service had about 140,000 employees.[55] NIA graduates also tended to serve in subordinate positions as deputies, while real power in local government continued to be wielded by captains and majors of the ARVN. Diem remained reliant on the military for consolidating his rule, especially when the Communist insurgency began to pick up speed. The decision to ally himself with the particular strata of the population who were most identified with French colonial rule and most influenced by its social and cultural legacy was perhaps inevitable but made it difficult for him to change the dynamics of relations between the GVN and its rural citizens.

The bulk of the GVN's officials had come of age serving a French governing apparatus whose main means of intercourse with the rural population had been the use of force, not the two-way exchange of ideas. There was little communication between villagers and local government officials, and little active support for the GVN. Most GVN officials had spent the past decade battling the Viet Minh. This gave them a security-oriented approach to their jobs and also meant that they tended to view all former sympathizers of the struggle against French rule as potential threats, even though the Viet Minh enjoyed wide support for their nationalist credentials.[56] After Diem launched an "Anti-Communist Denunciation Campaign" in 1956, province officials cast the net widely over their old enemy, targeting many former Viet Minh. One province chief told a Western visitor in 1957: "When you have an official who will deal sternly with the Viet Minh, it is of secondary importance whether he is honest or otherwise capable. It is better to have a district chief who steals than a district full of Communists."[57] Tran

Ngoc Chau, a South Vietnamese official who was unusually sensitive to the plight of villagers, complained that those who had formerly had connections with the Viet Minh were automatically assumed by GVN officials to be Communists.[58] Villagers who had supported the Viet Minh found it incomprehensible that they were now supposed to side with former collaborators against the resistance. It is not surprising that a widespread rumor held that when Ho Chi Minh heard that a large contingent of pro-French officials had fled Hanoi to seek refuge in the South, he remarked: "Good! That is the best news I have heard in a long time. With that crowd in the South, how can we lose?"[59]

Given their backgrounds, training, and predilections, most South Vietnamese officials lacked the ability to understand rural society, and especially the strengths and motivations of the Vietnamese Communist movement. These facts proved difficult to grasp for a class of administrators and soldiers who had benefited from French rule and experienced it mostly from the vantage point of the prosperous cities. Tran Van Don, who was a leading general under Diem before turning against his regime, would later write of this period that Vietnam had "no peasants exploited by rich landowners," and "the bulk of the land was held by individual Vietnamese who owned only small parcels on a highly democratic basis."[60] This comment rates as frankly bizarre, given that large-scale landlordism in the south dated at least to the Nguyen, who had ruled the region through powerful landholding intermediaries. This tendency had only increased under the French, and by the 1930s only a third of the land in Cochinchina was owned by those who farmed it.[61] But Tran's belief was widely shared among his colleagues.

Diem and Nhu were aware of the shortcomings of the GVN's traditional civil service and military and never fully trusted their nationalist zeal, given that so many had been trained under the French. They accordingly attempted to supplement their regime's political base of support by building organizations and paramilitaries that owed their loyalty directly to the Ngo family itself. Both Nhu and Diem admired how proficient the Communists were at political mobilization, and they attempted to emulate the Communists' techniques in setting up these extra-constitutional organizations.[62] Just as the Communists had done through the Viet Minh, the Ngo brothers sought to construct a series of fronts, mass movements, and associations that would mobilize support for their rule and allow them to spread their influence throughout rural society. At the heart of this network was the Can Lao, a clandestine party headed by Nhu whose members— like those of the Communist Party—were the ideological and political elite of the regime. The party's members even penetrated the military and governing institutions of the South Vietnamese state inherited from the French, where they attempted to steer policy in the direction desired by the Ngo brothers and sniff out disloyalty. The brothers sought to use the Can Lao and its fronts to create a broad network of loyal supporters and agents throughout South Vietnamese society, just as the Communist Party had done.

Yet lacking a clear ideology beyond boosting the power of the Ngo brothers, the Can Lao and its fronts had little success at achieving pro-regime mobilization. Tram Kim Tuyen, one of the early architects of the Can Lao who later became disillusioned with the Diem regime, commented later that "those who want to build parties like the Can Lao . . . start from the premise that the Communist Party is the source of strength in communist regimes, and that this example should be copied. Whereas the Communist Party is created first, develops, then seizes power, and finally establishes an administration as an extension of its power, those who established the Can Lao . . . think they can reverse the sequence."[63] Rather than following this bottom-up process of mobilization and organization, the Can Lao instead became an instrument of top-down coercion. In the words of an official CIA history, the true aim of the Can Lao was not to win popular support, but to "act for the new government where the bureaucratic legacy of the colonial regime was found inadequate."[64]

With the Can Lao as its steel spine, Diem's regime maintained the essentially coercive relationship with the rural population that had typified the colonial period. One aspect of this was the brutal crackdown he directed against alleged Communists and their fellow travelers, which culminated in the infamous Law 10/59 prescribing capital punishment for any "offense to national security."[65] The regime also embarked on a number of ambitious schemes to remake rural society altogether and make its rural citizens easier to control. Diem began by abolishing village elections and appointing what his critics called "hand-picked henchmen" to oversee village affairs instead.[66] These attempts at controlling rural society through coercion would eventually culminate in the Strategic Hamlet Program of 1962–1963, in which a large part of the population was to be relocated to new villages where they could be physically separated from anti-regime guerrillas and locked into ties of mutual obligation with the GVN. Although the program called for the reinstatement of village elections and a social and economic reform agenda intended to take the wind out of the NLF's sails, the officials who implemented it found it easier to forcibly regroup the population behind a barbed wire fence and declare their job done.[67]

Even as Diem seemed to score successes at increasing the coercive and administrative powers of the GVN, his failure at the other side of nation building— ensuring that those powers enjoyed legitimacy and popular support—was proving to be his undoing. His repression of anyone perceived to be an opponent of his regime was generating huge rural discontent and providing fertile conditions for the Communist movement to reconstitute itself. Those who feared GVN repression understandably turned to Communist cells for protection.

FIGURE 2. President Diem receives a loyalty oath from personnel of the Vietnamese Air Force, 1962. Diem's regime relied heavily on police and security forces to impose control over the countryside.

National Archives identifier 542330, Color Photographs of U.S. Air Force Activities, Facilities and Personnel, Domestic and Foreign, Record Group 342, National Archives II at College Park, Maryland.

More broadly, the millions of villagers who had experienced rule by the Viet Minh councils during the war against the French chafed at the return of the old socioeconomic order to their villages. These events, as well as the pressure being placed on the remnants of the Communist movement in South Vietnam, caused Hanoi to reappraise its policy of restraint. Diem's anti-Communist campaigns did grave damage to the remaining party infrastructure in South Vietnam, and the late 1950s have often been called the "darkest" period for the Communists in the South.[68] The leadership in Hanoi was split over how to respond to Diem's repression and refusal to hold reunification elections, but faced mounting pressure from its lower echelons to take the offensive against the GVN. Facing annihilation at the hands of Diem's security forces, cadres in the South began to arm themselves and commit targeted acts of violence against GVN officials. While this initially went against the party line being promulgated from Hanoi and angered some party elders, it also demonstrated how the party's decentralized decision-making procedure provided internal checks and balances. Attempting to follow Hanoi's line had led to absurdities such as party members with guns in their hands refusing to fire on GVN agents pursuing them. After the Communist cells began fighting back out of necessity, Hanoi gradually changed its line to reflect local realities. From 1957 onward, official armed units began to form, and an "elimination of traitors" campaign claimed the lives of hundreds and eventually thousands of GVN officials. In response, Diem ratcheted up his repressive measures. By 1959, the Politburo in Hanoi was reporting that Diem's regime had "increased the reactionary quality" of local authorities, and was even "consolidating [governing] organs" in the villages, staffing them with security personnel, Catholics who backed the regime, and anti-Communists who had fled North Vietnam following the Geneva Accords.[69]

In 1959–1960, a popular uprising swept much of South Vietnam, encouraged by the Communists but spreading further and wider than their own damaged infrastructure could ever have reached on its own. In late 1960, Hanoi directed the creation of the NLF in an attempt to harness the wave and transform the rebellions into a revolution once more.[70] As in the war against the French, party cells began to replicate themselves by recruiting cadres and attracting support to the new front, which like the Viet Minh aimed to "unite all people who can be united."[71] As the countryside rang to the sound of the wooden tocsins that had long announced the arrival of rural uprisings in Vietnam, the Communists worked to painstakingly reconstitute the revolutionary village councils, the militia, and the politico-military structures that sat atop them.[72] As they did so, their apparatus, which had already driven the French from the country, became the bane not just of the Diem regime but also of its superpower ally.

American Nation Building under Diem

On May 11, 1962, a forty-two-year-old American named Albert J. Fraleigh stepped off a cargo plane in Saigon. This was only his latest posting in a long career for the U.S. government and the United Nations. In World War II, Fraleigh had supervised the construction of airfields in Alaska and on the Aleutian Islands before working as part of U.S. Navy civic action teams persuading Japanese civilians to refrain from committing suicide after the defeat of their armed forces on Saipan and Okinawa. Managing UN port facilities in Shanghai after the war, Fraleigh become a close friend of future Chinese Communist premier Zhou Enlai. When the Communists took over the city in 1949, he was held under house arrest and harshly interrogated, escaping only with the aid of Zhou. Fraleigh then moved to Taiwan, where he worked for an American aid mission and became an adviser to future Taiwanese president Chiang Ching-kuo. Recognized as a result of this experience as the U.S. Agency for International Development's "most experienced man in civic action, rural development and Asian communism," Fraleigh had now been summoned to Saigon to help strengthen Diem's embattled government. It was his first time in South Vietnam.[73]

When Fraleigh arrived in South Vietnam in May 1962, the Diem regime was floundering. The Communist movement had reconstituted its politico-military infrastructure and spread its influence across much of South Vietnam, and was taking the armed offensive. A few weeks after Fraleigh arrived, NLF attacks reached an all-time high, targeting "health workers, teachers, and minor officials as well as village guards, local militia and the regular military." These attacks on anyone associated with the regime were forcing the retreat of GVN authority from much of the countryside, prompting military counteroffensives that did little to restore it. American officials were anticipating a long war against what they conceded to be "experienced, well-organized, and competently led guerrilla fighters."[74]

In response to this challenge, Fraleigh and his partner, a former CIA officer named Rufus Phillips, created the framework around which the wartime nation-building effort would eventually be built.[75] In late 1961, President Kennedy had dispatched former chairman of the Joint Chiefs of Staff Maxwell Taylor and deputy national security adviser Walt Rostow to the country to assess the U.S. effort there. One of their recommendations was for a new push to develop links between the Diem regime and the rural population by strengthening and legitimizing local governments. The United States Operations Mission (USOM) was to be the vessel for this effort, and Fraleigh and Phillips—who had worked on a similar program in Laos—its catalysts.[76] As so often throughout the war, this new nation-building push accompanied an increase in the U.S. military effort. The Military Assistance Command, Vietnam (MACV) was created in 1962 to coordinate military activity in the country, and American military advisers were assigned to all ARVN units of battalion size and above, and also to South Vietnamese province chiefs.[77]

The extension of a permanent official American presence into the South Vietnamese countryside, where it would remain until the American withdrawal in 1973, dates from the Taylor-Rostow report. Although USOM had deployed personnel to the provinces to help with the resettlement of refugees from North Vietnam in the 1950s, Diem had forced its withdrawal in 1958.[78] It was only the deteriorating military situation that led the president to reverse his stance. From late 1961 onward, the number of Americans deployed throughout the country increased steadily, their involvement in its political life growing along with the military presence. Phillips and Fraleigh's USOM personnel jostled for attention alongside Americans from other agencies, especially the CIA, who also began to become increasingly involved in rural affairs in the Diem period. This diffusion of agencies led William Colby to complain that Americans operated in "autonomous baronies," with little coordination between their activities. "Like the blind men around the elephant" he later wrote, "the [Americans] ... gathered about the Diem Government, each dealing with different pieces and sections of its problems and defining the animal accordingly."[79] This was problematic not only because it made it difficult for the Americans to speak with a single voice to the GVN, but also because each American agency had its own ideas about what that voice should be saying. This diffusion of effort and lack of agreement over the correct approach to nation building would continue to afflict U.S. efforts until the creation of CORDS.

The Washington policy makers who directed this nation-building effort provided little guidance on specifics. The Kennedy administration was full of officials who claimed expertise on guerrilla warfare and nation building in the abstract without having much knowledge of Vietnam in particular. One such official was Roger Hilsman, a close Kennedy adviser who served as head of the State Department's intelligence arm and afterward as assistant secretary of state for Far Eastern affairs. During World War II, Hilsman participated in guerrilla operations behind Japanese lines in Burma. He then returned to the United States and obtained a PhD in international relations before holding a series of academic posts. He met Kennedy while working in a senior position at the Congressional Research Service and was brought into the new administration in February 1961. Regarded as an expert on guerrilla warfare because of his service in Burma, Hilsman was called on to contribute to the administration's understanding of the emerging insurgency in Vietnam.

In a major report in 1962, Hilsman assured his colleagues that the basic desire of the peasants was that the GVN provide "security" against the NLF. But this was a simplistic view that ignored the extent to which many Vietnamese peasants viewed the GVN and not the NLF as the primary threat to their security and socioeconomic interests. A misunderstanding of how deeply the conflict was rooted in Vietnam's colonial legacies also led American officials to produce wildly inaccurate estimates of the strength of NLF support. Hilsman wrote that the organization had only one hundred thousand "supporters and sympathizers," but both the documented reach of the Viet Minh and the fact that the GVN claimed to be killing twenty thousand members of the NLF a year indicated this number was undoubtedly too low.[80]

Lacking clear guidance from Washington, American nation builders diverged in their approaches. American attempts at nation building in South Vietnam in this period can be split into three broad categories. The first category of project addressed itself to the central institutions of the Saigon regime. These nation builders took a top-down perspective, working on national plans for internal security forces, the training of civil servants, and the running of government ministries. Personnel concerned with these issues were drawn from the U.S. Agency for International Development (known locally as the United States Operations Mission, or USOM) and from a group of experts and technicians from Michigan State University (MSU) who operated under a contract with USOM. Diem had met the leader of the MSU group, Wesley Fishel, while in exile and had subsequently requested that Fishel head up a program of technical assistance to GVN ministries. The MSU group provided advice on public and police administration to the regime, as well as helping to run the NIA.

The MSU team's ability to have a meaningful impact on nation building was limited both by the narrowness of its aims and the approach that it brought to its work. MSU team members were experts in public administration in the abstract and not Vietnam itself; furthermore, their expertise lay specifically in *Western* public administration. This led them to attempt to graft lessons from the United States inappropriately onto the Vietnamese context, as historian Jessica Elkind has shown.[81] Dang, who frequently received their advice, complained that although their reports "were written by experts, some of whom had long practical administrative experience, in most cases their value was largely academic, because they brought out theoretical and technical problems, and lacked factual knowledge of the Vietnamese context."[82] The MSU team was constantly frustrated by its inability to persuade the Diem regime to introduce what it considered professional standards into the GVN civil service. Eventually, after a falling out with Fishel, Diem ejected MSU from the country altogether.

The second group of Americans who worked to strengthen the Diem regime were CIA officials who worked with province chiefs to attempt to increase the efficiency and legitimacy of GVN rule. Agency personnel had a keen interest in what they called "political action," the countering of the Communist movement's rural apparatus and the building of support for the GVN in its place. Colby, who served as deputy chief and then chief of station in Saigon between 1959 and 1962, was typically bullish about the CIA's expertise in this area. "Uniquely in the American bureaucracy," he later wrote, "the CIA understood the necessity to combine political, psychological, and paramilitary tools to carry out a strategic concept of pressure on an enemy or to strengthen an incumbent." Colby and his colleagues closely studied both the deficiencies of the GVN and the organizational strengths of the Communist movement and modeled their remedies accordingly. Colby believed that the GVN needed to copy the Communist model by "organizing the population into political groups, articulating a cause that would attract their participation and support, developing leadership and cohesion at the local rural community level, etc."[83] This was in contrast to MSU, who focused on pushing the central regime in Saigon into economic and political reforms. Instead, CIA officers began to work with local South Vietnamese officials on a joint rural nation-building agenda.

Tran Ngoc Chau, a former Viet Minh battalion commander and political officer who had rallied to the anti-Communist cause, did more to influence the CIA's efforts than any other individual. Born in 1924 into a mandarin family in Hue, Chau had joined the Viet Minh to oppose the Japanese occupation of Vietnam in the 1940s and then participated in the war against the French. Taken in by the Viet Minh's front policy, it was only as he was promoted through the ranks that he came to understand—and despise—the Communist ideology that lay at the core of the movement. After being the subject of repeated unsuccessful attempts to recruit him into the Communist Party, he defected to Bao Dai's pro-French government in 1949. He transferred his allegiance to the GVN when it was created in 1955, and by the early 1960s had attained the rank of major in the ARVN.[84]

In 1962, Diem appointed Chau chief of Kien Hoa, a province in the Mekong Delta. Chau's sympathetic participation in the Viet Minh had given him a largeness of vision that was unusual among other individuals in his class, as Americans who met him soon realized. Chau had seen firsthand how the Communists operated and how they responded to the genuine grievances of the rural population to win support for their movement. While he had been turned off when he realized that the Communists ultimately planned to establish a "dictatorship of the proletariat" that would abolish all property and religion—something rarely mentioned in their propaganda to the peasantry—he continued to see the value of their approach to local mobilization and politics. He also felt sympathy and "compassion" for rural villagers who felt it necessary to take up arms against their own government, "people whose duties were to provide them security and peace." This "villager-enemy" was one who should be won over to the GVN's cause rather than targeted in a brutal security crackdown, as the Diem regime did. "Since I always preferred to win over a living person than a dead one," Chau later wrote, "my ideas basically were aimed at converting the enemy, thus eliminating the need to kill him."[85]

To convert the enemy, Chau drew heavily on his experiences in the Viet Minh. His nation-building idea was based around the concept of the cadre, and what Stuart Methven, one of the Americans who learned from him, would later call "parapolitics." In the Viet Minh and the NLF, the word "cadre" (*can bo*) referred to an operative in a revolutionary organization, not necessarily a party member. While cadres had different functions, Chau focused on those through whom the Communist movement attempted to solidify its influence among the rural population. Mobile groups of specialist agitprop cadres toured the countryside, making contact with sympathetic villagers and combining to orchestrate the overthrow of the old village authorities and the installation of ones allied with the front. They had been instrumental in consolidating the revolutionary wave that swept South Vietnam in the early 1960s. Because of their temporary but decisive political presence, Methven referred to their activity as parapolitical, or "political action."[86] A witness to the same methods when they had been deployed on behalf of the Viet Minh, Chau now hoped to replicate them for the benefit of the GVN. "It was, in my understanding," he later wrote, "a revolutionary process to build the power from the grassroot peasants to change the colonial and mandarin system that most of the Vietnamese leaders, military and civilian inherited."[87]

Chau set about recruiting mobile cadre teams from among the local peasantry. This made a stark contrast to Diem's rural mobilization teams which were usually composed of moonlighting civil servants.[88] Chau's cadres formed what he called Census-Grievance (CG) teams. Like the NLF agitprop teams, they roamed the villages of the province, inquiring about rural grievances. Chau was adamant that the teams inquire about grievances caused by local GVN officials as well as the NLF, and in the early stages of the program about 70 percent of complaints concerned the Saigon regime. Chau could then use his power as province chief to address GVN abuses, and USOM contributed material aid in response to grievances. In addition, the CG teams also took a census in the villages, attempting to discover who was working for the NLF. A mixture of persuasion, cajolery, and attempted compromise would then be used to persuade them to defect to the GVN. In the last analysis, "counter-terror" teams could be sent to kidnap or assassinate them.[89]

Chau's methods were based on an assumption that the traditional GVN bureaucracy would never be able to win over and mobilize the peasantry as effectively as the Communist movement did. This was a belief shared by the CIA officials who learned from his methods and later attempted to replicate his program beyond Kien Hoa.[90] The paradox of Chau's position was that although he denigrated the GVN bureaucracy and hence constructed parapolitical structures to circumvent it, his influence depended on his position as province chief within this same bureaucracy. For the Americans, it hardly constituted a nation-building strategy to hope that similarly talented leaders amenable to American advice would emerge in all forty-four of South Vietnam's provinces. As Daniel Ellsberg, another American influenced by Chau, ruefully recalled, there were barely a handful of like-minded individuals across the GVN.[91] Chau complained that "the Saigon generals ignored my success in Kien Hoa," and without the involvement of higher-ups in the GVN, the program could not be extended to other provinces.[92] Neither did Chau possess the resources or personnel to have a decisive impact even in Kien Hoa, where the Communist movement continued to advance. Both the replicability of Chau's efforts and their ability to have a decisive impact were in doubt, and as late as 1964, the CIA's efforts consisted of only a few dozen officers trying to do "something, anything" to bolster local government.[93]

The third group of Americans who worked toward nation-building goals in South Vietnam under the Diem regime were those who worked out in the villages in daily contact with Vietnamese peasants, often focusing on economic development projects. The first Americans to do so on a sustained basis were those working for International Voluntary Services (IVS), an NGO that placed young Americans into development projects throughout the world. While MSU focused on the GVN's central institutions, IVS volunteers—or "IVSers," as they were known—lived and worked deep in the South Vietnamese countryside. Although the IVS presence in South Vietnam was fully funded by the U.S. government, many of those working for it saw their mission as separate from that of both the United States and the GVN. Don Luce and John Sommer, two prominent IVSers, were so focused on stimulating economic development for the sake of rural inhabitants that "even as late as 1963 and 1964 it often seemed" to them "as though the war itself hardly existed." They likewise felt remote from the Diem regime, seeing themselves as "more observers than participants in the affairs of the Vietnamese government."[94] IVS personnel worked on tasks such as helping villagers build agricultural improvements and spreading improved seed and crop strains. Many IVSers did not perceive their work as political, while those who did were often surprised to find that their assistance and material aid rarely translated into support for either the GVN or the U.S. presence. Such small efforts might help individual farmers, but they did nothing to address the reality of systemic political and socioeconomic repression that fueled resentment of the GVN and support for the NLF.[95]

After the 1962 arrival of Fraleigh and Phillips, USOM itself began to develop an official network of American representatives that would match and eventually exceed the reach of the IVSers. Prior to that year, USOM had run a "traditional" economic aid mission that focused on advising central political and economic policy-making institutions in Saigon, much like MSU. Even though the local governments that actually had contact with the rural population seemed to be the GVN's weakest link, USOM officials resisted involvement in the provinces. As for the guerrilla crisis, they believed that was best left to the military.[96] Instead, Fraleigh and Phillips pushed for the permanent deployment of American representatives in each province of South Vietnam, where they could act as conduits for U.S. influence over province chiefs. Although Diem had previously been opposed to having American representatives influencing civil government in the provinces, the deepening guerrilla crisis eased his reservations. Diem was also reassured by his trust in Phillips, whom he had met when the latter was deployed in Saigon as a military adviser in 1954.[97] Phillips and Fraleigh's efforts amounted to a revolution in the way USOM operated. When the pair arrived in Saigon, USOM had 120 employees, and only 3 were stationed outside the capital. They set about recruiting a new breed of provincial representatives who would act as American eyes and ears in the provinces, as well as providing advice to province chiefs on matters of civil government. Unable to elicit any volunteers from within USOM, Phillips and Fraleigh recruited a diverse bunch of Americans from outside the agency. The group included former military officers, personnel from other American agencies, and Peace Corps volunteers who had served in other countries. The first provincial representative was a former IVS volunteer who was dispatched to Phu Yen, a province on the central coast, in September 1962. Another early recruit was David Hudson, an NBC stringer who fancied his hand at rural reform. Duly hired, he was dispatched to the southern tip of the delta, a redoubtable NLF stronghold.[98] Some of the Americans who worked in the program would later go on to storied careers in the executive branch of the U.S. government, including Richard Holbrooke, John Negroponte, Hamilton Jordan, and Anthony Lake.

The new organization was known as the Office of Rural Affairs, and it eventually grew to have a representative in every province. Unlike the CIA, whose cadre program attempted to emulate the Communist movement's focus on propaganda motivation, the Office of Rural Affairs focused on the provision of social and economic benefits to the rural population. But while USOM had traditionally operated by attempting to influence the GVN in Saigon, Phillips and Fraleigh believed that "the best plans in the world dreamed up in Saigon or Washington, won't mean a thing unless they really reach the rural population." After gaining the trust of the province chief to whom they were accredited, the representatives were supposed to influence him to explore the "felt needs" of the rural population and then respond to them. Ideally there should be a "two-way street," with top-down projects such as the Strategic Hamlet Program and agricultural improvements being imposed from above, and suggestions for "hamlet self-help projects" being passed up from below. A special fund, which could be signed off at province level without reference to the interminable bureaucracy in Saigon, was set up. The aim was to decentralize the power and resources needed to carry out local development projects. As the *Provincial Representatives Guide* put it, the "hamlet people must and can be convinced by your quick action that their government has become responsive to their needs."[99]

While the CIA effort was based on a specific doctrine and idea of the role of Americans in supporting GVN officials who were particularly insightful and energetic in battling the insurgency, Fraleigh and Phillips built their effort on what they referred to as the American "'Can Do' spirit." Rather than being dispatched with detailed instructions on what they were supposed to accomplish, the Office of Rural Affairs representatives were exhorted to use their "dedication, common sense and imagination" to improve the lot of the rural population.[100] Fraleigh explicitly modeled what he wanted in a recruit on the young "BA generalists" favored by the Peace Corps, which he would later claim to have had a hand in founding.[101] The focus of the representatives was overwhelmingly on fulfilling the perceived material needs of the population; indeed, it is as a provider of "barbed wire and other materiel for community efforts" that Colby remembers the Office of Rural Affairs in his memoirs.[102] Representatives could act as a conduit to the central GVN and USOM agencies in Saigon, expediting the delivery of agricultural inputs, technical advice, and aid with schools and dispensaries. With this material backstop, they were exhorted to "feel proud of yourselves as Americans" and "make the seemingly impossible work successfully."[103] This early group of young and idealistic representatives became known as "the Tigers" because of Fraleigh's stock motivational phrase: "You can do it, Tiger!"[104] Through this combination of American élan and materialism, the Office of Rural Affairs aimed to make the GVN's local organs a match for those of the NLF.

Although USOM's provincial representatives had a broad remit to attempt to make provincial government both more effective and more legitimate, like the IVSers before them they had little ability to alter the fundamental dynamic between it and the rural population. The Communist movement's success did not derive simply from the provision of material benefits to the villagers. Instead, it had a political strategy to win them over, and offered them opportunities to achieve their own local aims as part of the movement. It cultivated local leaders and promoted peasants into positions of responsibility. Increasing the material resources available to GVN province chiefs could not alter the fact that they continued to treat the peasants as objects rather than subjects of governance. Most province chiefs were field-grade ARVN officers who were unlikely to change their behavior or views simply because an enthusiastic young American came into their orbit. Even when USOM representatives were successful in prodding GVN officials to carry out limited economic development projects, their involvement was unlikely to change the basic structure of relations between the GVN and the peasantry. Nor were the Tigers in a particularly good position to assess the impact of their own efforts. Although some of them stayed in one province for years and came to know it well, in general they were recruited and dispatched without any specialized knowledge of South Vietnamese history, governance, or politics. As we shall see when we turn to consider the experiences of CORDS advisers in subsequent chapters, this severely handicapped their ability to make a meaningful contribution to nation building. And like their counterparts in the CIA, what exactly the USOM representatives could accomplish was ultimately determined by the province chief to whom they were accredited.

FIGURE 3: Children gather at a market built with the help of USAID. Villagers might appreciate such projects, but they delivered few long-term political benefits to the GVN.

National Archives identifier 541851, Miscellaneous Vietnam Photographs, Record Group 306, National Archives II at College Park, Maryland.

This problem of comprehending and influencing rural society would bedevil American nation builders for the entire conflict. Americans who considered the position of the rural peasant during the Diem years frequently came to the conclusion that, as one put it, "lack of rapport between him and the central government" was the crucial problem facing the country. The solution, they believed, was to "strengthen the political and administrative bases of the government."[105] Yet few Americans in South Vietnam had the language skills or understanding of rural South Vietnam to be able to accurately observe how "strong" these "bases" were, let alone to strengthen them. In 1959, only 9 of the 1,040 Americans working for government agencies in the country could speak Vietnamese.[106] Despite an ever-growing number of military advisers, the United States lacked its own network of agents who understood South Vietnamese rural society. As a result, U.S. officials complained that all they knew was "what the government of Vietnam knew that we wanted [to know]."[107] John Vann put it more colorfully to an American visitor in 1962: "Hell, I don't even know what is going on across the river at night."[108] American officials hence complained of a "shadow of uneasiness" when they turned their thoughts to popular attitudes toward the GVN, conceding that it was "difficult, if not impossible, to assess how the villagers really feel."[109] A CIA report on the attitudes of peasants in fifteen provinces was unable to establish much beyond their hatred of province, district, and village officials.[110] Washington officials reported not finding field reports on the topic "particularly informative or encouraging."[111]

American observers had initially been hopeful that the Saigon regime might make a concerted effort to gather support in the villages and construct a genuine mass basis for the regime. But they soon concluded that the Ngo brothers only intended to use their parties and fronts as instruments of control, not to widen political participation. As career advancement and even survival became dependent on joining the Can Lao, it became clear that it and similar organizations were "actually formed by coercion—that is, people join because they are afraid not to—rather than being genuine organizations rooted in the hearts of the Vietnamese people."[112] Even worse, heavy-handed, top-down schemes like the Strategic Hamlet Program failed to achieve political mobilization for the GVN or to bind the population into ties of mutual obligation with the regime. In fact, they were mainly successful at mobilizing support for the NLF, driving more peasants into the arms of the front than they suppressed.[113] Rural communities had been given little reason to identify their interests with a regime composed of colonial holdovers and Diemist parvenus, and Saigon's attempt to reshape rural society in its own interests had paid little heed to the desires of the peasantry.

This points to yet another problem in early U.S. efforts: it required the resources and active interest of the central government in Saigon to carry out such a sustained nation-building effort across South Vietnam. There was only so much that province chiefs or other local figures could do on their own without national support. The situation became even more dire after the overthrow of Diem. Local officials and their schemes were subject to the capriciousness of national politics, as there was always a risk that each new junta would feel the need to appoint its own loyalists to positions in local government. A case in point was the Force Populaire, an extensive cadre program run by Diem's brother in northern South Vietnam, which was summarily disbanded after the 1963 coup and the Ngo family's fall from grace.[114] Parapolitical efforts such as those of Chau could look suspiciously like attempts to build local power bases when viewed from Saigon. Indeed, the frequent turnover in Saigon did encourage the emergence of such bases. Given the weak institutional basis of the Saigon regime, local politics in South Vietnam were prone to warlordism, as they had been throughout Vietnamese history. After the 1963 coup, the four commanders of South Vietnam's military regions—known as corps commanders—took over responsibility for civil government as well as military matters within their area. This included the hiring and firing of province chiefs, giving them the ability to build up local fiefdoms that were generally free from central oversight.[115] Centrifugal tendencies made it even more difficult to construct a nationwide effort to reform local governance. Colonel Robert M. Montague, a key figure in the creation of CORDS, castigated the resultant "44 separate province wars" as "ridiculous" because "you didn't have the leadership down at the province; you didn't have the resources to go around; and the enemy could have defeated you piecemeal, because he was operating under a centralized strategy."[116]

Diem, who remained a hardheaded nationalist even as his own government's incapacity to deal with its problems became clear, refused the deep collaboration with the Americans that would have been necessary to create such a centralized strategy. To do so would necessarily have increased the influence of the foreigners over the GVN, diminishing its claim to independence and validating the Communist propaganda that labeled him "My-Diem"—American Diem. Those Americans who managed to influence Diem the most were ones who developed a personal connection with him, such as Fishel and Phillips. But much like the CIA's relationship with Chau, theirs were temporary and partial arrangements that never managed to change the fundamental dynamic of the GVN's relations with its rural citizens or to provide an effective counterpoint to Communist rural mobilization. After Diem's overthrow and murder in 1963, the GVN collapsed into even greater chaos as the civil service was purged of his loyalists and a succession of coups rocked Saigon. Under these difficult circumstances, the Johnson administration set out to reorganize America's nation-building machinery in South Vietnam in search of an effective and centralized strategy that might change the dynamics of the conflict.

2

THE JOHNSON ADMINISTRATION
AND NATION BUILDING

Lyndon Johnson assumed the presidency just three weeks after Diem's overthrow in November 1963. He could hardly have been more different from the man he replaced. Whereas John F. Kennedy had oozed youthful, even naïve, optimism about America's capacity to do good through an activist role in the world, Johnson's priorities were domestic. He pursued the most ambitious legislative program since Franklin Roosevelt's New Deal, advancing civil rights, federal aid to education, and health-care programs for older and poor Americans. Despite his desire to stay focused on this domestic agenda, which was dubbed the Great Society, Johnson was tormented by the deteriorating situation in Vietnam. Faced with a choice between allowing the collapse of South Vietnam and paying a steep political price at home or risking becoming mired in an unwinnable conflict that would undermine his domestic agenda, Johnson chose the latter.[1]

Johnson came eventually to leave a heavy imprint on U.S. nation-building efforts in South Vietnam. But his appreciation of the importance of the GVN developing strong and legitimate institutions developed only slowly over time. He also came to realize that nation building enabled him to frame the war at least in part as a constructive, positive activity—one in which the United States would strive, as he told his aides, "to build as well as to destroy."[2] Although some critics have argued that Johnson interfered with the war effort by attempting to export his Great Society domestic programs to Vietnam, it was in fact an inescapable part of U.S. strategy to focus on the GVN's relationship with its rural population.[3] As the war ramped up in the period 1963–1966, Johnson and his aides orchestrated a nation-building escalation alongside the military buildup. Although the president had initially pictured the nation-building effort as focused on meeting the material needs of the Vietnamese poor, he and his close aide Robert Komer eventually came to focus on what the French had dubbed pacification—the spreading of GVN control and coercive power across as much of the South Vietnamese countryside as possible. It was this agenda that led to the decision by the administration to create CORDS in May 1967, setting the stage for a unified and comprehensive nation-building effort for the remainder of the time that American forces were in South Vietnam.

Embracing the "Do-Gooders"

When Johnson assumed the presidency in November 1963, he was by no means an ardent crusader for increased U.S. involvement in the internal affairs of South Vietnam. At the first meeting Johnson held on Vietnam, Defense Secretary Robert McNamara brought up the topic of economic aid to South Vietnam. Johnson said that he supported aid, "but at the same time he wanted to make it abundantly clear that he did not think we had to reform every Asian into our own image. . . . He was anxious to get along, win the war—he didn't want as much effort placed on so-called social reforms." CIA director John McCone noted afterward that he detected a "President Johnson tone" that contrasted with the "Kennedy tone" in that the new president had "very little tolerance with our spending so much time being 'do-gooders.'"[4] McNamara came away with the same impression.[5] Johnson believed the coup against Diem had been an example of unwise U.S. meddling in South Vietnam, and instead wished to focus on taking action against North Vietnam. His first significant policy initiative was to order stepped-up covert action against the North.[6]

Johnson's concern about the post-Diem situation in South Vietnam was well placed. After the November coup, Saigon entered an era of profound political instability that would not come to an end for nearly two years. Coup and countercoup were launched by various factions in Saigon, each distinguished not by its nation-building vision but by its plan to divvy up the spoils of office to its followers. Lacking any central impetus, rural nation-building efforts remained marginal or nonexistent. Meanwhile, the U.S. military effort to seek a partner for nation building in the GVN's central institutions was providing little relief. In 1964, the U.S. military command prodded the GVN to adopt a military pacification plan called Hop Tac, aiming at reasserting a GVN presence in the provinces around Saigon. It is illustrative of the disjointed efforts of the U.S. agencies in South Vietnam, and the limitation of their efforts to areas where they happened to find talented South Vietnamese partners, that Kien Hoa, the scene of the CIA's most promising effort, was not viewed by Westmoreland or by the ARVN as a priority province at that time.[7]

The Hop Tac campaign itself achieved results that can be described as minimal at best, and which in turn showed the ARVN's unsuitability as a nation-building partner at this time. ARVN generals remained absorbed in Saigon politics, an obsession that both fueled and was a by-product of the repeated coups that occurred throughout 1964. At least one Hop Tac mission was aborted only for the forces assigned to it to next be spotted back in Saigon participating in a coup.[8] Most Vietnamese military commanders considered the campaign to be American in conception and hence showed little interest in making a success of it, exposing the limits of American influence. The commanders of the units involved in Hop Tac saw few benefits in risking the wrath of their superiors by incurring casualties in pursuit of a cause that was valued by the Americans but of little apparent interest to any of the rotating cast of generals sitting in the Presidential Palace in Saigon. In November 1964, the director of the U.S. office supporting Hop Tac reported frustration at "the general lack of motivation and drive" shown by ARVN officers who saw the war as "a way of life rather than something to finish off quickly." Because the slow progress of the program was determined by the national political situation and the general attitude of ARVN officers, factors the United States did not have sufficient leverage to alter, a "marked increase in [the] rate of progress" was believed "beyond the control of the U.S. unilaterally."[9]

Meanwhile, the overthrow of Diem led to a decisive shift in policy in Hanoi. In early 1964, the Communist Party adopted Resolution 9, which shifted North Vietnam from a posture of assistance and aid to southern revolutionaries to one of a full-out push for victory. The NLF, which by now had mobilized substantial military might, began driving ARVN forces out of large areas of the countryside. A far greater number of North Vietnamese Army (NVA) advisers arrived to professionalize the guerrillas, along with draftees to buttress their numbers. In late 1964, Hanoi decided to deploy and maintain multiple NVA regiments in South Vietnam for the first time. By the time they entered combat at the end of the year, the Communist movement had already established a "liberated zone" stretching from the Central Highlands down to the northwestern reaches of Saigon. About half of both the population and territory of South Vietnam were under some form of Communist control.[10] "Throughout the countryside, we moved to consolidate our control in liberated areas and accelerate the establishment of NLF governmental entities in disputed regions," an NLF guerrilla later wrote. "The object of this effort was not to take land, but to create a strong and continuous NLF administrative presence, which villagers would accept as their valid government."[11]

As the Communists consolidated their own administration, minds were focused in Washington on the weakness of their ally in Saigon. For Johnson, this included a quick realization that "getting along and winning the war" was inseparable from addressing the perennial ineffectiveness of the GVN. Doing so did not require remaking it in America's own image, but it certainly seemed to require doing something. "From all that I have heard," Johnson cabled Saigon in January 1964, "I could not be more in agreement that political energy is at the center of the government's problem in South Vietnam."[12] Again later that year he reemphasized "the importance of economic and political actions having immediate impact in South Vietnam," which was "governed by a prevailing judgment that the first order of business at present is to take actions which will help to strengthen the fabric of the Government of South Vietnam."[13]

What exactly to do was less clear. The period between the fall of Diem and the final decision to dispatch U.S. combat forces in 1965 was characterized by a growing frustration with the state of drift in South Vietnam and the inability of U.S.-based officials to influence the situation.[14] Their counterparts in South Vietnam pointed out in response that there was little they could do unilaterally under present conditions to change the marginal character of their efforts.[15] Frustrated and facing increasingly bold Communist attacks on American installations in South Vietnam, Johnson returned to his starting place: attacking the North. From February 1965, the U.S. launched air strikes in North Vietnam. As well as deterring attacks against American assets, the aerial campaign had the goal of strengthening the morale of a GVN by finally taking the war to the North. But such a psychological fillip could go only so far, especially if it provoked Hanoi into greater escalation in the South in response.[16] Increasingly on the brink of military collapse and further than ever from being a viable nation-state, South Vietnam needed radical American intervention if it were to be saved.

From the middle of 1965, Johnson directed just such an intervention. Alongside the military escalation that began with Marines splashing ashore at Da Nang, he also launched an escalation of rhetoric and action aimed at reforming the GVN. Johnson's initial thinking on the issue was closest to the materialist and developmentalist USOM view, and this affected how he approached the problem. In a famous speech at Johns Hopkins University in April 1965, Johnson made clear that he considered economic and social development in South Vietnam a necessity on par with the war effort. "In areas that are still ripped by conflict, of course development will not be easy," he declared. "Peace will be necessary for final success. But we cannot and must not wait for peace to begin the job."[17] This was in contrast to an earlier draft of the speech that he had rejected, which relegated development to a task that would follow the war.[18] The Johns Hopkins speech has often been dismissed as rhetoric, given its call for large-scale development projects—such as constructing a Tennessee Valley Authority (TVA) on the Mekong—which were incompatible with the escalation in the war that Johnson was about to launch. Its claims were indeed fanciful. But it ought to be seen as one component of a broader nation-building push by the president and his subordinates. This push would eventually give birth to CORDS, which would have a much greater influence on the war than the stillborn idea of a TVA on the Mekong.

But in the chaotic conditions of mid-1965, neither the Americans nor the GVN was in the position to launch a nation-building push in any realm beyond that of rhetoric. In May, Johnson asked National Security Adviser McGeorge Bundy if there was "anything we can do with land reform at all." "Yeah, we can do land reform, but we can't do it until the government will say it," Bundy replied. "And . . . the government's goddamn busy doing other things."[19] The Americans were busy too, and they had few concrete ideas about nation building anyway. The debate over nation building at this time took place at a high level of abstraction without being enriched by detailed knowledge of the actual situation in South Vietnam, much as it had under the Kennedy administration. While Johnson stressed the importance of social and economic measures to improve the lives of South Vietnamese peasants, his advisers stressed alternative—but equally broad-brush—approaches. McNamara, Bundy, and Secretary of State Dean Rusk all agreed in September that it was necessary to stress "pacification," using the old French colonial term for establishing governmental control of the rural areas. As McNamara explained, this primarily meant helping the GVN develop an effective internal security apparatus: "You can't win it [the war] with American troops going out after Viet Cong terrorists—it just isn't going to be done that way."[20] U.S. proposals for pacification had in the past focused on the need to control the population through police measures, not by providing them with material goods or winning their active participation against the Communist movement.[21] Frank Scotton, an architect of the early cadre programs who visited Washington on leave from Vietnam around this time, remembered that "when I raised the need for political development from the ground up, eyes glazed." The priority now, he was told, was "stability at the top."[22] The Communist offensive of 1964–1965 had some administration principals wondering if it was premature to worry about anything but how U.S. divisions were faring in battle. Writing to Johnson in December, Bundy admitted: "We do not have a complete and fully developed political, economic and social program to match the major new military deployments proposed for 1966." Such a program could be developed in the fullness of time, he continued, "but we have to understand that unless and until there can be military victories, this program is irrelevant."[23] This was a stark but accurate assessment of priorities in wartime Washington in 1965.

As Johnson pressed for more focus on his "development" agenda, he was ill served by the bureaucratic system he had established for running the war. The main forum for the discussion of wartime strategic issues in the Johnson administration was the "Tuesday lunchtime" meeting of Johnson and his senior advisers. In keeping with the president's informal but demanding style, the meetings usually took place without the preparation of either a detailed agenda or minutes. The principals present were bound by the fierce loyalty that Johnson demanded of his subordinates to follow the path set out at the meeting, but their own subordinates were often in the dark about what had even been discussed. Conversely, the scope of views expressed at the meetings was strictly limited by their secretive and tight-knit nature. Johnson discouraged dissent, and he did not provide a forum for the discussion of detailed policy papers prepared lower down in the bureaucracy, as President Nixon's National Security Council system would later do. Management of the war was also hampered by the fact that throughout 1965, there was no individual in Washington above the rank of colonel (or its civilian equivalent, GS-15) who was working full time on the issue of Vietnam.[24]

In this system, nation building was a bureaucratic orphan. The regular attendees at Tuesday lunchtime were Johnson, McNamara, Rusk, Bundy, CIA Director William Raborn (succeeded by Richard Helms), and the chairman of the Joint Chiefs of Staff, Earle Wheeler.[25] USAID, which was overseeing Phillips and Fraleigh's fast-expanding provincial advisory network, was unrepresented at the meeting. And while the CIA had assets in Vietnam that were working on the task of strengthening the GVN, under Johnson the agency was relegated to the role of a provider of intelligence rather than shaper of policy. Helms recalled that there was "no occasion in all the meetings I attended with him" that Johnson asked for his opinion on policy.[26] The relatively small size of both CIA and USOM assets in South Vietnam made it difficult for them to contribute to a policy discussion that was dominated by military voices. As the military had come to dominate the American presence in South Vietnam, McNamara was Johnson's most important adviser on the war. But McNamara was consumed by the military effort, and to a lesser extent by "pacification." Both USOM and CIA personnel who got the opportunity to brief McNamara about their own nation-building approaches found him unresponsive and uninterested in following up.[27]

With other administration principals uninterested, the president was a key catalyst in pressing the national security bureaucracy to focus on nation building. Even if his own idea of "development" was a diffuse and unfocused starting point for a discussion of nation building, he continued to press the issue. The very day after Bundy sent his pessimistic memo about the "irrelevance" of such efforts, Johnson was again telling his aides that he demanded "more non-military action/ leadership of more senior rank and energy."[28] This presidential predisposition would soon be encouraged by Johnson's political needs to shift the domestic debate over the war onto more positive ground. Combined with the emergence of new and more stable leadership in the GVN, the ground was set for the creation of a comprehensive U.S. nation-building effort in South Vietnam.

The GVN and the Honolulu Conference

"On Thursday, February 4 [1966] I left the White House area for my first leisurely lunch in many weeks," recalled Chester Cooper, one of Bundy's deputies. "I returned to the West Basement at about 2:30 to find Bundy desperately trying to reach me." A summit between the American and South Vietnamese heads of government—the first time these two figures would meet—had been hastily called in the time it took Cooper to have lunch. It would begin just two days later. Cooper worked furiously to patch together a quick agenda for the meeting and reserve the required hotel rooms in Honolulu, which was at the height of tourist season. It was only late in the day that it occurred to one of the Americans to inform the South Vietnamese ambassador of what was about to take place. When they decided to invite him to travel with the presidential party at the last minute on Saturday morning, the ambassador "raced madly from his home in Chevy Chase to Andrews Field and barely made the plane."[29]

Despite its significance for the war, the Honolulu conference emerged in this chaotic fashion because it was conceived as little more than a short-term political expedient for Johnson. In early 1966, he was facing mounting domestic criticism of his war strategy. A Christmas pause in the bombing of North Vietnam and a related "peace offensive" had generated no results, leaving the administration red-faced as it resumed bombing. On February 3, the Senate Foreign Relations Committee announced it would hold televised hearings into the war, promising many news cycles of discomfort for the administration. Trying to find a way to divert media attention with a dramatic gesture, Johnson telephoned Rusk and suggested that the American and South Vietnamese presidents meet for the first time at Honolulu.[30] When Daniel Inouye, a senator from Hawaii and member of the Foreign Relations Committee, asked to attend the conference, Johnson rejected his request and declared that the meeting was only being held anyway because of the committee and its "goddamned report" on the war.[31] Cooper's lunch was interrupted shortly afterward.

Given how little preparation the American side made for the conference, it is unsurprising that during it they continued to talk about the need to strengthen the GVN in the same abstract and vague terms they had used so far. Henry Cabot Lodge Jr., the U.S. ambassador to South Vietnam, spoke of an "economic and social revolution, in freedom," while Johnson spoke of "better methods for developing a democracy." The president warned both the Americans and the

Vietnamese present that he would demand to see progress on these amorphous goals by the time of the next summit, including wanting to know "how have you built democracy in the rural areas? How much of it have you built, when and where?" The bizarre demand to quantify democracy was in keeping with an abstract American discourse on South Vietnam that did not engage seriously with either the inherited problems of the GVN or the roots of the NLF's appeal in the rural areas. Nor did the conference address the thorny problem of how to bring together the different approaches taken by the various agencies in South Vietnam, which were as divided and fragmented in their efforts as ever.[32]

However, the conference came at a particularly opportune time for the GVN, even if—given the meeting's origins in American political machinations—this was purely by chance. The U.S. military escalation ordered by Johnson from mid-1965 had finally brought an end to the revolving-door coups that had characterized GVN politics since the fall of Diem. In June 1965, a new junta had seized power, headed by Prime Minister Nguyen Cao Ky and Chief of State Nguyen Van Thieu. The two men could hardly have been more different. Ky, initially the dominant figure in the twosome, was not yet thirty-five years old. Flamboyant and impulsive, Ky, with his signature lavender flying scarf and ivory-handled pistol, was instantly recognizable. He had served for several years as commander of South Vietnam's air force, a politically sensitive position given its potential to swing the balance in the frequent coups that beset the capital. One of the first pilots to fly covert missions against North Vietnam, Ky still managed to get airborne every day by commuting the two miles to his office by helicopter. Politically naïve and hence malleable in the hands of the more experienced, he worked hard to cultivate a daredevil public image. His efforts were aided by his glamorous wife Dang Thi Tuet Mai, an air stewardess who was nicknamed Miss Air Vietnam and was reported to be just as handy with an ivory-handled revolver as her husband.[33] Thieu was older than Ky at forty-two years, was "married to Nguyen Thi Mai Anh, a shy and modest housewife," and was a much more cautious speaker and political operator. He had risen through some of the most prestigious combatant commands in the ARVN and cultivated a network of support in the lower and middle ranks during a long stint as superintendent of the Dalat military academy after South Vietnamese independence.[34] Considered by other personalities in the GVN as more conservative and less dynamic than Ky, Thieu, with his methodical style, would eventually eclipse his partner and rival.[35]

When Ky and Thieu first emerged at the forefront of the South Vietnamese regime, many Americans regarded them as "absolutely the bottom of the barrel."[36] Vietnamese observers were skeptical too. Bui Diem, who served Ky somewhat skeptically as an aide, reported that a common joke held that if Ky and Thieu were put in a blender, then "what came out would be a good deal better for the country than what went in."[37] The two ruled through a directorate of generals. In a further example of Saigon's aping of the techniques that had allowed the Vietnamese Communist movement to become so successful, Ky created an Armed Forces Council with sixteen hundred members down to the rank of colonel. The idea, Ky claimed, was to allow ideas to flow upward from those closest to the impact of decisions, much like the Communist movement's structure. Ky privately referred to the directorate as the "politburo," and boasted that it was "similar to that of the Communist party, which had proven remarkably durable." However, in deference to staunchly anti-Communist colleagues, he referred to it as his "politburo" only in private.[38] Apart from this organizational innovation, coming to power just as the United States began its military escalation also had distinct advantages for the new regime. American officials had made clear their displeasure at Saigon's repeated coups in recent years, but only now did they have the political leverage to discourage them. As the influx of American forces began to blunt the effect of the Communist offensive in mid- and late 1965, the political situation in Saigon also stabilized. There would never again be a coup against the regime's leadership.

FIGURE 4. The Honolulu Conference. *Seated around the table clockwise from right foreground:* Nguyen Cao Ky, Robert McNamara, Nguyen Van Thieu, and Lyndon Johnson.

National Archives Identifier 192497, Johnson White House Photographs, White House Photo Office Collection, Lyndon Baines Johnson Library.

By committing the United States so publicly to the regime of Thieu and Ky, the Honolulu Conference was instrumental in this political stabilization. The two were exhilarated to be summoned at such short notice to receive the American stamp of approval—unsurprisingly, given how effectively this reinforced their domestic authority. They and other members of the GVN delegation made sure they told the Americans what they wanted to hear, even when it became clear how detached from the realities of South Vietnam some Washington-bound Americans were. Ky "thought it strange" when Johnson pressed the GVN to put NLF defectors on the radio to denounce the movement, and when he suggested they "develop better contacts with the communists to gain increased understanding of the movement." As Ky knew but declined to explain to the president, "few Vietnamese, and fewer Vietcong, owned radios." Nor did Ky, whose father-in-law had been assassinated by the Communists, feel that he needed a lecture on understanding the movement. Nevertheless, he nodded along with the president.[39] Meanwhile, other GVN representatives made a host of highly specific promises, including building 913 kilometers of roads, encouraging village handicrafts, and promoting rural electrification.[40] These were expertly tailored to appeal to Johnson's desire to focus on rural "development" and show a benign side of the war to the American people, even if they bore little relation to the capabilities and intentions of the GVN in the rural areas. As Ky later wrote, the conference showed that the GVN and American "views of the world were quite different," a point echoed by Bui Diem.[41] Outside critics were also quick to point out that little would result from the conference. Dismissing the high-sounding words about reform spoken at Honolulu as nothing but a smokescreen, the NLF issued a statement noting how the United States had "summoned their servants in Saigon" for a "farce of a conference" aimed only at "further intensification and expansion of their aggression in South Vietnam."[42] The veteran French journalist Bernard Fall likewise predicted that the promises made at Honolulu would amount to little.[43]

More consequential was the communiqué issued by both parties at the end of the conference, which committed the junta to eventually promulgating a new constitution and instating civilian rule in Saigon. How seriously the South Vietnamese leadership took this commitment is unclear. Bui Diem, whose skepticism of working for Ky was partly fueled by his own desire for a return to civilian rule, was delighted to find both Ky and Thieu "too euphoric" about dealing with the president of the United Sates as equals at an international summit to worry too much about the specifics.[44] Although no timeline was provided for this transition—something the duo would have been unlikely to agree to—this represented a black-and-white commitment that both Americans and South Vietnamese could hold the regime to. In the short term, the disconnect between abstract American demands for "democracy" and "social revolution" and the

GVN's intentions meant the conference had virtually no impact on the GVN's activities in the rural areas. But in the long term, the regime was now committed to an activist agenda that would gradually—whether they liked it or not—take concrete form.

Robert Komer and the Origins of CORDS, 1966–1967

In early 1966, Robert Komer was a deputy to Bundy on the staff of the National Security Council (NSC). Born in 1922, Komer had escaped what he seems to have considered an uninspiring future in Saint Louis by means of a scholarship to Harvard, where he completed undergraduate studies and an MBA. Along the way he was drafted, entering the war in Europe as a private assigned to write operational histories of the war in the Mediterranean theater. In January 1944, he was stranded on the Allied beachhead at Anzio in Italy, enduring months of heavy bombardment before a successful breakout. Rising steadily through the ranks, Captain Komer was discharged after the war and entered the employ of the newly formed CIA in 1947. As a midwesterner of modest means in the patrician and refined environment of the early CIA, Komer relied on intellect and brashness in equal measure, much as he had in the similar social environment at Harvard. Throughout his career, he proved adept at cultivating his politically and socially better-connected mentors. His success as an intelligence analyst led to his being assigned as the CIA's liaison to the NSC, and at the start of the Kennedy administration he was asked to join its staff full time. Here he came to know Johnson, who recognized him as an able and reliable subordinate. For his part, Komer showed the same affection and fierce loyalty to Johnson as he had to the other mentors who had catapulted him from the banks of the Mississippi to the heart of American policy making.[45]

After the Honolulu Conference, when Johnson wanted to appoint an aide to drive progress on the ambitious agenda agreed there, he turned to Komer. The president was not picking Komer because of his expertise or enthusiasm for the war. Komer was—in his own words—a "tabula rasa on Viet Nam," and he had discouraged more junior colleagues from getting their careers entangled in what he saw as a distraction for the United States.[46] Rather, Johnson valued Komer's loyalty and reputation as a brash expediter, the latter of which earned him the nickname "the Blowtorch." In the aftermath of Honolulu, Johnson continued to conceive of nation building in South Vietnam as primarily involving economic development that would win the allegiance of the rural population through addressing their material needs. He told Komer that henceforth he would be in charge of "the other war . . . a war to build as well as destroy." Komer was told to focus on "generating a massive effort to do more for the people of South Vietnam, particularly the farmers in the rural areas."[47] Komer recalled that Johnson continued to see this "other war" as "largely being a sort of building of TVA [Tennessee Valley Authority] and REA [Rural Electrification Administration]," transplanting his knowledge of large-scale American development initiatives to Vietnam.[48]

Johnson had a rhetorical preference for these "high modernist" development schemes that promised sweeping transformations through centralized plans.[49] But despite the president's focus, U.S. personnel on the ground continued to favor decentralized approaches that sought incremental change through alliances with province chiefs and village communities.[50] The fragmentation and decentralization of resources still prevalent among U.S. civilian agencies in South Vietnam made any other approach impossible. Lacking high-level relationships with members of the new junta in Saigon and eclipsed many times over in resources by the growing American military machine, the efforts of the civilian agencies seemed more marginal than ever. American civilians also seemed out of touch with the war effort and unsure of the relationship between the military effort and their own activities. In January 1966, U.S. officials from the agencies interested in nation building had reached a consensus that it would take "several years' more fighting at least on the current scale before the GVN will be in a position to exercise effective control over substantially all of South Viet-Nam except over Viet Cong base areas." But even Ky had recently told McNamara that he expected to control no more than 50 percent of the country's population in two years' time.[51] U.S. nation builders in South Vietnam were as far as ever from a comprehensive and coordinated plan to strengthen the GVN and come to grips with the NLF's hold on the countryside. Richard Holbrooke, who joined Komer's staff in the White House, reported as late as February 1967 that a visitor to South Vietnam could "visit ten provinces and you will get as many concepts and methods for pacification; not field expedients being tested but just different concepts about what the program is about."[52]

Komer pronounced the situation to be "a mess!" and pledged to bring "order out of chaos."[53] Komer later said that the nonmilitary aspects of U.S. involvement in South Vietnam—what was then called "the other war"—had "never really been satisfactorily defined." "So I worked up my own definition," he recalled. "After all, nobody else knew what it was either."[54] His lack of background knowledge does not seem to have overly perturbed him. Instead, the Harvard MBA focused on what he later called the "fascinating" issues of bureaucratic management involved.[55] As for the intrinsic problems of nation building in South Vietnam, Komer "borrowed liberally from the people and studies which impressed me."[56] These included Sir Robert Thompson and Victor Kru-lak, the commanding general of the Fleet Marine Force, Pacific. But Komer's desire for quick results, reliance on others for policy ideas, and unfamiliarity with the situation in South Vietnam could sometimes get him into trouble. Not long after starting his job, he conceded to Johnson that he had "just pushed the town [Washington] hard on the new land reform program Lodge so enthusiasti-cally endorsed till I found it so vague and half formed that it will require com-plete redoing."[57] Komer's efforts would continue to be dogged by an enthusiasm that was often not tempered by knowledge.

As he began to travel frequently to South Vietnam and learn more about the situation there, Komer was quick to realize that Johnson's grand developmen-tal schemes were unrealizable. Instead, Komer had to focus much of his early attention on trying to cope with the monetary inflation and port congestion that accompanied the U.S. military buildup.[58] Beyond that, he saw that the Com-munist movement's military offensives had eroded even the pretence of a GVN presence across much of the country. Having been launched into the job because Johnson wanted to stress transformative rural reform in South Vietnam, Komer instead came to focus on the much narrower topic of establishing the GVN's physical control of the countryside.[59] By May 1966 Komer was reporting that he had "progressively lowered my sights from the desirable to the do-able."[60] He told Johnson in the same month that "I have on my desk many imaginative ideas for urban reconstruction, industrial development, people-to-people projects, educa-tional schemes. These make sense in time, but not until we control inflation and pacify more of the countryside."[61] This brought Komer to the conclusion that it was a "military failure" to loosen the Communist movement's military grip that was the most immediate problem, not the failure of the civilian agencies to strengthen the GVN. In September, he told McNamara that "60–70% of the real job of pacification is providing local security." "If the military will only clear and hold the hamlets," he told Johnson, "I'll produce plenty of lollipops."[62]

Komer had arrived at a view of nation building that blended elements of the military and USOM approaches. Like McNamara, he had come to see "pacifica-tion"—the physical control of the countryside—as primarily a coercive task. It would be accomplished by soldiers and police, not CIA agents or USOM person-nel whispering in the ear of a GVN province chief. But Komer also conceived of a role for "lollipops," the provision of social and economic aid to the rural popula-tion, in the aftermath of the imposition of control by GVN security forces. With this emphasis he was fulfilling the mandate originally given to him by Johnson, even if he did so in a way that was more commensurate with the realities of the conflict. The result was a sequential "clear and build" policy that tied the U.S. mil-itary and civilian efforts in South Vietnam together into a coherent whole. Even so, Komer did not engage with the broader problem of how exactly the United States was supposed to prod the GVN into overcoming the deficiencies that had led to the birth of the NLF and the explosion of the conflict to begin with.

Having formulated this understanding of the conflict, Komer took the next logical step: advocating for the absorption of the responsibility for nation building by the military. Early on in his new role, Komer had worried that "we are not thinking big enough." He reached the conclusion that giving the job to the military, with its vast resources in South Vietnam, would force an enlargement of vision.[63] He was determined, he told McNamara, on "bringing the military fully into the pacification process."[64] Komer had also come to see the military as a more promising vessel for implementing the presidential will. "Soldiers go where they are told," Komer complained to Johnson, "but about three key civilians turn us down (funny how they develop physical disabilities) for every one who accepts."[65] Especially with difficulties getting the right personnel, Komer believed it could "take at least eighteen months in my judgment to get a civilian management structure which might handle pacification as effectively as MACV could today."[66] By October, Johnson seemed to have come around to this point of view and now recognized the immediate primacy of security in South Vietnam, and of the military's role. "I don't think AID can run anything anywhere," Johnson told McNamara. "I don't think they have personnel. I think what personnel they have is generally not too competent—ex-schoolteachers and things of that kind. They're a third of their people short out there. They advertise and trying [sic] to get them—I don't think they have the type that can take over when the troops move out." Johnson went on to add that "I do have a respect for the military, or I would have respect for a chief of police that's had some training in protecting people from coming in with terror at night and things of that kind."[67]

Komer's vision of nation building as a combination of security and lollipops sat uneasily with CIA, USOM, and State Department personnel who had been focused for years on the problems of nation building on the ground in South Vietnam. Having watched the NLF grow from its origins as a popular uprising against Diem, many of these Americans had been uneasy with Johnson's military escalation. The idea that their nation-building efforts might now be subordinated to the soldiers made their heads spin. The CIA, whose efforts had focused on painstakingly cultivating South Vietnamese leaders like Chau and supporting them through cadre programs patterned on the NLF, believed any attempt to scale up their efforts could only be accomplished at the expense of the political sensitivity and local knowledge that made them successful. George Carver, who was special assistant for Vietnam affairs to the agency's director, Richard Helms, was particularly scathing of Komer's proposals in a memo to his boss. Criticizing Komer for his "gee whiz" style and "tone of activist omniscience which masks some fundamental misconceptions," Carver argued that although management and resources were important, "the *essential* aspect of pacification is one of doctrine." Carver believed that the CIA's cadre programs had found the right formula for success, and needed time to show it. To "give this program a military cast . . . would ruin its chances of success."[68] Helms emphasized this himself to Komer, saying that greater MACV control could threaten the "irregularity, local characteristics and individuality of leadership" that were "the essentials of our pacification effort." Stressing "the political heart of the pacification program" as opposed to a narrow focus on "security," Helms was keen to point out that the goal of the program was a "motivated population, not merely an administered one." An overemphasis on "statistical successes" and standardized organization, especially when it interfered with the work of "political motivation" that the CIA claimed to know so well, would threaten the program. But ominously for his own argument, Helms admitted that he "cannot contest your statement that we cannot match the MACV presence throughout the districts."[69]

Opposition to Komer's proposal from the State Department and USAID primarily contended that placing all nation building under MACV would undermine the prospects of stable, civilian government appearing in South Vietnam. Dean Rusk's own Vietnam experts were concerned about the "impression" the move might make, making it look like pacification had "become a civil affairs / military government matter, with all the overtones of the US taking over in an occupied country." They also feared that the move might impact the balance of forces within the Saigon government itself, complicating efforts to move toward civilian rule. They worried that putting American military officers in charge of strengthening the GVN would only reinforce the ARVN's dominance over the GVN, and particularly its rural governance. It would also reinforce the position of the four ARVN corps commanders, who had come to exercise far-reaching control over rural government in their zones. Rusk wrote to McNamara that his "principal problem" with the proposal "was that we seem to be moving toward military govt."[70] AID director William Gaud shared this reservation.[71] State and AID believed that a civilian central government would be more responsive to the needs of the South Vietnamese populace and thus better able to establish the ties of mutual obligation between state and citizen that were at the heart of nation building, and that civilianization should therefore be encouraged over the long term. At the CIA, Carver viewed the point as "valid," although, perhaps in deference to the bureaucratic division of labor that he was in the midst of chastising Komer for not respecting, he advised Helms that "we feel it is a consideration we should let them [State] argue."[72]

Komer, backed by McNamara and ultimately by Johnson, did not view any of these objections as decisive. His need to demonstrate tangible success to the president was too great to place his faith in South Vietnam's national political process, which was not due to produce a civilian government through an election for over a year. As he told McNamara, "the fact remains that the bulk of GVN pacification assets are under military control." As for the nefarious role of the corps commanders, "I agree, but doubt it will be politically feasible to push the ARVN corps commanders out of the picture for a while. If so, let's use them, not deplore them."[73] Even though Komer later told Johnson that "the political plus from an elected government would far outweigh any likely loss of administrative efficiency," encouraging such an outcome was not his short-term priority. He remained wedded to pragmatically working with the current, military-dominated GVN.[74] Indeed, Komer believed that military personnel on the U.S. side would be more effective at motivating and advising ARVN personnel than civilians could be, a belief that seemed more compatible with maintaining ARVN influence within the GVN, given that the bulk of resources and personnel on the U.S. side were also from the military.[75] Komer's view stemmed from his belief that it was essential to begin a much more comprehensive push to increase GVN control of the population imminently. This desire for quick progress was at odds with the careful incrementalism that underlay the objections of the civilian agencies.

Nor did Komer share the CIA's preoccupation with doctrine and the conceptual underpinnings of nation building. Komer did not believe that a successful program relied on "a sophisticated concept centrally orchestrated," but rather on "good" local GVN leadership that was provided with "adequate resources."[76] By eliding what was meant by "good" government in the context of South Vietnam—a problem that had clearly vexed the GVN itself—Komer placed his faith in an increase of scale. Unwilling to wait for the chance emergence of exceptional Vietnamese leaders like Chau, Komer hoped somehow to substitute American resources and know-how. Holbrooke, who had worked for USOM in South Vietnam, worried that his boss did not appreciate the difficulty of turning local policies that had been found to work in one area into larger, national schemes without a commensurate loss of quality.[77] Unlike officials in the civilian agencies, Komer was more concerned about quantity than quality. Though acknowledging that there was "great confusion, and widely differing views, on what pacification . . . means and how to carry it out," he was more impressed with the "*massive*" resources that would be available in 1967. "*By sheer weight alone, this mass application cannot help but produce significant results in 1967*," he told Johnson.[78]

Johnson was won over, and had decided by October 1966 that nation building should be placed under MACV.[79] Yet he was still reticent to ride roughshod over the civilian agencies or to make it appear that he was rushing to militarize nation building. Johnson therefore mandated that civilian agencies be given a ninety-day trial period from November to consolidate their own operations in South Vietnam and show results before nation building would be turned over to MACV. There is little evidence that anyone in Washington saw this arrangement, known as the Office of Civil Affairs (OCO), as more than a sop.[80] Johnson had come to understand that MACV's involvement and an emphasis on local security were necessary prerequisites to his larger ambitions, and to demonstrating progress in the war to the American public. General Harold K. Johnson, the secretary of the army, astutely judged the direction the political winds were blowing in this regard when he cabled Westmoreland to say that "the more I ruminate about the rate of progress in Vietnam and the inevitable relationship to our own elections in 1968, the more convinced I am that you will be given full responsibility for the program sometime after the first of the year [1967]."[81]

General Johnson turned out to be correct. In January, after the OCO had been in existence for several months, Westmoreland reported that detailed pacification planning, ARVN involvement in pacification, and the coordination of military and civilian assets in the field were all still problems.[82] By April, Major General William DePuy, Westmoreland's special assistant for pacification, was still reporting that pacification was "regressing" in I Corps, showing only "limited progress" in II and II Corps, and at a stalemate in IV Corps.[83] In late February, as the civilian agencies continued to fight what seemed an inevitable drift toward military control, Helms had the CIA prepare a paper for the State Department on the prospects for nation building in 1967. While again criticizing the "administrative, imposed connotation" of MACV's approach to nation building as against the more politically minded doctrine of the CIA, the paper warned against "undue expectations of rapid success" and stated that the goals set for 1967 were "modest," with a further million civilians to be added to "secure areas."[84]

With this implicit confession that although the CIA disapproved of the military's approach, it was not able to promise success either, Johnson took the final step and placed nation building entirely under MACV in May. He also decided to dispatch Komer to Saigon to head the new organization, and later in the month Komer followed Fraleigh and so many Americans before him in stepping off a plane into the Saigon heat. It had taken nearly two years since the war started, but America finally had a dedicated nation-building agency—and a man to run it—in South Vietnam. It now remained to be seen what it was capable of.

3

SETTING UP CORDS

When briefing the interminable stream of visitors who came from the United States to hear about the progress of the war effort in 1967, Brigadier General William Knowlton liked to show them a map. It depicted in red and green shades the areas of South Vietnam controlled by the Viet Minh and the French colonial regime at the time of the Geneva Accords in 1954. "Every Vietnamese government since 1954," he told one delegation, "has had to deal with the aftermath of this map." In parts of what used to be northern Annam—now the South Vietnamese military district of I Corps—children had grown to be adults while knowing nothing but rule by the Communist movement and its fronts. Even when Diem had the movement on the ropes in the late 1950s, there had still never been any effective GVN authority in these areas. Other large, densely populated provinces on the central coast—places like Binh Dinh, Phu Yen, and Quang Ngai—remained Communist bastions. Farther south, the Mekong Delta was a patchwork of red and green, and a menacing band of red hung like a noose around Saigon, from where ARVN's Hop Tac operations had failed to dislodge the Communists. And no map based on a concept as crude as physical control could account for the hidden allegiances of the rural population or the places where an underground Communist infrastructure still owned the night.[1]

It was telling that Knowlton could use a map from 1954 to illustrate the situation at the time of his briefing in late 1967. Despite the U.S. military escalation and a stabilization of the political situation in Saigon, the GVN had still made few inroads in the country's rural areas. But 1967 also brought the final creation of the Office of Civil Operations and Revolutionary Development Support (CORDS), which many American nation builders hoped would allow them to overcome the fragmented nature of their previous efforts to assist the GVN. An American nation-building agency that mirrored the GVN's own governmental organs from Saigon to the remotest district, CORDS was designed to allow the United States and the GVN to work together on joint plans to strengthen the South Vietnamese regime, build links with the rural population, and undermine the Communist movement's grip on the villages. But as 1967 drew to a close, it became increasingly clear that even as the Thieu-Ky regime proved more effective than its predecessors and the Communist movement was under pressure like never before, both the Americans and Vietnamese most committed to reform faced tough—and perhaps insurmountable—challenges.

War Comes to South Vietnam

When American combat units first arrived in South Vietnam in the summer of 1965, their immediate task was to stave off an imminent Communist victory. Both the NLF and regular North Vietnamese Army units had carried out increasingly audacious operations aimed at inflicting serious defeats on ARVN forces. Despite South Vietnamese operations around Saigon, the NLF military machine had continued to mobilize manpower in the area. In the waning days of 1964, it unleashed its newly created Ninth Division in the battle of Binh Gia near the capital. For four days the NLF occupied a government stronghold, repulsing counterattacks by the ARVN's strategic reserve, made up of elite ranger, airborne, and marine units. The South Vietnamese suffered hundreds of casualties, leaving two ranger companies and a marine battalion operationally ineffective. The NLF claimed to have suffered only a few dozen casualties, and they did not leave a single body on the battlefield. After achieving the NLF's greatest victory yet over the ARVN, the Ninth Division melted back into the countryside. An attempt to pursue them, named Operation Nguyen Van Nho after the slain commander of the marine battalion, turned up nothing.[2]

Although the Ninth Division was equipped with heavy weaponry infiltrated from North Vietnam, its manpower was drawn from Cochinchina. With the NLF's own forces capable of annihilating entire formations of the ARVN's strategic reserve, the entry of NVA units into the battle in the South promised even worse to come. As 1965 progressed, the NLF and NVA launched a general offensive. Le Duan, the Communist movement's paramount leader in Hanoi, hoped that the movement's forces could cause the collapse of the ARVN before the United States would have a chance to react and intervene. The movement's administrative infrastructure in South Vietnam moved into high gear, mobilizing peasants into the NLF's main force units. In a series of large operations in and around the Central Highlands, the NVA and NLF moved to force the government to deploy its strategic reserve and then annihilate it. Once these reserves had been worn down, the path would lay open for Communist forces to enter Saigon, hopefully accompanied by a mass civil uprising against the GVN and the Americans. By early June, Communist offensives were chewing through multiple ARVN battalions per week, presaging the imminent collapse of the force's cohesion and will to fight.[3]

These were the conditions in which the first American combat units arrived in 1965 under General William Westmoreland. U.S. forces had to spend considerable time establishing their bridgeheads, constructing an enormous logistical system, and managing the influx of troops before they were able to go on the offensive. By October 1966, there were about 350,000 American military personnel in theater. While the arrival of U.S. forces stiffened the resolve of the ARVN and allowed for spoiling operations to be launched to stave off imminent defeat, it was not until late 1966 that Westmoreland was equipped for a nationwide offensive. The search-and-destroy operations he launched throughout 1966 were mainly intended to keep Communist forces off balance and prevent them from massing for attacks on American or GVN strongholds. Nevertheless, poor American intelligence—compounded by the GVN's lack of supporters in the rural areas where battles were fought—meant that the Communists controlled the tempo of the fighting, and American units nearly always fought on the tactical defensive after suffering ambushes.[4]

The political situation in Saigon likewise settled into a stable but inconclusive and uninspiring pattern. The Thieu-Ky regime brought an end to the era of revolving-door coups, but there were few initial signs it would be able to restore even naked physical control of much of the country, much less win the complicity of the rural population. GVN local authorities had largely retreated to district towns and other fortified positions in the face of the Communist movement's growing administrative and military might. As James C. Scott has pointed out, the tendency of landlords and officials to flee and seek the protection of a distant state power that was so despised in many rural communities underscored their distance and alienation from the peasantry.[5] Even to reassert its presence sufficiently to rebuild the reviled apparatus of local government that had existed prior to the coup against Diem would be a huge task for the Thieu-Ky administration.

Between the start of the U.S. buildup and the creation of CORDS, American nation builders in Vietnam continued to operate in their previous stovepipe fashion. Governmental stability in Saigon, an increased availability of resources, and slightly improved coordination between military and civilian efforts enabled

American actions to have greater impact. But there continued to be widespread disagreement among Americans in different agencies about whether the impact they were having was the right one. These disagreements had only grown more heated in the precarious environment of the last few years. The analysts who wrote the *Pentagon Papers*, who were intimately familiar with American policy debates, noted that those interested in what was called pacification were "often in such violent disagreement as to what pacification meant that they quarreled publicly among themselves and overlooked their common interests."[6] As we saw in the previous chapter, this made the creation of CORDS controversial. But it also affected how pre-CORDS nation-building efforts developed, something that had an impact on the eventual workings of CORDS itself.

After 1965, nation-building efforts took place in a new military context. As American forces established themselves and began to push outward from their bases, they took on most of the burden of fighting large enemy units. ARVN forces, meanwhile, adopted the tasks of providing static defense to populated areas and—at least in theory—"pacification." As Westmoreland explained in July 1965, the United States would focus on "large, well organized and equipped [enemy] forces," which they would locate through search-and-destroy operations. Westmoreland hoped the United States could do most of its fighting in remote, sparsely populated areas, like the Ia Drang Valley, in which the first major clash between the United States and the NVA occurred in November 1965. Meanwhile, it fell to the ARVN to provide South Vietnamese villagers in the populated areas with security "from the guerrilla, the assassin, the terrorist and the informer." Westmoreland was cognizant of the need for nation building, but his concept of operations left undefined how exactly it was supposed to be achieved behind the military shield provided by the United States. As the military emergency of mid-1965 eased, both the CIA and USOM attempted to work with the GVN to provide an answer to this question.[7]

The CIA sought to capitalize on governmental stability in Saigon to transform the local cadre efforts discussed in chapter 1 into a national effort. In doing so, it worked with a number of key figures in the GVN. The first was Chau, who became head of a national cadre program established in November 1965 on Thieu's initiative.[8] The second key Vietnamese figure was Nguyen Duc Thang. Born in Cao Bang Province, a traditional home of rebels and independence fighters on the border with China, Thang entered a Viet Minh youth organization at the age of sixteen. Like Chau, he claimed to have left after the awe he felt toward his Communist superiors turned to unease and then disgust at their brutal actions. His family's social status was high enough to allow him to enter the University of Hanoi, and in 1952 he graduated from a French officer-candidate school as a classmate of Ky. After independence, Thang rose to the rank of major general in the ARVN, and Ky made him head of the GVN's Ministry of Rural Development (MORD) in late 1965. At Ky's insistence, MORD then assumed responsibility for the cadre program, with Thang as Chau's superior.[9]

The nucleus of the GVN's new cadre program was a training center at Vung Tau, a beach town near Saigon. By centralizing training and direction of the numerous local cadre programs that had sprung up over the previous years, both the Americans and Vietnamese involved in the effort hoped to produce a program with nationwide impact. Thang hoped to overcome the problems inherent in the patchwork nature of previous, local initiatives, arguing that "the principal problems in the situation are the lack of clear doctrine and definition of pacification; lack of a pacification plan since 1963, with military plans backing up a nonexistent pacification plan; no clear chain of command for pacification; and lack of clearly defined techniques for pacification."[10] Control by the central government also meant that Saigon would not have to fear that the cadres were being used to create local political bases or undermine the central state. As a result, existing local cadre programs were ordered dissolved and their personnel screened for aptitude and loyalty before being sent to Vung Tau to be molded into instruments of the GVN's nation-building agenda.[11]

The first class of what came to be known as the Revolutionary Development (RD) cadre matriculated at Vung Tau in February 1966, around the time of the Honolulu Conference.[12] Like their predecessors in Kien Hoa, the RD cadres were charged with befriending the villagers whom they served among, carrying out agitprop for the GVN, directing small-scale economic aid projects, and ferreting out NLF cadres and supporters. As an American who worked closely with the major Vietnamese figures behind the RD program said, they were "quick to admit that they have adopted and adapted to the RD Program much of the dogma and techniques of the Vietnamese Communists."[13] ARVN chief of staff Cao Van Vien himself described the RD concept as "Communist-inspired," whereas Don Luce and John Sommer called the cadres "imitation VC."[14] In this, the RD program followed the example of Chau's cadre effort in Kien Hoa.

On the one hand, the emergence of the RD program signaled that with the military and central political situation becoming less desperate, the GVN was ready to begin an effort to establish a rural political base. As the U.S. Mission wrote in its campaign plan for 1967, "Revolutionary Development is the integrated military and civil process to restore, consolidate, and expand government control so that nation-building can progress throughout the Republic of Viet-Nam."[15] The RD cadres were to be the "vanguard elements" of this process.[16] But on the other hand, attempting to achieve this goal via a cadre program modeled on the NLF was paradoxical. Chau had designed his cadre system in Kien Hoa on the assumption that the regular GVN bureaucracy was irredeemable. Like the

NLF, he aimed not to improve that bureaucracy, but to supplant it. The result had been the system of "parapolitics" described by Chau's CIA handler Stuart Methven, who became an acolyte of the approach he learned from his Vietnamese colleague. According to Methven, parapolitics was an emergency measure taken when the regular government could not be reformed quickly enough to deliver necessary results, as was the case in South Vietnam. Although it was hoped that the cadres would "provide the bridge for the government to cross over so that it can establish itself among the broad base of the population," this was by no means guaranteed, especially if the government remained unreformed. In fact, the recourse to parapolitical measures could actually delay the reform of the regular government because the province and district leaderships were not themselves required to build support among the people.[17] As an emergency measure, parapolitics could hence retard the ultimate goal of nation building.

A further problem with the RD program was the relationship of the cadres to local GVN authorities. The Communist movement's cadres became the leaders of the villages in which they served, and were at the bottom of a chain of command that passed through NLF district and province leaderships until ultimately terminating in Hanoi.[18] This created a structure of authority that paralleled the GVN and competed with it for the complicity of the peasantry and to mobilize their resources for the war effort. Like the NLF, the RD cadres also paralleled the regular GVN authorities at the villages and hamlet level. But this made much less sense when their ultimate aim was to reform and proselytize for the GVN rather than to destroy it, as the Communists sought to do. Furthermore, the parapolitical structure of an RD cadre was extremely shallow, having no presence above the village level. RD cadres were ultimately responsible to the local GVN province chief, meaning they had little practical authority or capacity for independent action. There was no guarantee that the province chiefs would be interested in addressing GVN abuses that the RD cadres reported, which were mostly the result of the province chief's own actions. This system had worked in Kien Hoa because Chau was the province chief, providing the cadre with a link to an individual who could address the grievances of the population. But Chau had been a rare kind of province chief, and mostly the RD cadres were either ignored or used as a regular paramilitary without any political function. At best, they might build sympathy for the GVN through their personal actions, but they could not systematically reform it.[19]

The RD program was riven by disagreements, both between the Vietnamese and the Americans and on the GVN side itself. Chau was convinced that nation building in South Vietnam could be successful only if the idea of South Vietnamese nationhood was fostered. He had learned from his time observing how the Viet Minh functioned that there needed to be a "sense of nationalistic conviction and motivation on the part of everyone involved" to rival the impetus provided by the Communist movement. Only then could the "colonial and postcolonial legacy" of the GVN be overcome.[20] Like Colby and Methven, he placed a high premium on the indoctrination of cadres and the ideas they would espouse in the villages. Chau wanted the cadres to operate in teams of eighty each, with half dedicated to the political work of proselytizing for the GVN, mapping out the aspirations and allegiances of local villagers, and reporting grievances. The remaining forty would provide paramilitary functions, both protecting the team and training village militia after the fashion of the NLF's local guerrillas. But with Colby back in Washington, Chau found that the local CIA leadership had different ideas. Chief of Station Gordon Jorgenson pushed for fifty-man teams, with forty assigned to paramilitary duties and only ten carrying out the political tasks that Chau considered the heart of the program. The CIA's offer to house his headquarters in their own facility in Saigon also convinced Chau that the Americans did not understand the GVN's need to protect its nationalist credentials. The figure of fifty-nine-man teams was eventually agreed, but this was much closer to the American position and led Chau to react angrily by attempting to marginalize Americans involved with the effort.[21]

Chau and the CIA managed to maintain a working relationship, however fractious. But Chau eventually fell victim to the still-unstable political situation within the South Vietnamese government itself. Although Thieu and Ky had brought an end to the era of continuous coups, their regime remained beset by internal fissures and conflicts of personality. Chief among them was the conflict between Thieu and Ky themselves. The two men both suspected that the other was attempting to build a personal power base and relationship with the Americans in order to eventually sideline his rival and emerge as the paramount leader of South Vietnam. Chau's position at the forefront of an effort to build a rural political base for the GVN made him a natural target of suspicion for Ky loyalists, who suspected that this base might ultimately serve the interests of Chau's patron, Thieu. The situation took a surreal twist when Chau discovered that Vung Tau's commander, Captain Le Xuan Mai, was an adherent of the Dai Viet, an anti-Communist Vietnamese political party that had been involved in the disputes and coups of the post-Diem years. The party was much more radical even than Chau in its desire to overthrow the Vietnamese social and political order, and vehemently opposed to Ky, whom it considered corrupt and licentious. Like most non-Communist Vietnamese nationalists, the Dai Viet had never been able to advance beyond its urban, educated base. Now it appeared that Captain Mai and a band of like-minded instructors had been using the Vung Tau center to indoctrinate cadres to spread not only anti-Communism but also the Dai Viet's heavily antigovernment and anti-Ky beliefs in the rural areas. Chau and John

Paul Vann believed that CIA personnel, having never bothered to translate the training material used at the center into English, had not noticed.[22]

Whether this was true or not, the issue blew into the open when Chau attempted to have Mai dismissed and take over the operations of the center himself. In response, a large number of instructors at Vung Tau distributed weapons and organized their students to put up armed resistance to Chau's appointment. Perhaps hoping he would mishandle the situation and so could then be dismissed, Thang placed a battalion of paratroopers at Chau's disposal and told him to do whatever was necessary to restore order. Chau instead managed to restore order peacefully and persuade Mai to move on through unclear means. Shortly afterward, he quit the government to seek office as a legislator, apparently in disgust at political infighting in the GVN. The affair showed that even if the ARVN generals had stopped launching coups against each other, political and personality clashes still hampered the emergence of GVN institutions at the center, much less in the rural areas.[23]

The Office of Rural Affairs started by Rufus Phillips and Bert Fraleigh was also afflicted by conflict in the years prior to the creation of CORDS. The duo's attempt to transform USOM by building up a network of provincial government advisers had run into opposition among more traditional USAID personnel who believed the aid mission should focus its efforts on the central government in Saigon. In 1964, James "Big Jim" Killen, former head of USAID's mission in South Korea, became head of USOM. In Seoul, Killen had pushed hard for USAID to avoid taking on too many of the functions the South Korean government should have been performing for itself, and he brought similar priorities with him to Saigon. Questioning whether provincial agents tended to sap the autonomy of GVN local government by "institutionalizing an excessive dependence on the USOM representative to do things they should be doing for themselves," he took steps to reduce the influence of Fraleigh's young Tigers in the provinces.[24] Somewhat paradoxically, Killen also took aim at the system of providing province representatives a per diem to live off the local economy, arguing that they should be provided with a higher standard of living as a means of inducing respect from the Vietnamese. He eventually launched security investigations against a number of Tigers—including, in some cases, on the spurious grounds that they had homosexual relationships with their Vietnamese counterparts—and in late 1964 had Fraleigh and thirty of the Tigers recalled to Washington.[25] Fraleigh eventually resigned from USAID altogether in 1967, disgusted by what he viewed as the gutting of the program he had helped establish. Back in Washington, one Tiger penned a ballad titled "The Legend of James D. Killen" to lament the changes. "The moral of the story, is plain with A-I-D," it read, "You don't work for the people, you work for bureaucracy!"[26]

Although Killen's moves seemed to go against the trend of increased American involvement in South Vietnamese rural affairs, his opposition to the Tigers won him support in some quarters. Both the philosophy behind the program Fraleigh had established and the personnel he had recruited to staff it came in for criticism as American involvement in South Vietnam grew and the problem of nation building drew the attention of other agencies. As we saw in the previous chapter, Fraleigh had sent his young charges forth into the provinces with a general remit to make provincial government run more smoothly, develop links between it and the rural population, and enthuse the Vietnamese with American can-do spirit. But other Americans increasingly began to question whether "BA generalists" recruited from the Peace Corps and IVS could effectively advise the grizzled ARVN majors and colonels who made up the majority of South Vietnamese province chiefs. "You couldn't get a province chief to listen to a boy of 22 or 23," said one USOM official who served in South Vietnam in 1966, summing up a common perspective. "He knew he wouldn't have the experience."[27] Chau remembered that the first time he saw the American sent to be his adviser in Kien Hoa Province, he thought "I don't need any babies down in this province; I've got enough problems."[28] One adviser even wrote a ditty that mocked the pretensions of his youthful colleagues. "Now Colonel, you're forty, I'm just twenty-two," it began, "but I've been to college, so I'll advise you!"[29]

Others took aim at the materialistic philosophy that lay behind USOM's activities, focusing as they did on hoping that villagers would be so grateful for minor economic aid projects that they would abandon a Communist movement whose bread and butter was nationalism, revolution, and social empowerment. One older American who worked alongside the Tigers was openly contemptuous of what he regarded as a "pathetic reliance on the belief that good works like fertilizer and improved rice seed are an end in themselves without regard to the political implications these things involve."[30] Colby was likewise concerned with having USOM involved in village cadre efforts, believing they were "technical adviser[s] ... [and] not, as a rule, operationally oriented."[31] As the war escalated, more and more Americans were in a hurry to see concrete results from their nation-building efforts, and dismissive of the idea that simply providing economic goods to the villagers was enough. While Fraleigh had stressed that the Tigers' goal was to help the Vietnamese people, the generation of advisers who served during the military buildup were more inclined to believe that, as one put it, "your primary purpose in going overseas is the interest of the United States government. It is not the interest of Vietnam—this is *our* foreign policy that we are implementing."[32] Altruism would not be enough to achieve U.S. goals.

In the northern reaches of South Vietnam, the U.S. Marine Corps was carrying out its own program to attempt to strengthen the GVN. These were known as the Combined Action Platoons, or CAPs. The CAPs aimed to expand a zone of security around Marine installations and populated areas in I Corps, the Marine Corps area of operations in South Vietnam.[33] Integrating closely with an ARVN unit and living in close proximity to South Vietnamese villagers, the Marines trained the GVN soldiers and carried out civic action projects in an attempt both to provide security and to win over the villagers to the GVN's cause. One recent writer has declared CAPs to have been "the conflict's best example of American COIN [counterinsurgency]," and other authors have argued that they should have been extended beyond I Corps to other parts of South Vietnam.[34]

But while the CAPs had limited success as a tool of counterinsurgency, they were no more capable of nation building than any other U.S. initiatives in the war to date. William R. Corson, the Marine Corps officer who was in charge of the CAP program at its height, considered the CAPs mainly a means of protecting Marine bases. It was explicitly not a program that aimed at preparing the GVN to be self-sufficient in the event of U.S. withdrawal, or to establish ties of mutual obligation between the GVN and its citizens that would enable the GVN to meet the challenge of the Vietnamese Communist movement. Corson viewed the GVN as a predatory institution that it was best to cut entirely out of the process of providing for local security and economic benefits to the Vietnamese people. Instead, he focused on direct interface between Marine units and Vietnamese villagers, and on winning support through manipulating what he called the "acquisitive bent of the Oriental."[35] The CAPs hence combined the "parapolitical" weaknesses of the RD program with the excessive materialist focus that marked USOM's efforts. As Colonel Robert Montague, Komer's military aide and later an official in CORDS, pointed out, the impact of the CAPs was not "permanent" because "everyone knew the Marines weren't going to be there very long."[36] Lacking any answer to the problem of reforming the GVN in a holistic manner, Corson was instead reduced on one occasion to punching a corrupt district chief in the face.[37]

The deficiencies and failures of these previous American nation-building efforts formed the background for the creation of CORDS. The bureaucratic rivalries and ideological disagreements that had afflicted them did not disappear when they were amalgamated into the new agency. And despite CORDS's clever bureaucratic structure, mirroring as it did the GVN at every level from Saigon to the districts, there was no guarantee that Americans and Vietnamese would be able to work together in harmony, or that they even ultimately shared the same goals. A punch in the face was unlikely to improve matters, but would CORDS do any better?

Setting Up CORDS

By May 1967, many of the individuals who would be key players in the U.S. nation-building effort until the end of the war were in Saigon. At the beginning of the month, Ellsworth Bunker arrived to take up the post of ambassador, and General Creighton Abrams arrived to serve as Westmoreland's deputy, charged with overseeing the development of the ARVN. Komer arrived to take over as head of CORDS, which was established in late May.[38] In Saigon, Komer became a civilian deputy to Westmoreland with the personal rank of ambassador, equivalent to a four-star general. As the deputy for CORDS (or DepCORDS) to Westmoreland, he had at his disposal the resources of all civilian U.S. agencies concerned with nation building, and a sizable military contingent as well. L. Wade Lathram, who had been director of the transitional Office of Civil Operations, became Komer's deputy. His deputy in turn was Knowlton, who had been head of MACV's Revolutionary Development Support division.[39] Komer also obtained responsibility for U.S. efforts to develop local militia forces to counter the NLF, and for rooting out the NLF's administrative and political infrastructure in the villages. CORDS hence took responsibility for the war in the villages in all its civil and military components. Such an organization was unique in American history. As an official history noted: "To have civilians fully operating in a military chain of command was extremely rare in the history of the United States; it had certainly never before occurred on such a scale."[40]

At the level of each of the four military corps commands in South Vietnam, the OCO director for each region became the corps DepCORDS, charged with overseeing advice to the GVN's civil government. He then assumed control of an integrated military/civilian staff that paralleled that of CORDS in Saigon, along with the ability to supervise the chief U.S. adviser to ARVN forces in the corps areas on matters pertaining to the support of nation building.[41] At the province level, the current civilian and military teams were consolidated into one organization with a single manager. Either the senior civilian or military officer was elevated to the position of overall manager, known as province senior adviser (PSA), with the other as his deputy. This led to a "sandwich" management structure in which a civilian boss always had a military deputy, and vice versa. The decision as to which arrangement to adopt in each province was taken on "the basis of security in the province, civil-military balance in the RD effort and [the] qualifications and experience" of the personnel involved.[42] In areas where security was poor, the PSA was more likely to hail from the military, and the initial balance saw twenty-five military PSAs versus twenty-two civilians.[43] Finally, the arrangements at the district level largely mirrored those at province, with the exception that owing to the severity of the security situation in 1967 and the fact that not all districts had OCO representatives at the time CORDS was created, in most cases the officer serving as MACV district adviser was appointed the district senior adviser (DSA), with a civilian deputy.[44]

The result was a nation-building organization of unparalleled reach and size. Tens of thousands of Americans would join CORDS to work on nation-building tasks during the remainder of the war. Although it has often been alleged that the United States failed at nation building in South Vietnam because key figures failed to be interested in the problem, the CORDS system won the full support of Bunker, Westmoreland, and Abrams. Komer had no complaints about his relationship with Bunker, which he characterized as "intimate."[45] Using a phrase that would later be associated with Abrams's tenure as commander of MACV, Bunker told both U.S. civilian and military leaders in South Vietnam in May 1967 that he favored a "one war" approach to the conflict that combined military and civilian assets both to fight the war and strengthen the GVN. Though his call to facilitate the GVN in carrying out a "social revolution" was vague and contrary to Komer's focus on local security, he gave Komer wide latitude to work as he wished.[46] Bunker's backing was important, as under a system that had first been established by a grant of authority from President Johnson to Ambassador Maxwell Taylor in 1964, the ambassador was the senior American in South Vietnam, to whom even the commander of MACV was subordinate. Bunker chaired the Mission Council, a policy-making body that consisted of the local heads of the various American agencies in the country along with the ambassador's deputy and the MACV commander. With the creation of CORDS, Komer took a chair in the council, and he also attended Westmoreland's leadership conferences with his top subordinates. Despite the allegation by Lewis Sorley that Westmoreland was uncomprehending of nation building, Komer found Westmoreland highly supportive and believed that "the way Westmoreland handled the thing was one of the basic reasons why CORDS worked."[47]

As well as giving all of the Americans interested in nation building one high-ranking voice in American councils, CORDS also finally eliminated the problems created by the "autonomous baronies" of the various U.S. agencies that Colby had described. The U.S. presence in the provinces and districts was now unified under one chain of command and spoke to its South Vietnamese counterparts with one voice. With the inclusion of military assets, CORDS was also able to have a presence in every district throughout South Vietnam. This was of particular importance to Komer, who had brought with him from Washington his belief in the importance of the primacy of local security for nation building. There was now a single organization, stretching from Saigon to the remotest districts, which had the capacity to coordinate all necessary resources on the U.S. side in support of nation-building plans and programs and then to work with the GVN to see them implemented.

Komer set to work on the same "fascinating" management problems that had captivated him in Washington. For CORDS to work, the GVN would need to develop central institutions capable of conceiving a nation-building strategy and implementing it throughout the country. The ministry would develop national concepts for nation building, decide on priority areas for their implementation, and then allocate the resources accordingly and direct the local personnel involved. As well as helping conceive the plans at the center, CORDS would also help to execute them at each level of government down to the district. In theory, this top-down cooperation between Americans and South Vietnamese would allow for sweeping reforms of the GVN directed from the center.

CORDS could be viewed as a bureaucratic scaffold erected around the GVN's organs of governance, allowing American workmen to access all parts of the regime from top to bottom. In theory, they would work in harmony with their South Vietnamese counterparts in the structure itself to improve the regime. It would also make it easier for Saigon to control and reform its own structure of rural government, as the central regime could work with the Americans manning the scaffold to intervene in district and provincial governance. This would allow the United States and the GVN to jointly move beyond the stopgap measures of the RD cadre program, which after CORDS was set up came to be viewed as a "transitional" step. RD had led the way by being "the first GVN program that had truly national scope," but now the focus was on developing the GVN's "normal processes of government." Parapolitical emergency measures would become a thing of the past as CORDS enabled a wholesale, top-down reform of the GVN.[48] As Frank Scotton later wrote, "reform, unlike revolution, must start at the top."[49] But as we shall see, there was always the potential for disagreements between the American and GVN workmen scurrying around the scaffold, and no guarantee that the measures CORDS pushed would be beneficial in any case. However well designed in theory, CORDS in practice would require a complex process of compromise and negotiation to work.

Making this work involved avoiding a number of pitfalls of which the American nation builders who had come before CORDS, and their Vietnamese counterparts, were well aware. One was ensuring that the new, more muscular American organization did not undermine the very GVN capacities it was designed to develop. CORDS was, as its name implied, a *support* organization. CORDS officials were not supposed to run village governments, distribute rice to refugees, or personally root out the NLF's political cadres. Rather, they were to help develop the GVN's capacity to do these things for itself. As Komer put it, the nation-building effort had "room to breathe behind the military shield" created by Westmoreland's offensives in 1966–1967, but it was a "GVN responsibility, with the U.S. providing advice and resources."[50] This made the sustainability of any strengthening of the GVN critical. As Montague had pointed out in his critique of the Marine CAPs, CORDS was not going to be around forever. Bunker put it like this in January 1969: "My yardstick of success here is what the Vietnamese can do themselves, because that eventually is the ultimate test. They've got to take over someday. It's quite clear that we're not going to be here forever. And what *we* can get them to do—through instruction, through persuasion, through pressure, in whatever way—to do the job themselves is the ultimate yardstick of success."[51] Yet this was not the whole story. CORDS personnel did not generally perceive their role as merely to unthinkingly support whatever the GVN wanted to do, but rather to influence the GVN to reform in ways the Americans believed conducive to its long-term survival. In this respect, CORDS had more of the spirit of Fraleigh and his young Tigers than of the traditional USAID bureaucrats represented by Killen. According to Fraleigh, an off-color joke that did the rounds among more action-oriented Americans in South Vietnam concerned a bull brought in by USAID for "stud purposes" who "refused to perform because he was there as an 'advisor' only." It is no wonder this joke was popular among the province and district advisers of CORDS, many of whom came from the military and believed along with Fraleigh in the need to offer "positive solutions" to the GVN's problems.[52] This meant that CORDS aimed to influence and change and not just "support" the Saigon regime. Few Americans in South Vietnam had any illusions about the deficiencies of the GVN by 1967, and there was widespread understanding that reform might often involve making the South Vietnamese act in ways they did not want to. As Chau had discovered in the conflict over the size of his cadre teams, the fact that the United States was providing resources for a program often gave it a lot of influence over its design. As Komer described in 1970:

> The Vietnamese ran every single operating program. Pacification was and is 99 percent pure Vietnamese in its staffing. Now, we did an awful lot of advising, managing, prodding, cajoling, and where necessary, pressuring from behind the scenes. We were the bankers. We provided the bulk of the logistics support. We were the shadow management. Most of the new initiatives in pacification, most of the program design, the management techniques, were ours, but transferred to the Vietnamese. I think that pacification stands as a model of U.S.-Vietnamese rapport.[53]

In this passage, Komer describes many of the different ways that U.S. officials interacted with their GVN counterparts. Because CORDS staff were not directly in the GVN chain of command, they always had to operate via the indirect exercise of influence. "The totality of our U.S. effort is inserted into the society of [South Vietnam] at thousands of key points—each one is referred to as a

Vietnamese counterpart," a U.S. Army report titled *A Program for the Pacification and Long-Term Development of Vietnam* (PROVN) had asserted. "Whether, and how, he can be influenced is crucial to the achievement of U.S. objectives."[54] The means of influencing GVN officials ran the gamut from persuasion and flattery to the threat of sanctions or the application of some other form of pressure.

The correct amount of pressure or "leverage" to place on the GVN was one of the issues that had long divided U.S. nation builders. Too direct an involvement in South Vietnamese affairs was controversial in the USAID mission. The extent of USOM's deployment in the rural areas of South Vietnam was unprecedented in its history, and was resisted by some officials.[55] In late 1966, a journalist who covered USOM's activities in South Vietnam wrote that it was "axiomatic in the United States mission that you must 'get along with your Vietnamese counterpart' or get out."[56] Even after the creation of CORDS, Komer believed that this attitude "lasted on in USAID, those parts that were not under our control."[57]

At the other end of the spectrum of the debate on leverage were the military authors of PROVN, all of whom had extensive experience in South Vietnam. The study's authors considered "nonfunctioning Vietnamese officialdom" to be "the crux of the matter and the harsh reality of our situation" and called for a high degree of involvement by U.S. personnel in the affairs of South Vietnam. "If we lose in Vietnam," the report noted, "we pay the price no matter how carefully American officials rationalize the need to respect Vietnamese sovereignty." PROVN painted a picture of a GVN that was unable to save itself and would need the United States to "stimulat[e] social reform as required" if it were to survive. Paraphrasing the Serenity Prayer, the authors said that U.S. personnel must possess "the courage to become directly involved where we must, the patience to abstain when appropriate and the wisdom to know the difference."[58] Colonel Volney Warner, who had worked on PROVN and then joined William Leonhart's White House office, continued banging the drum during 1967. Warner called for a "scaffolding of influence" that allowed for the exercise of leverage by relatively low-level personnel in CORDS, including the ability for PSAs to withdraw support from GVN provincial programs that were not performing. He also raised the issue of "an explicitly negotiated U.S.-GVN influence relationship" that would lay down obligations on both parties and allow for the exercise of sanctions on the GVN, such as the withholding of funds for key programs, if necessary.[59]

Komer had his own ideas about how leverage ought to be used to improve GVN performance. Eschewing grand theories of leverage, Komer was insistent that its exercise was an art of the possible and that it be used discriminately rather than as part of a formal framework. Komer would have agreed with White House advisers who exulted that "for the first time the Mission structure is sufficiently integrated to permit its influence to be properly focused."[60] By unifying the U.S.

nation-building effort, CORDS had created the capacity to coordinate the exercise of leverage against all levels of GVN officialdom, from Saigon down into individual villages. But Komer continued to believe that the best way to exercise influence over the South Vietnamese was informally and quietly. Many of the South Vietnamese officials involved in attempting to reform the GVN—especially Chau and Thang—were particularly sensitive to the charge that they served American masters, especially when they went against the preferences of their own countrymen. Komer hence wanted to retain tight control over the exercise of leverage rather than devolving it to lower levels.[61] As he explained in January 1968, "I do not want leverage considered as an advisory tool available to all our field personnel. It should only be applied at certain key power centers and only when other advisory techniques have not brought results. Even then, as few people as possible should know that we imposed our way and what methods we employed to do so."[62] This did not mean that CORDS personnel in the provinces were not supposed to try to influence their GVN counterparts; that was in fact the sum total of their job. What it did mean was that the direct imposition of the U.S. will or the use of coercion was to be limited. Komer was willing to go only so far away from the old USAID admonition to get along with your Vietnamese counterpart or get out. Given that the work of CORDS depended on a good relationship with GVN officials, threats to remove American support or resources would jeopardize the daily functioning of CORDS if they caused a GVN official to "lose face by knuckling under to his advisor."[63] Komer directed that if disputes arose at the provincial level over the actions of GVN officials, then PSAs should get the official to agree to an action plan and hold him accountable for implementation. But if cooperation was not forthcoming, then the PSA's only recourse was to report the incident up the chain of command. Komer, Westmoreland, and Bunker would then decide what action was to be taken in light of overall U.S. interest.[64] Westmoreland also favored a "low key, behind the scenes" approach to influencing the GVN.[65] How much change could be leveraged out of the GVN under such conditions would be a key question for CORDS.

Komer had once been in favor of a greater use of leverage but believed that he had "mellowed" since arriving in-country and realizing "that the practical problems just look a lot different when you're out there on the implementing end."[66] While he acknowledged that the United States had to pressure the GVN into reforms, this pressure had to be carefully calibrated so as not to undermine the independence of the GVN in the long term. It was also crucial to avoid a nationalist backlash that would make the GVN's task of winning over the rural population even more difficult. For the thousands of Americans who now came to South Vietnam convinced they could leverage useful reform from the country's regime, doing so both effectively and sensitively became the key challenge ahead.

CORDS's First Year

It was in Komer's hard-pushing nature to hit the ground running. After CORDS was established in May 1967, he set about trying to have an immediate impact on the effectiveness of the GVN's local government. As during his time in Washington, he seemed to place his faith in the mass application of American resources to achieve this end. He had little to say about long-running disagreements between U.S. agencies over how best to pursue nation building, for instance whether the provision of economic goods or the intangibles of motivation and ideology were more important. Komer's general message was for everyone to push harder on all fronts, and eventually the GVN would muddle through. But his efforts were frustrated by two long-running problems in South Vietnam: the rural security situation and the return of governmental instability in Saigon. Faced with these challenges, Komer and CORDS appeared to be as helpless as their predecessors.

Komer's attempt to have an immediate impact on GVN performance was known as Project Takeoff. He named it for Walt Rostow's theory of economic takeoff, which held that developing countries passed through a number of stages of economic development before taking off into self-sustaining growth.[67] In a vivid demonstration of the impossibility of applying large-scale visions of modernization to wartime South Vietnam, Komer's goals in the project were considerably more limited.

While Thang had attempted in 1967 to impose on provincial and district governments an overall national plan for strengthening the GVN, based largely on the RD cadre effort, he had failed. Corps commanders and province chiefs continued to operate as they wished, with little fear of punishment if they did not follow central direction. As was typical in South Vietnam, the program had also been slow to begin until after the Tet celebrations, which fell at the end of January.[68] In the words of CORDS officials, the GVN's reform efforts for the year remained hampered by an adverse security situation, "a general lack of enthusiasm among officials at all levels of GVN participation," and the limited ability of central GVN officials such as Thang to coordinate and influence local government around the country.[69] These were the perennial bugbears of South Vietnamese rural governance. Security problems continued, and no major improvement appeared to be on the horizon if the war remained within its current dynamics. A major CORDS report in August concluded: "The VC have the capability to counter pacification throughout SVN with few exceptions. The strength of the infrastructure and local VC units has not changed substantially despite successes . . . against main force units."[70] In other words, the struggle for security, much less nation building, was only just beginning. It was around this time that Knowlton was briefing visitors from Washington with a map that showed how little progress had been made in controlling the countryside since 1954.

A fundamental problem faced by the GVN as it attempted to spread its administrative control throughout the country was a lack of resources. Even with U.S. forces fighting the bulk of the main-force war, the GVN did not have the military or administrative assets to control all of the countryside at the same time. Even where an ARVN presence could be established, South Vietnamese soldiers were frequently abusive toward the local population and defined their goal narrowly as preventing the visible movement of enemy units. This meant that an ARVN presence might appear to provide "security" while doing nothing to challenge covert NLF administration, much less the population's allegiance to it. The main U.S.-backed attempt to bridge the gap between the people and the GVN's local organs thus far—the RD cadres—were often unwelcome in the villages as well. But even if they had been successful, there were not enough RD cadres to go around. This was especially the case given the high rate of attrition they suffered. In the summer of 1967, the political scientist Samuel Huntington arrived in South Vietnam for a six-week study of the GVN's nation-building program. After visiting fifteen provinces in all four corps areas, Huntington concluded that "improvements in security produced by the introduction of a governmental presence last only so long as the presence lasts." After government forces left, the NLF's administration resurfaced. Noting that the United States and the GVN did not have "sufficient military forces, administrative personnel, or RD cadres to saturate the entire countryside simultaneously," Huntington concluded that *"pacification by itself cannot produce comprehensive or lasting rural security."*[71]

Project Takeoff was CORDS's attempt to improve the situation against this grim background. The project was, according to one briefing, "designed to focus attention on the top priorities and to marshall the effort and the resources to make pacification work."[72] It did not involve any new projects or initiatives, but rather was designed to emphasize the activities that Komer felt were most important at that stage. Project Takeoff accordingly set eight priorities: improving 1968 planning, accelerating a program called Chieu Hoi aimed at encouraging defections from the NLF, mounting an attack on the NLF's infrastructure, expanding and improving ARVN support of pacification, expanding the RD effort, increasing refugee-handling capabilities, revamping the police, and pressing land reform.[73] These were all goals the GVN was already pursuing. Nation builders who had been in the country longer than Komer were quick to note the lack of originality in the plan. John Paul Vann wrote to Daniel Ellsberg in August that "Komer has been a big disappointment to me" and sardonically questioned the value of a plan that was a mere "intensification of current efforts."[74] Others shared Vann's skepticism. Corson, the Marine officer who was handy with his fists, stated: "Komer made it plain to the CORDS people that they were going to do better and were going to operate as a team, but then he neglected to make clear exactly *what* they were to do."[75] Much as the attempt by Washington officials to urge forty-one different programs on the GVN in the summer of 1965 had shown they lacked a coherent plan, Project Takeoff was a sign that Komer had no clear sense of priorities or idea of how to deliver a radical departure in U.S. efforts.

Nor did Komer manage to make headway in winning the cooperation of key figures in the GVN for a joint program in 1967. Without the involvement of the Saigon leadership in drawing up the CORDS programs, there was little incentive for provincial and district officials around the country to follow them. With the Americans remaining outside the chain of command and acting merely as advisers, GVN officials had nothing to gain by following a program that their own bosses in Saigon seemed to regard as unimportant. Even if Komer had possessed a clear and incisive vision for how to achieve nation building, rather than a vague list of priorities, he would have been stymied by the continued infighting and lack of focus on rural nation building that continued to characterize Saigon politics.

The problem started with Thieu and Ky. Bolstered by the American support he had received during the Honolulu Conference, in early 1966 Ky tried to orchestrate the ouster of the Vietnamese commander of I Corps, Nguyen Chanh Thi. The son of a French mandarin from the old imperial capital of Hue, Thi had been one of the most independent of the corps commanders, running his realm as a personal fiefdom. Following the practice of local strongmen back to the days of the emperors, Thi aligned himself much more closely with local political forces in the northern reaches of South Vietnam than he did with the central government. In his case, this meant cultivating ties with the activist Buddhist movement, which was strong in and around Hue. Though this movement was extremely diverse, its core idea was a rejection of violence by both the Communists and the GVN and an embrace of what one activist called "the politics of reconciliation to bring peace and happiness to the country." The movement's leaders refused to take a stance in favor of either side in the war, viewing soldiers on both sides as helpless peasants who were "victims of society's ignorance and injustice."[76] The moral evenhandedness of the movement was interpreted by the GVN as tacit support for the Communists, and the movement was even suspected of being secretly directed from Hanoi. Thi's flirtation with the movement was hence extremely provocative to Saigon. When Ky finally moved against Thi, Buddhist leaders declared a "struggle movement" and attracted dissident ARVN units to protect them. After months of a tense standoff, loyalist ARVN units crushed the dissidents in street-to-street fighting in Hue and Da Nang. Thi was sent into exile and the Buddhist leader Thich Tri Quang put under house arrest, ending the struggle movement.[77]

From the perspective of Thieu and Ky, the removal of Thi was a necessary step to decrease the autonomy of a corps commander who had gone too far. It also meant crushing the last organized movement in South Vietnamese urban politics that was strongly anti-American, as the burning of the U.S. consulate in Hue during the struggle movement had demonstrated.[78] But it also had other consequences. During the course of quelling the movement, the duo felt compelled to agree to a timeline for the national constitutional assembly and subsequent elections they had agreed to in principle at the Honolulu Conference. This would mean a civilianization of the government, at least formally, with either Thieu or Ky leaving the armed forces and becoming the civilian president. Although the Thieu-Ky regime had seen off the last major non-Communist challenge to the Saigon regime until the end of the war, they now became absorbed in the question of what the outcome of the election would be. Until September 1967 when the elections were held, Thieu and Ky were engaged in a struggle for power with each other to determine who would emerge as the paramount figure in the GVN. They had little time to worry about CORDS. Project Takeoff was not briefed to GVN officials because "the attention and effort of the GVN has been so taken up with the elections that Takeoff would not have been understood or given the time it merits."[79] Komer nevertheless brought the subject up with Ky, who gave it a "vague blessing."[80] In these conditions, even with the best ideas in the world, CORDS could accomplish little.

According to Vann, it was "absolute madness" to expect programs drawn up unilaterally by Americans without the backing of Saigon to be followed by provincial and district governments throughout the country.[81] Local advisers were left to attempt to persuade their GVN counterparts on their own, a task made only marginally easier by the creation of CORDS. The new agency did at least put an end to what Bui Diem called the "rivalries and bureaucratic games" fought between Americans at the local level when their efforts had been split between various agencies. This had diluted American influence by overloading local GVN officials with conflicting advice, making it easy for them to ignore it.[82] Yet while the creation of CORDS did at least unify advisory functions on the American side, this did not necessarily make it easier for local advisers to exercise leverage over their counterparts.

The ability of CORDS advisers to achieve their goals was dependent entirely on how they managed their relationship with their GVN counterpart. Advisers communicated extensively with their GVN counterparts and often became aware of a gaping chasm in worldview and priorities. Advisers necessarily spent much of their time managing this relationship. They could not impose their will through coercion, and most believed it counterproductive to establish a belligerent or hectoring relationship with their counterpart. Instead, they likened their roles as akin to acting as diplomats, lobbyists, or confidence tricksters.[83]

Most province chiefs hailed from the urban, French-influenced class and had little understanding of the rural population. They had risen to field-grade ranks in the ARVN, meaning they had likely participated in the war against the Viet Minh on the side of the French, or been trained by officers who had. What contact they did have with the rural population thus far in their career had often been down a gun barrel. And having risen to respectable ranks in the byzantine politics of the ARVN without been killed or purged, province chiefs frequently went about their new jobs with an abundance of caution. Most American advisers found their counterparts difficult to persuade to change their established patterns of behavior just because an enthusiastic new American had arrived in their orbit. Americans were often struck by what they regarded as the lethargy of Vietnamese local officials, while others complained that the chiefs hardly knew their provinces better than the Americans did and refused to travel around them.[84]

How to manage their counterpart relationship correctly was the key task facing CORDS advisers, and often forced them into compromises. Having few methods of acting unilaterally, they had to accomplish almost everything in cooperation with local officials. "This is the Vietnamese country and we're advisors," explained one American who served in 1966. "This is one of the things we have to realize—we are nothing but advisors and when we act in any capacity other than advisors we are out of our element. I think that persuasion is the word that is necessary and I think that it is very necessary to be able to persuade by being knowledgeable and know what we're doing."[85] Another adviser, who served in I Corps in the same year, felt that doing anything against the wishes of the province chief was unwise. "The day when we start going this way and he wants to go the other way," he remarked, "our usefulness is terminated." The application of careful persuasion after gaining the chief's trust—which this adviser believed could take four or five months, or over a third of the length of an advisory tour—was the only way to go.[86] The creation of CORDS did little to change this dynamic. Most advisers operated circumspectly, believing that developing hostile relations with their counterpart would destroy their ability to operate. Guidance sent to all PSAs noted that advice should be given to the province chief "in privacy so that he will not *lose face* when passing it to subordinates."[87] Acting as a behind-the-scenes counselor and manipulator, advisers clearly had some power but still relied on their local partner. In 1970, an end-of-tour report by Louis F. Janowski, a Foreign Service officer who served in various advisory positions in IV Corps, stated that "too often good counterpart relations simply means letting your counterpart do exactly what he wants or raising minimal objects [*sic*] to his actions."[88]

SETTING UP CORDS   87

Virtually no adviser regarded his counterpart as a puppet who was easy to manipulate into doing what the adviser wanted. "Brad" described the handicaps that faced advisers in interacting with their counterparts on an equal basis. "In the first place," he began, "let's face it, you probably tower over the guy, you weigh twice what he does, you probably are enjoying a salary several times his, and you have all kinds of amenities that he probably does not enjoy, such as access to the PX and all the goodies therein." Given the fact that advisers could also leave the country if they had to, whereas GVN officials could not, Brad concluded: "You're starting the relationship under a hell of a handicap, and it's a miracle that the guy doesn't hate your guts on sight."[89] It was also incredibly difficult for an adviser to grasp the context in which his counterpart operated. An American adviser faced with the task of understanding the political, cultural, social, and economic intricacies affecting Phu Yen's province chief in 1968 confronted the same task that a Vietnamese would have faced if parachuted into California and ordered to understand the priorities of Governor Ronald Reagan. One document written by an experienced adviser and distributed for the edification of his PSA colleagues listed sixty-four separate questions about the counterpart's religious affiliations, business interests, sex life, political links, and educational background, the answers to which could bear on his behavior.[90] Few American advisers were equipped to understand even a fraction of these factors, and the language barrier only exacerbated the problem.

One of the main problems facing CORDS advisers on a daily basis was encouraging their counterparts to focus on the rural population even when this did not accord with their own interests or priorities. The fact that almost all province chiefs were ARVN officers with a limited background in understanding rural life meant that PSAs could find it difficult to get them to agree on the importance of such efforts.[91] By late 1971 a CORDS briefer reported that in rural South Vietnam, "the center of power rests with the province chief, who is by and large an Army Colonel, does not have an M.A. in Economics or Public administration, and has been fighting a war all his life." The chief's characteristic response to being told to involve himself in civil matters, the briefer said, was "to have nothing to do with it because he would have nothing to say."[92] Vann considered the GVN to be "dominated by military men who have to be coerced into performing civil functions, and it was a strange role for them to perform."[93] Cao Van Vien, chief of staff of the ARVN, likewise commented after the war that "most ARVN field commanders acted as if they were totally detached from the problems of pacification and concerned themselves solely with military matters." According to Vien, the fault lay with the Americans, who had trained ARVN commanders to fight conventional war and left them "woefully inadequate as contestants of the 'other war.'"[94] CORDS advisers faced the difficult task of undoing what decades of ingrained cultural and social biases and professional training had wrought on their counterparts.

In attempting to persuade their counterparts to focus on civil functions, the methods used by CORDS advisers varied. Most sought to see their counterparts at least daily, and also to develop social relationships with them. Because of their access to the technical knowledge on matters such as agriculture that American provincial organizations could supply, as well as access to the resources that CORDS was willing to invest in local development and reform programs, advisers could become valuable to their counterpart. Yet most advisers felt the need to not appear too indispensable, lest they undermined the appearance of the province chief's autonomy and sovereignty within his own province. One adviser commented that "it was very difficult to work in such a manner to try to get things done and to control things while, at the same time, presenting the facade that I was not manipulating anything."[95] Another described his job as akin to a lobbyist, but one who did not want to seem too close to the province chief lest it arouse suspicion that American interests were in fact governing the chief's actions. "Try not to give the overly [sic] impression that you are with him all the time," he advised, "because he either resents it or if he doesn't resent it, he starts looking like an American puppet."[96] With factors such as these limiting the direct influence that an adviser could have on a province chief, some sought indirect means such as developing closer relationships with the province chief's deputies. They could then plant an idea further down the GVN hierarchy and endorse it when it came across the province chief's desk, maintaining a facade of noninterference.[97] However, such interventions seemed to undermine the long-term goal of fostering an independent GVN.

Far from being the compliant puppets of NLF propaganda, GVN officials also actively sought to manage the relationship with their American counterpart in a way that benefited their own interests and in line with their own conception of their duties. As CORDS advisers were attempting to reshape the behavior of their Vietnamese counterparts, GVN officials were also attempting to shape and control the behavior of the Americans. The description by "Anh" of his handling of American officials is instructive. A self-confident son of the rural elite, Anh was born into a rich landowning family in Kien Tuong Province. Deprived of the ability to enjoy the family fortune by the coming of the revolution and war in the 1940s, he partook of the rural elite's traditional way out by fleeing to Saigon with his family as his home province became a Communist stronghold. Proud of his rural roots, Anh attended the National Institute of Administration (NIA) and began working in local administration under the Diem regime. Along the way he attended college courses in government administration in the United States, including at Michigan State University and the University of Connecticut.

Choosing to continue to work in government service despite the possibility of much higher salaries in the private sector, Anh was exactly the sort of socially conscious civilian that many Americans and Vietnamese leaders like NIA chief Nghiem Dang saw as crucial to strengthening the GVN.[98]

Anh believed that Americans had to be domesticated and taught to "think Vietnamese" if they were to be successful advisers, while one Vietnamese adviser to IVS despaired at whether this was possible, as his countrymen had "our own way of thinking, our own logic," which was difficult for Americans to understand.[99] Anh said that the Americans "should think that they work for the Vietnamese" and "never" give orders themselves. Instead, the only proper role of Americans was to "advise discreetly" while remaining invisible behind their counterpart. Vietnamese officials like Anh worried that an influx of thousands of American advisers would undermine the apparent independence and sovereignty of local GVN organs, and called for American contingents to place a focus on the quality rather than quantity of advisers. "I recommend very strongly that Americans be trained as advisors, not doers," he told USAID personnel, "as otherwise you will leave the impression of being a conqueror, a colonialist, or a capitalist"—in other words, the exact impression of American personnel that NLF propaganda aimed to create.[100] Another South Vietnamese official who had "known and worked with many Americans" also strongly believed that CORDS should stick to its role as a "support" organization rather than appearing to override the sovereignty of Vietnamese officials. In his view, good American officials were "humble" and only distributed material aid or advice through Vietnamese channels, so it could be clear to the population that "their local government helped them."[101] Vien likewise believed that "there was a requirement for US advisers to be modest and self-effacing in their life and work." They also needed to "exercise tact and persuasion instead of leverage to get things done, because no Vietnamese could stand a loss of face"—especially to a foreigner. For the Americans to act otherwise would give credence to the "vicious slanderings of Communist propaganda."[102]

Anh made clear that he viewed the balance of power in the relationship between him and his adviser as favoring himself. He mused about the possibility of having to "oust" a bad adviser, and boasted of another that "I made him behave the way he should, one way or another." Anh also believed it was crucial for the effectiveness of any GVN government official that he maintain his independence, as any Vietnamese who seemed too close to the Americans or who seemed to display what Anh regarded as American patterns of thought—"modern, scientific and rational"—risked being ostracized by the rest of the GVN hierarchy.[103] While Vien believed that the presence of U.S. advisers had led to "modern management techniques" and "scientific knowledge" diffusing throughout the GVN hierarchy, Anh's grassroots perspective suggests this cultural and organizational change was

limited in practice.[104] Anh also questioned the quality of many American advisers, and by extension the usefulness of their presence. He complained that while
the French had sent their best administrators to Vietnam, the Americans did not
seem able to muster a similar cohort of experienced and dedicated officials. "For
the sake and honor of the United States, which has very good administrators as
far as I know," he said, "they should send their good administrators, who should
impress the Vietnamese." Faced with the prospect of having to work with less
impressive Americans, he advised his Vietnamese colleagues to closely study the
weak points of their counterparts and work around them. He also complained
that younger Americans like the Tigers could give the impression of "lacking in
experience," and said he preferred middle-aged Americans who had technical
expertise rather than young generalists.[105]

An incident in 1966 demonstrated that even the vast amount of American
combat power deployed to South Vietnam could not protect U.S. advisers from
threats of physical violence at the hands of their counterparts if they went too
strongly against their wishes. A USOM province representative believed he had
discovered a corruption scandal with "implications all over the Delta." At the
time, the local corps commander was General Dan Vang Quang, whose financial
dishonesty was notorious. Believing that corruption needed to be rooted out
if the GVN was to become stronger and more legitimate, the American began
investigating. Then one night the local chief of police invited him to ride in his
car to inspect a remote outpost, only for the adviser to feel the cold muzzle of the
carbine pressed against his neck from the backseat. With the help of a "goon," the
police chief was attempting to intimidate the American to get him to stop asking
questions. When the adviser informed his superiors in Saigon, they told him they
were powerless to take action and offered him a transfer to another province.
They were unable to take any action against the police chief, and with Ky having
offered corps commanders the power of virtual warlords within their fiefdoms,
the central GVN would not act against him either.[106] Despite its reconfiguration
of the American presence in the provinces, CORDS could do little to address
problems and dynamics such as these without the cooperation of the central
GVN in ending the corps commander system. But with their attention elsewhere
and their reliance on the commanders undiminished, neither Ky or Thieu was
willing to take such a step in 1967.

Faced with these problems, long-serving nation builders like Vann believed
that Komer and CORDS had done little to help them. Having to deal daily
with corrupt or incompetent GVN local officials shielded by the corps commander system, they began to question the value of Komer's subtle approach
to influencing an apparently unmoved GVN. Advisers like Vann wanted much
more dramatic action from the center to radically overhaul the GVN's system

of rural governance. "What is desperately needed," Vann opined to Ellsberg, "is a strong, dynamic, ruthless, colonialist type ambassador with the authority to relieve generals, mission chiefs and every other bastard who does not follow a stated, clearcut policy which, in itself, at a minimum, involves the US in the hiring and firing of Vietnamese leaders."[107] Another American wrote that "Saigon has apparently given up all hope of regaining lost leverage over RD/pacification execution despite repeated pleas from field advisors and a history of program failure." Castigating what he saw as "supersensitivity for Vietnamese sensibilities," he added: "With 200 men dying each week to buy [the] GVN time, it is very difficult for me to agree that the RD program is primarily a Vietnamese affair."[108] But a heavy-handed U.S. approach is precisely what Bunker, Komer, and Westmoreland all ruled out, as likely to be too upsetting to nationalist sensitivities and risking derailing the constitutional process. Given the potential for anti-American unrest that the Buddhist struggle movement had revealed, their opinions appear valid.

Out in the provinces, the Communist movement remained largely unmoved by GVN nation-building efforts in 1967. Given the honesty with which the internal documents of the Communist movement usually addressed problems and shortcomings, this is notable. American military operations were placing pressure on its infrastructure, but observers in the movement saw little evidence that U.S. and GVN military victories were being followed up by nation building. In the central lowland province of Phu Yen, an NVA infantry division had been placed on the defensive by American search-and-destroy operations, and the number of people living in the Communist "liberated area" had shrunk to one-tenth of its peak size. Assessing GVN actions, the NVA observers correctly concluded that the operations had three phases: search operations to drive away large Communist units, police efforts to go after party infrastructure, and the effort to "re-organize their control" by reestablishing GVN village and hamlet administration. Whenever the enemy tried to move beyond stage one, "these occasional efforts were only temporary and would disappear as we redoubled our efforts," the NVA reported. Lacking the assets or policies to reoccupy the entire countryside, much less carry out nation building, the GVN was disrupting Communist control but doing little to establish its own.[109] An NLF agent reported from Phu Yen in June that although the RD cadres were spreading "demagogic" propaganda and trying to ingratiate themselves with the villagers, the GVN was having little success in reestablishing permanent hamlet governments.[110] Although enemy military operations were forcing Communist cadres to live an underground or mobile life and making it difficult for them to engage with the population, there seemed little indication the GVN was making inroads among the population either.[111]

Disillusioned with the Saigon regime—and reeling from his conflict with Thang—Chau had left its service in 1967 to run as a legislator. Still head of the Ministry of Revolutionary Development (MRD), Thang was hence the highest-ranking GVN official who kept his attention on rural reform. Thang hoped in 1968 to subordinate the corps commanders to the central government and to push a national reform effort, with benchmarks to be met and punishments to be dispensed if they were not. Yet he was unable to successfully curb the autonomy of the four "warlords" in the corps areas. The notes taken by a U.S. liaison officer of a meeting in late September 1967 reflected the fact that "at least two (if not all four) of the Corps had completed their 1968 RD plans long before coming to the meeting . . . MRD officers were not amused."[112]

More fundamental reforms of the structure of the GVN would be required if the autonomy of the corps commanders was ever to be reduced enough to allow the central state in Saigon to design and implement national programs of the sort Thang wanted. For the GVN to acquire the strength to contest the Communist movement, it needed to revamp the relationship of Saigon to its local organs of power. Thang devoted much energy during this period to pushing for reforms of the relationship between Saigon, the corps commanders, and province chiefs. He wanted to reduce the power of the corps commanders to appoint province and district chiefs, which the commanders used to shelter incompetent and corrupt officials. As one American wrote of the futility of economic aid delivered via a corrupt government, "too many Vietnamese counterparts see no value in the program and either have no desire to execute it or demonstrate an intolerable knack for converting the Self Help program into a Help Yourself program."[113] Thang believed the solution was to appoint province and district chiefs directly from Saigon, removing the ability of corps commanders to shelter corrupt officials in return for kickbacks. Under Thang's proposals, province and district officials would be selected by the Saigon authorities and trained at Vung Tau. Thang's proposals were thus a continuation of the task of centralizing the nation-building effort, removing its direction from the hands of the myriad local GVN actors who had come to prominence in the chaotic years since the coup against Diem and instead enforcing national plans and standards set in Saigon. Duly appointed by the central GVN, the new breed of province and district chiefs would be beholden to it.

The problem was that those local officials who stood to lose from such reforms did not intend to be passive throughout this process, and neither Thang nor the Americans had the power to bring about such an overhaul of the GVN. The fate of Thang's efforts revealed much about how little had changed in South Vietnamese politics even after Thieu won the presidential election of September 1967. Regardless of the veneer of civilian government,

Saigon politics remained military politics. Thieu was extremely reticent to undermine the power of the corps commanders, because he believed that he owed his position to them and because to challenge them would create, as he told an American interlocutor, "dissension and instability." Protesting that he had no independent power base to resist coups, Thieu said he had "no intention of standing against the entire army as President Diem did."[114] Even though Thieu had emerged as president after the 1967 elections, his ongoing rivalry with Ky also made him skeptical. Given that the proposals for the selection and training of province and district chiefs would allow Thang and Ky to select the individuals involved and then, as an American observer put it, to "control the countryside through the province chiefs" who were beholden to them for their jobs, this only compounded Thieu's problems by essentially demanding that he take power away from his own key constituency and place it in the hands of his opponents.[115]

As the dispute between Thieu and Thang raged, Komer and other high-level U.S. officials were forced by their own theory of leverage to tread carefully, even though they broadly favored Thang's proposals. Thang's own attitude limited what they could accomplish on his behalf. Like Chau, Thang was unwilling to ask for Americans to back him against figures in his own government, believing it would undermine his nationalist credentials.[116] Komer and other U.S. officials tried to use their access to Thieu to gently influence him in favor of Thang's proposals, but their results were limited. On January 2, 1968, Thieu tried to square the circle between his two main constituencies—the ARVN and the Americans—by announcing limited reforms to the structure of the armed forces. The corps commanders and commanders of ARVN divisions would have their power over the provinces diluted, Thieu announced. But the change would come only once a number of what a senior U.S. observer considered "crippling stipulations" had been met, including an improvement in the military situation, which was unlikely anytime soon.[117] Thang responded by submitting his resignation.[118] Bunker and the CIA believed that Thieu was right to move cautiously in curtailing the prerogatives of the military, and Westmoreland went so far as to tell Thang's military superiors that Thang "is old enough to know better" than to resign.[119] This split in the U.S. community was the final nail in the coffin of any attempt to use U.S. leverage at the center to make Thieu move more rapidly. Faced with the prospect of a governmental collapse and the central GVN's complete loss of control as in the period after the coup against Diem, Komer's preference for working with the corps commander system broadly as it currently stood, combined with the fear of the unknown, overrode any desire to push for radical change. Then, just as an apparent impasse loomed, it was broken—in the most violent and undesirable way imaginable.

4

THE "OPPORTUNITY"

As 1967 drew to a close, the war in South Vietnam was stalemated. In the dry season that lasted from October 1966 to May 1967, U.S. commander William Westmoreland had sent the formidable U.S. military machine that had been built up in South Vietnam on a series of offensives designed to win back the initiative and inflict heavy losses on Communist forces. U.S. brigades spread out in a checkerboard fashion over the countryside and sought out the enemy, drawing on their advantages in mobility and artillery. The main focus was the area around Saigon, where two massive U.S. operations code-named Cedar Falls and Junction City sought to annihilate the Iron Triangle, a Communist base area that had existed since the war against the French. Though they inflicted heavy damage on NLF and NVA forces, U.S. troops were soon forced to withdraw, ceding the sanctuary back to its occupants. Meanwhile, Communist forces maintained the initiative both in the northern part of South Vietnam and in the mountainous areas of what had formerly been Annam, and a grueling guerrilla war simmered on in the Mekong Delta. Westmoreland simply did not have enough troops to guard against enemy offensives in the north, destroy and occupy enemy base areas around Saigon, and drive the enemy from the delta. The result was stalemate.[1]

It would fall to Hanoi to break it. Throughout 1967, the Communist leadership was split into two factions. One, headed by party general-secretary Le Duan, believed the time would soon be ripe to launch a final military offensive in South Vietnam. Much like in the months before the U.S. intervention in 1964–1965, the Communists hoped they could break the ARVN with one decisive push and triumphantly enter the cities amid an anti-GVN and anti-American popular uprising. The presence of substantial U.S. forces in South Vietnam added a new layer of complexity that would be dealt with by diverting their attention to battles far from the cities, such as the famous siege of Khe Sanh. On the other side of the debate stood a group of officials headed by Ho Chi Minh and Vo Nguyen Giap, who argued that Le Duan's adherents misunderstood the state of the war and that the Communists needed to dig in for a long struggle. A premature push would waste revolutionary resources and make the final victory more difficult to attain. As the matter was settled by day in high-level debates dripping with Marxist-Leninist verbiage, by night the secret police rounded up journalists, academics, and mid-ranking officials opposed to Le Duan's approach and spirited them away. Ho and Giap left the country in unclear circumstances and remained there when the offensive began. Certainly not any more democratic than the Saigon regime, the dominant faction in Hanoi was more ruthlessly effective at imposing a strategic direction on its agents. Le Duan had won, and the orders for the offensive were carried south in August.[2]

The decisive push that North Vietnam's paramount leader wanted came on the night of January 30, when combined NLF and NVA forces struck nearly every major urban area in South Vietnam. Saigon, which had long existed in an insulated bubble punctured only by acts of terrorism, saw major combat for the first time. The attackers seized almost all of Hue, where they would remain until dislodged by bloody street-to-street fighting in early March. While neither the collapse of the ARVN nor the urban uprising that Le Duan had hoped for occurred as a result of the offensive, its impact on American policy eventually marked a turning point in the war. Under domestic pressure from a public and media who had been led to believe that the war was on the verge of being won, Johnson soon announced that he was halting almost all bombing of North Vietnam and seeking to open peace talks with Hanoi. Formal talks opened in Paris on May 13. Sensing weakness, Le Duan ordered a second wave of attacks, resulting in a May offensive that the Americans dubbed "mini-Tet." While the ARVN still held firm, Saigon again saw widespread destruction. Hanoi ordered a third wave in August, but by this point the Communist movement could summon only scattered ground attacks and the indiscriminate bombardment of the civilian population in Saigon by long-range rockets. After the August offensive fizzled, Communist main forces withdrew to base areas and cross-border sanctuaries to lick their wounds, allowing Bunker to report in October that allied forces had "more freedom of movement than they have had at any time since the start of the U.S. build-up."[3]

The year 1968 was hence one of dizzying and seemingly contradictory shifts. By its end, Le Duan's hope of a quick termination to the war lay in tatters, but apparently faltering American will had opened up a new possible path to victory through diplomacy. Meanwhile, the situation in the countryside had been rendered fluid by the Communist decision to mobilize all of its resources for the urban offensives. After an initial period in which they were stricken by despair, as the dust settled U.S. and GVN leaders in South Vietnam saw the opportunity to launch a nation-building offensive unlike anything they had attempted before.

TABLE 1. U.S. KIA by corps area, 1967–1968

	1ST QUARTER	2ND QUARTER	3RD QUARTER	4TH QUARTER	TOTAL
I Corps					
1967	684	1,604	1,348	1,006	4,642
1968	2,646	2,892	1,675	877	8,090
% change	286.84%	80.3%	24.26%	−12.82%	74.28%
II Corps					
1967	530	427	271	558	1,786
1968	512	447	300	170	1,429
% change	−3.4%	4.68%	10.7%	−69.53%	−19.99%
III Corps					
1967	773	647	367	688	2,475
1968	1,340	1,102	810	812	4,064
% change	73.35%	70.32%	120.71%	18.02%	64.20%
IV Corps					
1967	56	58	69	93	276
1968	326	250	142	161	879
% change	482.14%	331.03%	105.8%	73.12%	218.48%

This table is adapted from figures in Thomas C. Thayer, ed., *A Systems Analysis View of the Vietnam War, 1965–1972* (Washington, DC: OASD(SA)RP Southeast Asia Intelligence Division, 1975), 8:125.

TABLE 2. ARVN KIA by quarter, 1967–1968

	1ST QUARTER	2ND QUARTER	3RD QUARTER	4TH QUARTER	TOTAL
Nationwide					
1967	3,092	3,222	2,834	3,568	12,716
1968	9,424	6,241	5,147	3,453	24,625
% change	204.79%	93.7%	81.62%	−3.22%	93.65%

This table is adapted from figures in Thayer, *Systems Analysis View*, 8:217, 222, and 6:27.

Holding the Line: The 1968 Offensives and Urban Relief

Although some high-ranking Americans would claim in postwar accounts that they did not share the panic that struck U.S. media and political circles in early 1968, those involved in the nation-building effort were gravely shaken.[4] It is easy to understand why. As tables 1 and 2 show, "Tet" should be understood not as a singular event but as the beginning of a year of unremitting military pressure on the United States and the GVN that only began to tail off in the fourth quarter. There were only three instances over the whole year when any given part of the country was safer for allied forces than it had been at the equivalent time the previous year, and two of these came in the last quarter.

Physical damage was also widespread. Around 150,000 homes had been destroyed during the year's offensives, primarily in Hue and the greater Saigon area.[5] But smaller towns were not immune from the destruction either. In My Tho, the Mekong Delta hometown of President Thieu's wife, the firepower required to dislodge two regiments of Communist forces left 25 percent of the population homeless.[6] The fact that much of the damage was inflicted by U.S. firepower raised fears of rising anti-Americanism. As Saigon police chief Nguyen Van Luan, a close ally of Ky, complained: "The Viet Cong has no air force of its own, so it uses ours."[7] Playing on these themes, NLF propaganda attempted to drive a wedge between the Americans and their "puppets" in the GVN. Leaflets were distributed accusing "Thieu-Ky" of "lending a hand to the foreigner's colonialist mission ... destroying countless lives and properties, flooding our country with death, sorrows and sufferings."[8] With both U.S. firepower and Communist shelling of major cities bringing destruction to the urban population like never before, NLF propaganda could easily prove effective. Bui Diem had previously noted on trips to Saigon that the war had seemed very distant, and the population occupied with making a living and the twists and turns of the Thieu-Ky rivalry.[9] After the offensives of 1968, the war would never seem so distant. Nguyen Thi Thu-Lam remembered that "never again were we to feel safe on the streets of Saigon."[10] The steady military pressure during the first three quarters of the year also vastly complicated the effort of resettling the homeless and restoring a sense of normalcy.

The initial damage to the GVN's position in the countryside also seemed grave. Large numbers of RD cadres and local GVN officials had to be withdrawn from rural areas to aid with urban relief efforts and because of threats to their security, leading Komer to report in April that rural administration had been "seriously reduced."[11] As at other times of stress and insecurity, fleeing from the rural communities of

FIGURE 5.   Devastation in Saigon in February 1968.

National Archives identifier 558530, General Black and White Photographic File of the Department of the Navy, Record Group 428, National Archives II at College Park, Maryland.

which they supposedly were the leaders into the protective embrace of a distant state only underlined whom these officials really represented.[12] By August and September, the NLF was announcing the creation of "liberation committees" in areas it controlled, following the promulgation of a Provisional Revolutionary Government (PRG) in June.[13] Although little more than a rebranding exercise for its infrastructure in South Vietnam, these moves allowed the Communist movement to demonstrate to the world the extent of its political reach in South Vietnam and hence negotiate from a position of strength in the unfolding peace talks. Colby, now Komer's deputy at CORDS, briefed military commanders in September that "in the event of a cease-fire, the enemy might claim political control of about one-half of the population of South Vietnam."[14] As Komer recognized, it would require new military offensives into the countryside to dislodge this PRG infrastructure and restore GVN rule.[15] Thus, the military pressure placed on both the United States and the GVN in 1968 was matched by a new political challenge. Both the top civilian and military leadership in South Vietnam recognized its importance, but they first had to deal with the crisis in the cities.[16]

If Vietnamese civilians no longer felt safe in the streets of Saigon, then American officials no longer felt safe in their strategy. The relentless military and psychological pressure of the spring of 1968 led Bunker to write to Washington during a dark moment to question "how long this can be endured without threatening all that has been achieved here."[17] Komer was even more pessimistic. In a briefing to journalists in late February, he said that pacification had suffered extremely heavy setbacks in the Mekong Delta and I Corps, and that many hamlets previously considered "pacified" would now need returning to. While he noted there was a "vacuum" in the countryside after the heavy losses suffered by the Communist movement, he was pessimistic about the ability of the GVN to capitalize on it. And if the movement shifted its attention from the cities onto what was left of the GVN's rural infrastructure, then "we'll have problems, real problems," Komer concluded.[18] Several days after the briefing, Bunker dispatched Komer back to Washington to recuperate from the psychological strain placed on him by events. Bunker was so concerned about his subordinate's mental state that he sent a secret cable to the White House asking that Komer not be pestered to take part in official meetings during his time in the capital.[19]

Nor was Colby immune from doubts. In February, shortly before he left to take over as Komer's deputy at CORDS, Colby was one of several officials to place his name to a memo that seemed to ooze complete despair over current American strategy.[20] The proposal, dubbed Operation Shock, stated, "Over the years the current leaders of Vietnam have developed a complacent assurance that American support is immutable. Consequently, they have felt free to approach the war in terms of gradualism, favoritism among the limited circle of person-alities at the top and only a casual attention to mobilizing popular support and engaging the population actively in the war. . . . The Tet offensive can be utilized in a frontal assault on these attitudes and habits."

In the view of the memo, the GVN's inability to protect its own borders without half a million American troops and to keep the enemy out of the Ameri-can Embassy "demonstrated that the present GVN lacks some of the principal attributes of sovereignty." Faced with a weak state that was dependent on it for survival, the United States was justified in demanding that the GVN "follow U.S. direction" and allow its own structure to be remade according to U.S. wishes. The authors argued that Thieu should be compelled to give a greater role to Thang and Ky and that the GVN should then be given one hundred days to rein-vigorate the pacification effort, tackle corruption, and expand the government's base among the population. If it failed, unspecified but severe consequences were to be threatened.[21] Operation Shock was circulated by Director of Central Intelligence Richard Helms to several key figures in Washington, but without the authors being identified on the memo. It does not appear to have been cir-culated in Saigon.

Operation Shock was wildly unrealistic in assuming that the United States could simply snap its fingers and solve problems that had already failed to be resolved in nearly fifteen years of American involvement in South Vietnam. It also ignored political realities in Saigon. As a later CIA study noted: "No one can seriously have thought that President Thieu would consent to put his nemesis Nguyen Cao Ky in charge of both a mass corruption purge and a national political front."[22] Colby's contribution to the memo is curious because his actions after he became head of CORDS did not remotely reflect anything written in the docu-ment. Nor were the other authors—Helms's special assistant for Vietnam affairs, George Carver, and former Saigon station chief John Hart—bureaucratic gadflies. Consequently, it is hard to see the document as anything but the product of panic in the CIA in the immediate aftermath of the Communist offensives of early 1968.

American optimism was gradually restored as it became clear the Communist offensives would face military defeat, and as 1968 wore on, Komer turned to orga-nizing joint U.S./GVN relief efforts for the urban population. As well as hoping to restore confidence in the government among the ravaged urban population, Komer hoped to establish a model of cooperation between CORDS and the Sai-gon regime in the future. The United States and the GVN formed a joint executive committee to run what became known as Project Recovery.[23] Project Takeoff had failed because of a lack of GVN cooperation, but Komer and his colleagues "in effect operated as part of the Vietnamese government" during Project Recovery.[24] The Central Recovery Committee was initially chaired by Ky, with Komer acting as his U.S. opposite number and Thang serving as chief of staff. Komer and his deputies also began attending GVN cabinet meetings during this period.

Project Recovery's immediate focus was to provide for the vast numbers of evacuees created during Tet and the subsequent offensives. A CORDS report later noted that enemy offensives between Tet and August "generated over a million cases of people who, while they did not have to leave their homes for more than a few days, required assistance in reestablishing themselves after the death of relatives and/or the destruction of their homes."[25] Unlike rural refugees, the urban refugees generated during Tet usually moved only very short distances from their homes and maintained access to their livelihoods once normal economic life was restored in the cities. But many saw their homes destroyed in heavy fighting and needed to be rehoused. There was also a fear among Americans in Saigon that food shortages might quickly lead to riots, which the Communists could then misrepresent as the general uprising they had predicted.[26]

FIGURE 6.   Vietnamese refugees in northern South Vietnam, 1965. According to the U.S. Marine Corps photographer, "the wages of many years of war are reflected in the faces of this aged Vietnamese couple."

National Archives identifier 532436, General Photograph File of the U.S. Marine Corps, Record Group 127, National Archives II at College Park, Maryland.

Feeling unable to trust its bureaucracy to oversee the rebuilding of shattered urban centers, the GVN decided the effort would take the form of "a community action project, with the government furnishing funds and materials and the people building their own houses on presurveyed plots."[27] The plan was to provide direct, tangible aid to the refugees rather than relying on the GVN administration to supervise building projects. Thang won an argument with the Americans on the committee over whether the corps commanders could be made responsible for delivering aid to refugees. As well as not wanting the United States to completely supplant the GVN at the most basic task of providing shelter for its citizens, he also argued that officials could be observed and punished for corruption during the process.[28] As one U.S. official explained to a journalist, failure could have dire consequence for the GVN: "I think even the most corrupt official realizes what is at stake. The Government's best support comes from the cities, and if it lost this support because of corruption in the refugee program it would be in serious trouble."[29]

Komer was enthusiastic about Project Recovery, but his enthusiasm betrayed how limited was his grasp of the challenges of genuine nation building. It was one thing for the GVN to perform adequately in the distribution of American largesse to its citizens, and quite another for it to undertake fundamental reforms to build an active base of support and undermine the political appeal of the Communist movement. The need to focus on urban recovery had also meant a transfer of attention and resources away from rural areas, where the real battle for the allegiance of the population was still to be won.[30] In addition, the nationwide refugee caseload actually grew substantially over the course of 1968 despite Project Recovery's efforts. There were nearly eight hundred thousand refugees at the end of 1967, and this caseload had increased to over 1.3 million individuals by January 1969 despite the resettling of over a million temporary evacuees during 1968.[31] Where the GVN's rural administration was still functioning at all, it remained as sclerotic, centralized, and unresponsive as before. Local officials had to get permission from Saigon to take the smallest action, such as rebuilding a bridge or a classroom, and they could wait months for their requests to be answered.[32] Komer's earlier statement that he was lowering his sights "from the desirable to the doable" had now brought his sights very low indeed, admittedly through necessity. Project Recovery accomplished little more than helping the GVN stave off collapse in 1968, a necessary achievement but one that did not automatically promise a future of U.S.-GVN cooperation once the immediate emergency had passed. As the Americans stood eager to help, what happened next depended primarily on Thieu.

"A Great Opportunity to Be Seized": GVN Reform in 1968

The initial Communist assault had found Thieu celebrating Tet in his wife's hometown of My Tho, a fact unknown to the assaulting Communist forces. Had the rural cadres attempting to guide the attack not got lost in the unfamiliar streets, and had Thieu's personal guard of elite rangers not helped fend them off, the president might have been captured. As it was, he escaped My Tho in a U.S. helicopter on the second day of the attack to return to Saigon.[33] Absent from the political scene in Saigon in the first weeks of the offensive in unclear circumstances, the cautious general eventually emerged to take control. Over the course of 1968, he consolidated his grip on the GVN, never to relinquish it. "Little by little," Ky later conceded, "the balance of power between us swung in his favor."[34] Tran Van Don observes that during this time "Ky gradually lost power, much like American vice presidents, but remained in the government."[35]

Alongside this sidelining of his adversaries in Saigon, Thieu managed over the course of 1968 to strengthen Saigon's grip on the localities. Liquidating Ky's power also allowed him to bring to heel the corps commanders who were Ky's most important allies, and to appoint his own men in their place. Unsure of his own position when the Thieu-Ky regime started in 1965, Ky had given the corps commanders "total authority over local decisions" in return for their loyalty to the central regime.[36] If Thieu wanted to get a firmer grip on rural administration, he would have to rescind that authority. In consequence, Thieu worked with, and became reliant on, CORDS's network of provincial and district advisers to provide support to local GVN officials, but also to spy on them. Only by using the United States was he able to make inroads against the corps commanders and their traditional system of corruption and patronage. In this sense, Thieu turned the concept of leverage on its head and used CORDS as leverage against his domestic opponents. By October, Bunker was able to report back to Washington: "Thieu is in fact now close to exercising the full powers vested in him by the constitution, and the extra-constitutional power of Vice President Ky and the other generals has continued to decline."[37] Thieu's newfound reliance on the United States also made him appear more willing to listen to U.S. advice and engage in a genuinely collaborative relationship with CORDS to reform the GVN.

Amid the nerves of spring 1968, one word kept recurring to U.S. officials in South Vietnam. That word was "opportunity." Even since the creation of CORDS, top U.S. officials had struggled to gain traction for their reformist ideas inside the GVN. The 1968 offensives came to be seen as an opportunity to galvanize the GVN to achieve reforms that would ultimately strengthen the South Vietnamese state once the immediate emergency passed. Lansdale was urging Bunker to see the offensive in this light in a memo typed even before the first day of the attacks was over. He wrote that "the extraordinary events of the past few hours open up a rare opportunity for President Thieu to exhibit some extra leadership right now that can have most rewarding consequences."[38] Bunker quickly took up the theme. At a meeting with Thieu shortly after the latter returned from My Tho, he told the South Vietnamese leader that the attacks presented "an ideal moment for him to demonstrate his leadership and to galvanize the nation."[39] Days later he told Thieu that the offensive was "a moment of opportunity" for him and Ky to bury their differences and unite with other top GVN leaders to prosecute the war more effectively.[40] In a message back to Washington, Bunker said that the GVN faced a "crisis of confidence" caused by its inability to prevent the widespread destruction caused by the offensive. Nevertheless, he claimed the cloud had a silver lining: "It is to meet the crisis of confidence to which I have referred that I have been pressing, as strongly as I know how, on Thieu and other leaders in the government the idea that there is a great opportunity to be seized in this situation; that if the government moves quickly to help the victims, to move ahead vigorously with recovery and reconstruction, if it mobilized the potential support available to these efforts, it can score a very significant political as well as military success."[41]

As well as hoping that the GVN would be invigorated by the offensive, U.S. officials calculated that the new level of political and military threat felt by the GVN might allow the United States to exercise greater leverage over the government's behavior and structure. This had been the idea behind Operation Shock. Vann, who had been sharply critical of the softly-softly attitude toward leverage at the top of CORDS, likewise thought Tet and subsequent events provided an opportunity to change this approach. Cynical as he was of the GVN's capacity to reform itself, he believed there was a need for much greater U.S. involvement in South Vietnam's "so-called 'internal affairs.'" Following the Tet Offensive and Johnson's speech of March 31, Vann thought the GVN was more susceptible to such pressure than ever before.[42] He also thought that effective change would require it. In July, Vann was asked by Ellsberg to explain why he thought the GVN would "rise to this which you describe as their opportunity." "Well, we don't know that they will," Vann replied. "All I'm suggesting is that we try to force them to."[43] Bui Diem remembers that "in Saigon, strangely enough, the mood was exuberant" in government circles as the Communist offensives were easily beaten back.[44] Bunker's own sense that Tet presented an opportunity that could nevertheless be squandered was encapsulated in his invocation of a line from Shakespeare's *Julius Caesar* that he felt captured the moment well: "There is a tide in the affairs of men which, taken at the flood, leads on to fortune: omitted, all the voyage of their life is bound on shallows and in miseries."[45]

It remained to be decided how the United States could best help the GVN take fortune at its flood. Komer and Bunker were not of a mind to make dramatic gestures that undermined South Vietnamese sovereignty, as Operation Shock had called for, fearing that this would only vindicate Communist propaganda and undermine the long-term confidence and viability of the GVN. Instead, Komer and Bunker quietly pressured Thieu behind closed doors in the manner they had always considered appropriate. President Johnson set the tone in a message to Bunker a few days after the Tet Offensive had begun, instructing the ambassador to tell Thieu that the United States could no longer live with a "business as usual" approach and criticizing the GVN president for his previous "cautious approach to problems." Present events, Johnson suggested, were an "opportunity" for Thieu to act more boldly.[46] Bunker took the rare step of showing this presidential message to Thieu to demonstrate that the demand came from Thieu's supreme patron. Bunker also told Thieu that "it is of the highest urgency for the GVN to act vigorously to meet both the immediate problems, as well as those of longer range and more deep-seated in nature." In the latter category Bunker placed the incompetence and corruption of local administration, and the role of the corps commanders in perpetuating it. Rather than minimizing the scale of the problem as he had done previously, Thieu admitted that "probably some eighty per cent" of current province chiefs were incompetent or corrupt.[47] Even before the shock of Johnson's March 31 speech, Bunker and Komer attempted to scare Thieu into greater reforms by threatening him with a collapse in U.S. support on the home front.[48] Bunker reported by May that "the Vietnamese are really beginning to face up to the fact that the time will come when they are on their own."[49]

The operation of Project Recovery was initially beset by mutual recriminations in which both sides in the Thieu-Ky dispute appeared more interested in pinning blame for failure on the other than making the effort operate smoothly. Thieu at first absented himself from the committee, leaving Ky to chair it, and then Ky and Thang resigned, claiming that the rest of the government was not cooperating with them.[50] In a blueprint eerily similar to that of Operation Shock, Thang reportedly urged Ky to have the constitution amended "so that he, Ky, can hold the post of Prime Minister, or to have Thang appointed to that post." Thang claimed the corps commanders would back such a move. Ky dismissed the suggestion as "foolish talk," adding that he and Thang "must work within the existing governmental framework for present."[51] Another source of pressure on Thieu was the powerful commander of the III Corps region, Le Nguyen Khang. Like many generals in ARVN, Khang was suspicious of the U.S.-backed trend toward democracy and civilian rule in South Vietnam, and favored a strong military dictatorship.[52] Among the top leadership of the ARVN, he was far from alone in this point of view. As Bui Diem explained, the generals "stood to lose a great deal in the transition to civilian government . . . they would find themselves subordinate to political leaders with whom they carried no special influence. . . . Their attitude dripped with contempt for the very idea that a civilian government could rule effectively."[53]

Khang also controlled the crucial military region around Saigon, which would be vital in any coup attempt. But realizing that the Americans would not tolerate any further coups, Khang forbade to openly entertain them, instead hoping to parlay his position into leverage over Thieu.[54] On February 18, Khang led a meeting in which he, Thang, Ky, and Joint General Staff chief Linh Quang Vien blasted Thieu for the GVN's "weakness" and what they saw as the ineffectiveness of the civilian ministries. Khang offered his resignation at this meeting as a symbolic gesture, knowing Thieu did not feel secure enough to accept it.[55] Despite having initially chided Thang for his "foolish talk," Ky began to press Thieu to appoint a general as prime minister as the year wore on.[56]

To the seeming surprise of his opponents, rather than bowing to demands to give the military and the Ky faction a greater role in governance, Thieu instead flashed his steel. He opted to ally himself with the Americans against his domestic opponents. Only the strong support and cooperation he received from CORDS both in Saigon and the provinces made this feasible.

Thieu's first step was providing effective leadership to the relief effort. After Ky and Thang resigned from Project Recovery, Thieu leapt in and made a success of it, in the process demonstrating that it seemed to lose little through not having Ky and Thang's participation. Buoyed by this close cooperation with CORDS and eager to take advantage of the crisis atmosphere as new enemy offensives struck, Thieu then began to implement more structural reform. On March 1, he removed the commanders of both IV Corps and II Corps, citing their incompetence under military pressure.[57] Thieu appointed Major General Lu Lan, widely perceived as an apolitical general, to II Corps. Thang, still popular with the Americans and a key confidant of Ky, was sent to become head of IV Corps.

At the same time as replacing these two commanders, Thieu announced wide-ranging reforms in the relationship between corps commanders, province chiefs, and the central government. Province chiefs would no longer be appointed by corps commanders, but rather would be picked and supervised by the central government. Invoking the success of the Project Recovery task force, Thieu said that "province chiefs will act as the head of a task force in each province for the ministries' representatives there." They would be supported by CORDS. Meanwhile, civilian inspectors appointed by Saigon would oversee the province chiefs, whose ultimate responsibility would be to the interior minister.[58] This returned South Vietnam to the system that had existed under Diem, in which the corps commanders were not yet official warlords in their own domains but answered to the central government.

Thieu soon began to demonstrate that this shift in responsibility had not just taken place on paper. Ten days after his initial announcement, he dismissed seven province chiefs in the II and IV Corps areas, where he had just appointed new commanders. He also dismissed the mayor of Hue, who had also failed to distinguish himself during the Tet Offensive.[59] This amounted to a nearly 16 percent turnover in provincial leadership in one day. By the end of the year, twenty of the country's forty-four province chiefs had been removed for corruption or incompetence, and some placed on trial. Ninety-one district chiefs, out of 243 nationwide, had also been removed.[60] By September, Thieu had replaced nine of sixteen province chiefs and nearly half of the district chiefs in the Mekong Delta.[61] When turnover due to deaths and other causes were added, over 50 percent of the country's provincial leaders were changed during the course of the year. The replacements were handpicked by Thieu.[62]

The support of CORDS was vital in enabling Thieu to make these changes. Since the beginning of Project Recovery, CORDS officials had been observing GVN provincial and district officials to sniff out corruption and incompetence.[63] Thieu made use of dossiers of evidence and advice from CORDS officials in deciding which chiefs to change, generally but not always following U.S. advice. CORDS was also vital in providing support to province and district chiefs whom the corps commanders shunned because they had been appointed from over their heads and were not part of the traditional networks of patronage and corruption. When Bunker told Thieu that CORDS had received reports that the corps commanders were not cooperating with local government officials and providing them military support when needed, Thieu "grew visibly annoyed" at the situation. It was clear under his reforms, he said, that corps commanders remained responsible for providing military support to the local chiefs when needed, even if they no longer had civil responsibilities. He also conceded that "province chiefs must depend more on CORDS and USAID than on corps and subordinate commanders to help them do their various jobs" in the civil sphere, but the ARVN "clearly must help" as well when military support was required.[64] Thieu's annoyance notwithstanding, it was only the existence of CORDS's networks of advisers and the resources at its disposal that allowed province and district chiefs to declare any independence from the corps commanders at all. Had it not been for CORDS, province and district chiefs would have remained reliant on local ARVN units in both civil and military matters, with all the dilution of central government authority this had entailed since 1963. But the existence of CORDS gave Thieu an alternative to relying on the troublesome commanders and instead allowed him to align himself with the Americans, using their network to project his power throughout the country.

Thieu concurrently took steps to solidify his rule in Saigon. In May 1968, he felt secure enough to appoint Tran Van Huong to the position of prime minister, ignoring the growing military clamor for a general to get the job.[65] Unlike many of the top figures in the GVN, Huong was actually born in what would later become South Vietnam, in the delta province of Vinh Long. Huong had refused to take sides in the Franco–Viet Minh War, then entered Diem's service as the mayor of Saigon after South Vietnamese independence. Huong resigned the post after falling out with Diem and became a prominent oppositionist, eventually being jailed by his former patron for demanding liberal reforms along the lines of those favored by the U.S. State Department at the time. Being opposed to Diem did not stop Huong being critical of the generals who murdered him, even as he served in the short-lived regime that followed the 1963 coup. Huong later became prime minister in his own right in November 1964, only to be removed in January 1965 amid widespread Buddhist protests at his attempt to increase mobilization for the war effort. This clash with his co-religionists was only the latest episode in a career marked by independence, bloody-mindedness, and anti-Communist nationalism. Huong was also widely regarded as incorruptible. He had run against Thieu in the 1967 presidential election, coming fourth in a field of eleven.

In appointing Huong, Thieu was hewing closely to American advice. Bunker had personally indicated that he considered Huong, whom the CIA rated as the "most widely respected politician in South Vietnam," as the best candidate for the post of prime minister.[66] But Huong's reputation and the fact he was a civilian also helped Thieu bolster the image of his government. With Huong on board, it would be harder for Thieu's opponents to accuse him of sliding toward Diem-ist dictatorship as he centralized power. Bunker also hailed the new cabinet as "a considerable move towards civilian government," both because Huong was expected to be a strong civilian leader and because it represented another way in which Thieu was strengthening the constitutional government at the expense of the military's power.[67] Huong also brought back General Tran Thien Khiem, another southern Buddhist who was then in Taipei as GVN ambassador, to serve as minister for interior. This role was vital now that province chiefs were responsible to the Interior Ministry. Khiem had been out of the country since he was ousted from one of the revolving-door juntas of 1964, and was feared throughout the ARVN because of the grudges he was presumed to hold from this incident.[68]

Huong's appointment was opposed bitterly by Ky and Khang.[69] They continued to tell American officials about the perils of civilian rule and the need for a military strongman, but they did not receive a sympathetic ear.[70] A number of factors were by this time working to undermine the power and influence of Ky and his allies. The first was the simple fact that as Thieu's government became more effective at carrying out reforms while working closely with the Americans, the space for criticism became more limited. Ky and Khang were increasingly unable to point to the GVN's ineffectiveness as justification for their standpoint. The dilemma of the Ky faction on this point was illustrated when Khang held forth to Samuel Berger, the U.S. deputy ambassador, on his favorite topic: that South Vietnam "could not afford democratic institutions at this time" and that the United States "had made a major mistake in forcing them" on the country. Khang again questioned whether Thieu's rule was "clear and firm" enough.[71] But for the Americans, it increasingly was, and any deficiency did not stem from a surfeit of military involvement. It was precisely the trend toward the increased "civilianization of the government" that Bunker praised as the year wore on.[72] What Bunker and other CORDS officials wanted was a GVN that was coherent enough to work with as a nation-building partner, and which had a network of responsive officials in the localities. Because Khang and Ky refused to participate in the GVN constructively, it began to look like their complaints stemmed purely from factionalism rather than valid ideological or policy concerns. It was not the form of government they objected to; it was their own declining power within it.

Ky's entourage had limited options in response. The Americanization of the war in 1965 had put an end to the series of coups that had characterized Saigon politics since the fall of Diem, and Americans in both South Vietnam and the United States were in even less of a mood to tolerate them now. As Komer had stressed to Thieu upon his return from visiting the United States in March, American public opinion could not countenance internal strife in South Vietnam. Even Khang, considered by Bunker to be an "avowed opponent of constitutional democracy," realized that acceptance of the GVN's constitution was a prerequisite for continued U.S. support.[73] With the seizure of power not an option, Ky and his allies could only access it through cooperation with Thieu and his American patrons. As CORDS allowed Thieu to expand his own power both by supporting his reforms of the GVN's rural apparatus and by the advice its leadership provided to both him and his ministries, Ky's faction found themselves increasingly irrelevant to the main concerns of the Americans. They hence became not only expendable but also to be seen mainly as potential spoilers by South Vietnam's U.S. backers.

A third factor in the declining fortunes of the Ky faction was a series of deaths in May and June of 1968 that thinned the ranks of Ky's supporters and close friends. On the first day of mini-Tet in May, National Police chief Nguyen Ngoc Loan sustained serious injuries while hunting snipers in the back alleys of Saigon. Then, on June 3, an errant U.S. helicopter missile badly wounded the mayor of Saigon and killed seven other officials, including Luan, the Saigon police chief who had made the apposite remark about the NLF "using" U.S. firepower. All the dead and wounded were allies of Ky, among them his "closest supporters."[74] Thieu moved quickly to appoint his own men to the now-vacant positions.[75] The sudden loss of so many close allies and hence influence was dizzying for Ky. He seemed to vanish from the political scene, and newspaper reports placed him "out of Saigon, depressed and tired."[76] While his mental state was said to have improved by September, Berger still found him "subdued, pensive, and intro-spective"—adjectives that previously had rarely been applied to the flamboyant and belligerent former fighter pilot.[77]

A fourth factor that undermined the position of Ky's faction was their repeated resignations, which only enhanced the impression that they were more interested in their faction's power than in the effective running of the GVN. Both Ky and Thang had left the Central Recovery Committee before a month was even through, and Ky subsequently adopted and then abandoned a key role in the raising of territorial defense forces.[78] Nor was Ky the only one who couldn't hold down a job even when it was one the Americans considered vital. With the decline in Ky's fortunes only accelerating, both Thang and Khang jumped ship in late June. Thang resigned from his position as head of IV Corps, claiming that Thieu did not trust him. This was the final straw among Thang's American backers, and the general was left without effective supporters in either the GVN or on the U.S. side. He played no further role in the war.[79] Khang also offered his resignation to Thieu as a token of responsibility for the rocket attack in Saigon that had killed so many prominent GVN officials. The offer was widely inter-preted as a protest against the installation of the Huong government and the dilution of the Ky faction's power in general.[80] Thieu accepted the resignation and brought his close ally, Do Cao Tri, back from the ambassadorship to South Korea to become the new commander of III Corps.[81]

Thieu had emerged on top through a combination of his own cunning, chance events such as the rocket strike that killed Ky's closest allies, and American sup-port. The military and political challenges of 1968 had finally spurred the noto-riously cautious general into action, and he had moved quickly to consolidate both American support for his regime and his own power within it. Attempting to ensure that American support would remain over the "long haul," he moved to seize the power that was technically his under the constitution and use it to adopt reforms that pleased the Americans.[82] The result was almost the opposite of what had been proposed in the Operation Shock memo earlier in the year. Rather than stepping aside and ceding power to Ky, Thieu had emerged in charge and had sidelined his rivals. It was a remarkable turnaround in Saigon politics. Now it remained to be seen if a similar turnaround might be produced where it really counted, in the villages.

Seizing the Nation-Building Initiative

For Komer, Colby, and other top CORDS officials, the most important item of business in the GVN's in-tray was the need to reassert its rural presence. Komer had become increasingly concerned as 1968 wore on that Project Recovery was diverting the GVN's attention from "rural recovery."[83] The Communist movement's success at bringing the war to the cities had put the GVN on the defensive and forced it to spend nearly a year concentrating on its own base areas, to the detriment of rural nation building. The unremitting enemy military pressure and the need to consolidate the GVN's control over the broadly pro-government cities made Thieu cautious and unwilling to embark on a counteroffensive for much of 1968. Back on the up and up following his convalescence in Washington, Komer told Thieu as early as March that he thought a "vacuum" was developing in the countryside. While the United States and the GVN had withdrawn to defend the cities and oversee Project Recovery, the NLF likewise had to weaken its grip over the countryside to generate the manpower for its continued offensives. While Komer said that a spirit of "offensive-mindedness" was needed, Thieu was much more cautious. He said that the GVN had to abandon grand ambitions for 1968 and cut back pacification activities to "oil spot areas around cities, towns, prosperous villages, and vital roads and canals." Emphasizing the spirit of consolidation, he summed up by saying: "We should know what to sacrifice."[84]

By October, Thieu came to accept the need for the GVN to reassert its rural presence. The starkly deteriorating military position of the Communist movement in the countryside was becoming apparent by this time. As a Communist history puts it, by late 1968 "our offensive posture began to weaken and our three types of armed forces suffered attrition. The political and military struggle in the rural areas declined and our liberated areas shrank. . . . Most of our main force troops were forced back to the border or to bases in the mountains."[85] A new GVN offensive seemed especially important, given the formation of the PRG and the Communist promulgation of its "liberation committees." With its military campaign petering out, the movement seemed to be shifting to focus on political struggle.[86] "By surfacing this apparatus," Komer told the Mission Council, "they could attempt to validate a claim to 'rule the countryside'—thus justifying either partition or a coalition government."[87] GVN officials were likewise concerned that the Communist movement's network of village committees would allow it to assert "extravagant claims of political control."[88]

CORDS and the GVN set out to work together on a counteroffensive. At a U.S. military conference in September, Colby issued the previously noted warning that the enemy might be able to claim control of nearly half of the South Vietnamese population in a cease-fire as things stood.[89] He also displayed a map showing the extension of the liberation committees over South Vietnam and argued that, as he recalled, "a vigorous extension of security and political presence by the Government, with American support," was necessary both to preempt the spread of NLF control and to penetrate areas they currently claimed.[90] With the blessing of Abrams, what became known as the Accelerated Pacification Campaign (APC) was then developed by CORDS and the GVN. In early October, a series of bilateral meetings were held at which the Americans put the proposal to top GVN officials including Thieu, Huong, and a brooding Ky. On the U.S. side, Bunker, Abrams, Komer, and Colby were among the participants. These large bilateral meetings became the norm for developing strategies through which to bolster the GVN's strength in the local areas. GVN cooperation with CORDS was spurred by the repeated emphasis that Thieu put on the need to win over the rural population.[91] Following the pattern of Project Recovery, the United States and the GVN were working closely on joint campaigns.

As well as the influence gained by their close working relationship with the central GVN, CORDS officials up and down the chain of command were newly empowered by the APC and the interest that Thieu showed in it. In the early stages of presenting the plan to the GVN, Komer had sent word down to the Dep-CORDS in the four main corps areas to sell the concept of the APC to the corps commanders. When the commanders were asked by Vien whether the program was feasible, they said it was.[92] Now that Thieu had made it clear that the corps commanders served at his pleasure and that he was aligning himself more forcefully with the Americans and with CORDS specifically, it behooved the corps commanders to follow American advice. Another key factor in boosting the influence of CORDS personnel was the fact that the APC relied on an American system called the Hamlet Evaluation System (HES) for measuring progress. The 1,084 hamlets selected to be part of the APC all had HES ratings of D or E, indicating that they were considered insecure by American advisers. Under the plan, success would be defined as upgrading them to category C or greater. The APC set specific numerical targets in every corps and province to be upgraded in this manner. As it was CORDS advisers who filled in the reports that determined what HES ratings were ascribed to each hamlet in South Vietnam, this gave them enormous influence over the central government's perception of both the plan's success and the performance of individual officials. HES had previously been criticized as a means of making false claims of progress in the war. But developments during the APC and thereafter showed that HES had another use—as a means by which CORDS advisers could focus the minds of their counterparts on the issues that they considered important in a local area, and then pass judgment on their performance up the chain of command via the HES ratings. As a GVN briefing noted, "President Thieu, in order to gauge progress more accurately and to provide a common basis for planning, chose to use the American Hamlet Evaluation System."[93] In this context it was more important as a tool of leverage than as an objective measure of progress. CORDS officials were careful not to make a public fanfare about the campaign and especially not to make a public relations issue of the numerical targets. Though the broad outline of the plan was revealed in the press, even the detail of its name was not widely known. Three weeks into the campaign, the veteran *New York Times* correspondent Charles Mohr erroneously reported that the APC was called "Quick Fix."[94]

HES was hence not being used to create an illusion of progress. It had instead become a tool both in reinforcing Saigon's rule over the provinces and in solidifying the role of CORDS advisers in acting as the central government's eyes and ears to assess the performance of its own officials. Unlike during the 1968 planning process, when Thang had not even been able to get the corps commanders to alter their plans, the APC was centrally conceived from the start. To further demonstrate his commitment to the APC and to nation building more broadly, Thieu established a Central Pacification and Development Committee. Chaired by Huong and often attended by Thieu, the committee met to consider policy issues and oversee cooperation on plans for 1969, in which the GVN would try to build on the gains of the APC.

Using leverage of the form that Komer had long advocated—behind the scenes in Saigon—combined with the newfound ability of U.S. officials to use their influence in the localities, CORDS finally seemed to have a chance to work as intended. It is little surprise then that Komer stated shortly after leaving his job that he was "perhaps prouder of the APC than anything else."[95] Even Vann, who had been so critical of Komer's leverage concept and his understanding of nation building in the past, was impressed. The situation in Vietnam, he stated in January 1969, is "better . . . than I have ever before seen it." He continued: "The changes in province chiefs and district chiefs have generally been good, and in retrospect, I attribute Bob Komer's initiative in securing leverage, establishing management tools such as HES and TFES (and initiating the Accelerated Pacification Campaign), to mark him as the greatest single American contributor to progress in Vietnam."[96] Given that Vann had previously been critical of both Komer and his "management tools," this was high praise indeed. Berger evinced similar optimism in September, when he told a chastened Ky that "many long term observers say the Huong government is the best one in a decade."[97]

Yet the events of 1968 also contained a cautionary tale. It was initiatives by the Communists that had changed the dynamics of the war. The nation-building effort, which had barely begun to be implemented at the grassroots, would be vulnerable to similar shocks in the future. And in 1969, there was a new administration in Washington—one determined to put its own stamp on the war.

5

THE NIXON ADMINISTRATION AND NATION BUILDING

When he heard that Richard Nixon had been elected president in late 1968, the British counterinsurgency strategist Sir Robert Thompson had severe misgivings about what lay ahead. Although he had become highly critical of the way the Johnson administration was prosecuting the war, he never doubted that it placed a high priority on the containment of communism in the Far East. But the new president was an unknown quantity. It would be easy for him to declare that Vietnam was a war that had been started by Democrats and lost by Democrats, and that all an incoming Republican administration could do was get out. Thompson was not the only one who thought Nixon might take the easy option. According to Thompson, the staunchly anti-Communist Singaporean prime minister Lee Kuan Yew took much the same view shortly after Nixon's election, bursting out to the Brit: "They've lost, haven't they?"[1] At the other end of the political spectrum, Daniel Ellsberg, by this point an ardent skeptic of the war, recalled that he felt no special alarm at Nixon's electoral triumph over Hubert Humphrey: "I knew no reason to think that Nixon would prolong the Democrats' failed war longer than Humphrey; if anything, as a Republican, he might do the contrary."[2] Buoyed by such hopes, Ellsberg even agreed to work with the administration in its early days.

His disillusionment, however, came quickly. Everything hinged on how Nixon reacted to the two key legacies of 1968: an increasingly inflamed and antiwar public discourse in the United States and an altered strategic situation in South Vietnam. Confounding expectations of a quick withdrawal, Nixon and his key national security aides—particularly National Security Adviser Henry

114

Kissinger—aimed to pull out slowly and cautiously. By doing so they hoped to prevent withdrawal from harming either their domestic political position or U.S. credibility abroad.

Historians have tended to be transfixed by Kissinger's diplomatic activities in Paris and Nixon's military ventures into Laos and Cambodia, which were two cornerstones of this strategy. Less attention has been given to the administration's attitude toward strengthening the GVN. Alongside the policy of strengthening the ARVN, which came to be known as Vietnamization, the Nixon administration also showed a keen interest in the development of GVN rural governance. They did not carry out any dramatic interventions in policy in this area, as Johnson had through the creation of CORDS. Nor did they share the reformist impulses that had led Johnson to first place a focus on the need to improve the lot of the South Vietnamese peasant through economic development. Instead, the new administration was focused on what Kissinger sometimes called "the control war."[3] It stressed the need for the GVN to exercise effective control over its population both to strengthen its hand at the negotiating table and to be able to stand up to the Vietnamese Communist movement after an agreement. Dismissing the idea that providing material benefits to the population was the key to success and unconvinced by the necessity of active as opposed to passive support for the GVN, Nixon and Kissinger came to stress "security" and physical control of the rural population, much as Komer eventually had. There was as a result substantial continuity between the two administrations, a fact that has been missed either because historians have overemphasized Johnson's initial reformist impulses or underemphasized Nixon and Kissinger's concern with "pacification."[4] Communist histories, on the other hand, emphasize the importance of "pacification" in the latter years of the war.[5]

While not ordering any dramatic departure in nation-building policy in South Vietnam, the administration did bring about a revolution in the White House's ability to understand its progress. While Komer and Johnson had been preoccupied with the herculean task of creating CORDS and had little time left over for asking larger strategic questions about its chances of success, Nixon and Kissinger inherited a mature policy and then subjected it to withering analysis. Through the creation of a Vietnam Special Studies Group (VSSG) dedicated to the task, Kissinger brought a sophisticated understanding of the limits of nation building in South Vietnam to the White House. The fact he did so shows how important he considered the effort. But the group's sobering conclusion that the GVN was unlikely to survive U.S. withdrawal undermined a key requirement for the success of a strategy that the administration had inherited but never truly believed in. If the Vietnam War was "effectively" won by the early 1970s as some have claimed, then this was far from apparent to Nixon or Kissinger.[6]

Nixon, Kissinger, and Nation Building

The inauguration of Richard Nixon as president in January 1969 brought to an end the period in which the making of Vietnam policy had been dominated by the now tired men who John F. Kennedy had brought to Washington nearly a decade earlier. The main members of Nixon's national security team—Kissinger, Secretary of Defense Melvin Laird, and Secretary of State William Rogers—were not personally committed to the policies of the past. Kissinger especially was known to be highly skeptical of the way the war had been conducted, and especially of U.S. nation-building efforts. In an article for *Foreign Affairs* written before he was selected to serve in the White House, Kissinger had criticized Johnson's strategy for the war and especially weaknesses in the "so-called pacification" program. In the article, he highlighted two key weaknesses of U.S. efforts to strengthen the GVN, pointing out there was "no concept as to how to bring about a political framework relating Saigon to the countryside," and that current strategy resulted only in "military successes that could not be translated into permanent political advantage."[7]

Like Nixon, Kissinger placed great emphasis on the manner in which withdrawal from Vietnam took place. In a widely cited passage in his *Foreign Affairs* article, Kissinger argued that the United States could not simply abandon the GVN: "The commitment of 500,000 Americans has settled the issue of the importance of Viet Nam. For what is involved now is confidence in American promises."[8] Keeping that confidence alive throughout the world, Kissinger thought, depended on ensuring the survival of the Thieu government after American withdrawal. This sometimes brought Kissinger into conflict with other members of the administration. Laird, a nine-term congressman who had served on the Defense Appropriations Subcommittee, was highly attuned to domestic politics and the strains that the continuation of the war was placing on the U.S. military in a time of budget constraints. This often led him, along with Rogers, to push for a faster withdrawal of U.S. forces than Kissinger thought wise.[9] Laird's ability to manipulate the Pentagon budget in a way that forced a certain pace of troop withdrawals from Vietnam meant that even though Kissinger was the most influential of Nixon's courtiers on matters pertaining to Vietnam, he did not always operate in circumstances of his own choosing.

There was no individual at the top level of the Nixon administration who placed the same emphasis on reforming South Vietnam as Johnson had done, nor did the administration order a dramatic restructuring of the U.S. nation-building apparatus that had taken shape in CORDS. But this did not mean that the administration had lost interest in strengthening the GVN. Despite their military escalations, Nixon, Kissinger, and Laird were not inclined to believe

FIGURE 7.   National Security Adviser Henry Kissinger set up a sophisticated system in the White House to monitor the progress of nation building in South Vietnam.

Photograph GRF-WHPO-A4263(26), Gerald R. Ford White House Photographs, White House Photographic Office Collection, Gerald R. Ford Library, Ann Arbor, Michigan.

that a "military victory" was possible in Vietnam, especially after Nixon abandoned plans for a dramatic escalation in the first year of his presidency.[10] As Laird told Nixon when the latter requested that maximum pressure be put on the enemy, Communist attacks could be "repulsed with heavy [enemy] losses," but there was little that could be done to "produce any significant change in the military situation over any short run period of time."[11] The lack of any unilateral military option was worrying because, as Laird told Thieu during a trip to Saigon, "time had run out on the last administration in terms of public support for our Viet-Nam policy." The administration had to stay ahead of the American public by ordering troop withdrawals and shifting the burden of fighting to the ARVN.[12] At the end of the trip, Laird recommended the withdrawal of from fifty to seventy thousand U.S. troops from South Vietnam in 1969.[13] While he later backtracked officially from this high figure and settled on twenty-five thousand, Rogers continued the pressure for an even larger withdrawal. Thus began the steady drumbeat from both the Pentagon and Foggy Bottom, which would continue throughout the administration.[14] Nixon would prove receptive, and he eventually announced the withdrawal of sixty thousand troops in 1969.

The withdrawal of U.S. forces without the abandonment of the goal of maintaining the Thieu regime naturally placed a large burden on U.S. efforts to strengthen the GVN, as the Saigon regime could now foresee the day when it could no longer rely on U.S. forces to defend it. The thought that this day would come too soon "torment[ed]" Kissinger.[15] As he told Nixon in July 1970, he feared "a crunch point where we are caught between an ally that cannot withstand any further American withdrawals and a public that will not stand for any further involvement."[16] Nixon likewise wrote in his memoirs that he agreed that the "central problem" was "whether the South Vietnamese were sufficiently confident and prepared to defend themselves against a renewed Communist offensive at some time in the future."[17] Kissinger was concerned that the pace of U.S. withdrawal was being determined by budgetary and political considerations rather than an objective assessment of the situation in South Vietnam. He was also concerned that what seemed to be steady gains in the GVN's strength depended on a U.S. security shield that was being steadily withdrawn, and not Saigon's intrinsic strength.[18] When Tony Lake and Roger Morris, two members of Kissinger's staff who were to resign over the Cambodian incursion, warned their boss that the United States was on course to withdraw from South Vietnam faster than was prudent, Kissinger was receptive and continued to mention his concerns to Nixon.[19]

Lake and Morris eventually went even further, warning that they did not believe there was "any option" that could achieve "an eventual political solution in South Vietnam in which most of us could take comfort."[20] This, however, was not a viewpoint that Kissinger expressed to the president. Instead, Kissinger placed his faith in two parallel tracks: negotiations with Hanoi, and the policy of "Vietnamization," which focused on developing the military capabilities of the ARVN through training, expansion, and equipment transfers. In the negotiations, Kissinger perceived that the United States had three bargaining chips. One was the rate of withdrawal of U.S. forces from South Vietnam. The second was the level of coercion that could be brought to bear against North Vietnam's assets. The third was the extent and durability of the GVN's control of the South Vietnamese population. If Vietnamization allowed Saigon to durably establish control over much of the rural population, the allies would be strengthened at the negotiating table. Hanoi might be forced to settle faster if it felt it was faced with a situation in which the GVN was continually strengthening and improving its relative position.[21] The more the GVN was able to accomplish without American support, then the more durable its position would appear. The strength of the GVN was hence a crucial bargaining chip in the negotiations with Hanoi. As the negotiations deadlocked over demands by the North Vietnamese delegation that the United States overthrow Thieu as the price for a peace agreement, it became

in fact the key point in the negotiations; this was not surprising, as the governance of South Vietnam was the central issue of the war.

The strengthening of the GVN was thus central to both the policy of Vietnamization and U.S. negotiating strategy. It was also implicated in the administration's coercive strategy in Cambodia and Laos. Both when U.S. forces invaded
Cambodia in 1970 and when they backed an ARVN assault into Laos in 1971,
the main aim was to clear out NVA supply and logistical networks. As raids,
they could set back impending Communist offensives and buy more time for the
GVN to strengthen itself, but without fundamentally altering the balance of the
war. Kissinger listed the benefits of the Laos operation as including "very important" blows to the NVA logistical network and the deterrent effect that would
compel the NVA to maintain combat forces in Laos in the future, meaning "these
forces (a portion of which were formerly in South Vietnam) cannot be used to
threaten Vietnamization in South Vietnam."[22] The Cambodian incursion had
been deemed to have a positive impact for the same reasons.[23] But even though
these temporary escalations could divert North Vietnamese resources and alleviate pressure in the South in the short term, it remained the case that developments in South Vietnam itself would decide whether the Nixon administration's
strategy was a success. This was so whether the war was "doomed always just to
trickle out the way it is," as Nixon believed in a pessimistic moment in September 1971, or whether a negotiated settlement could eventually be reached.[24] As a
result, efforts to bolster the GVN remained central to the success of U.S. strategy.

The Vietnam Special Studies Group and the War

If Komer had been a doer, then Kissinger was, especially at the outset of the
new administration, an analyzer. Kissinger had received his PhD from Harvard in 1954 and had spent the decade and a half since in the academic study
of international relations. He brought a sophisticated view of the complexity of
the Vietnam War—and especially of nation building—with him to the office.
"Throughout the war, criteria by which to measure progress have been hard to
come by; this problem has continued during the negotiations," Kissinger wrote in
his *Foreign Affairs* article of January 1969. "The dilemma is that almost any statement about Viet Nam is likely to be true; unfortunately, truth does not guarantee
relevance."[25] Kissinger was skeptical of the accuracy and relevance of the statistics that were used to measure progress in the war.[26] The first communication
that Kissinger sent to William Colby, Komer's successor as the head of CORDS,
stressed "the need for realism in reporting on the pacification program."[27] Laird
and Nixon felt likewise. After hearing an optimistic assessment from Johnson

administration holdovers about the declining morale of enemy forces in South Vietnam and their apparent willingness to surrender, Nixon pointed out that "I think there is a tendency to get skeptical of these optimistic reports," while Laird interjected: "I have heard these briefings each year and each year they get more optimistic and, therefore, I hope that we will be very careful in digesting the material which is put forth."[28] When Nixon met Abrams for the first time in May, Kissinger suggested that he inquire whether "the *apparent* progress in pacification is significant and whether or not he estimates that GVN control of the countryside is *actually* progressing."[29]

Kissinger set in motion an internal White House effort to measure progress in nation building, down to the analysis of individual provinces. Like much of the broader reshaping of the NSC and the policy-making process that Nixon and Kissinger embarked upon, this was done in a conscious attempt to improve on the informal style of the Johnson administration, which had made its policy at secretive and much-derided Tuesday lunchtime meetings. The NSC system that Nixon and Kissinger constructed has often been viewed as a cynical means of expanding White House control over government agencies and narrowing the channels of debate and dissent. On Vietnam, at least, this is only a partial impression. Nixon personally made some of the most controversial decisions of his term—such as the Cambodian incursion—against the wishes of almost all his advisers, but the new NSC system was not integral to his ability to do so. Similarly, Kissinger's ability to conduct negotiations with the North Vietnamese without the knowledge of most of the rest of the government did not depend on the new NSC system and would have been just as possible between Tuesday lunchtimes. While Nixon and Kissinger may have carried out a lonely policy at the negotiating table in Paris or in the Oval Office during the Cambodian incursion, the regular NSC machinery they set up actually served to widen the debate and information flow within the government on more routine matters. The new system provided multiple forums in which periodic and detailed assessments of the situation in South Vietnam could be presented as papers by the relevant agencies and then discussed, something never possible under Johnson. One typical meeting in January 1972 had twenty participants from State, Defense, the Joint Chiefs of Staff, the CIA, Treasury, and the NSC and debated matters such as enemy intentions and capabilities, the accuracy of intelligence, and the progress of Vietnamization.[30] The wide variety of agency input provided for a much greater degree of debate about the progress of the war and of nation building in particular than had been possible under the Johnson administration.

Johnson had created Komer's office as a means of bringing White House influence to bear in shaping the development of the nation-building program in South Vietnam. But he had never grappled in a holistic fashion with what exactly he wanted from the program and how it could help achieve U.S. war aims. Inheriting a mature program, Kissinger instead organized his own office specifically for the purpose of assessing that program's effectiveness. Kissinger's NSC machinery included two forums specifically devoted to the study of issues related to Vietnam. The first of these, the Ad Hoc Group on Vietnam, was created in February 1969 to prepare papers for consideration by the wider NSC.[31] In recommending its creation to Nixon, Kissinger told him that while the group would be useful to coordinate responses to Communist offensives, "it will not preclude the type of planning we conducted on Tuesday with Mel Laird and [Air Force Chief of Staff] General McConnell"—in all probability a reference to planning for Operation Menu, the secret bombing of Cambodia. Such sensitive matters, Kissinger assured the president, could be kept out of this channel. Nixon duly signed off on the recommendation to create the group.[32] This demonstrated that while Kissinger and Nixon did indeed work together against other agencies and government officials, this was not the purpose of the regular NSC machinery.

This also applied to the second group that Kissinger created, the Vietnam Special Studies Group. Its purpose was the "systematic analysis of U.S. policies and programs in Vietnam."[33] The group was chaired by NSC staff members, first Laurence Lynn and later Wayne Smith.[34] Until he left the administration after the Cambodian incursion, Lynn was considered by Kissinger to be a rigorous analyst, and the VSSG continued to impress him under Smith.[35] The memo that Kissinger sent to Nixon suggesting the creation of the VSSG—which was drafted by Lynn—cited numerous "preconceptions" that were said in the past to have led officials "astray even though a careful and objective analysis of readily available facts would have told them differently." It cited the failures of the Strategic Hamlet Program, optimistic assessments of the impact of bombing North Vietnam, the shock of the Tet Offensive, and "our excessively optimistic expectations for the various 'revolutionary-development' type cadre programs." Once constituted, the memo continued, the group could help to guard against such misconceptions by considering the progress of Vietnamization, land reform, territorial control, and other aspects of the war and nation-building effort in South Vietnam.[36]

Kissinger was receptive to these proposals. From the beginning of the new administration, he had displayed skepticism toward reporting systems inherited from the Johnson administration. He was also dissatisfied with the quality of analysis available on the strength of the GVN and progress of the war in general. Despite Ellsberg's reputation as a well-established critic of the war, Kissinger brought him into the administration to help him define broad policy options.[37] While working for Kissinger, Ellsberg suggested that the White House should issue each national security agency involved in Vietnam with a series of questions designed to expose inconsistencies and gaps in knowledge and interpretations of the war among the agencies. Ellsberg thought this would be especially useful in temporarily wresting the monopoly of interpretation on certain issues from the agencies and showing the wide variety of interpretation that existed within the government.[38] Kissinger took this advice and set Ellsberg to work developing a set of questions that would most accurately reveal where the bureaucratic bodies were buried. Kissinger's use of outside experts both to increase his own knowledge and bolster the White House's position set the tone for an administration that would be both much more intellectually curious about the war and more dedicated to setting up an independent analytical capability in the White House to understand it. When Lynn wrote to Kissinger suggesting the creation of the VSSG, he noted that Ellsberg's project was the first time that many granular details of the war, including those related to nation building, had been discussed at the White House level. He proposed the VSSG as a way to institutionalize this process.[39] Although Ellsberg became a strident critic of the administration, the early example he had set with National Security Study Memorandum 1 of how to best challenge the national security bureaucracy hence lived on through Lynn's proposals and the creation of the VSSG. The group was created on September 16, 1969.[40] Ellsberg thus contributed to the running of the Nixon administration's Vietnam policy in a way not appreciated by historians to date.

Despite their interest in strengthening the GVN, Nixon and Kissinger viewed this task mainly through the lens of increasing its military capabilities. At the very first NSC meeting on Vietnam, one of Nixon's priorities was Saigon's internal security forces. Echoing Johnson's words from late 1966 about the ineffectiveness of civilian nation builders, Nixon stated that he believed that "the AID people are totally unsuited to supervise the development of local security forces, stating it is like the blind leading the blind, adding AID is incompetent to handle this mission." Nixon also inquired about the leadership of the Chieu Hoi program, which was designed to encourage defections from Communist forces in South Vietnam. When told that the job fell under the remit of CORDS, headed by Colby, Nixon asked "is he a specialist, does he have any idea of what he is doing?" He seemed satisfied to hear that Colby's qualifications included having previously served as CIA chief of station in Saigon. Nixon was not similarly satisfied, however, with the answers he received on local security forces—and so he ordered a "complete report on the whole program to include who is doing it, whether he is qualified, what system he is employing."[41]

This concern with measures that either increased Saigon's coercive capacities or cut directly into the insurgency—but not on those that aimed at increasing popular support for the GVN or reforming local governance—prefigured the administration's focus. It was a preoccupation shared by Kissinger. In his *Foreign Affairs* article, Kissinger had drawn an explicit link between the negotiations and territorial control, complaining that U.S. and GVN assets were spread too thinly to produce durable gains for the GVN in extending its control of the rural population. "For purposes of negotiating, we would have been better off with 100 percent control over 60 percent of the country than with 60 percent control of 100 percent of the country," he explained—a viewpoint he continued to repeat in almost the exact same words throughout the Nixon administration.[42]

Unlike the Johnson administration's early moves toward promoting social and economic reform, or the CIA's concept of participative nation building, Nixon and Kissinger focused on the physical control of the population. Like Komer, they were dismissive of those with a wider view that differentiated between nation building and mere pacification. When Johnson had moved to put CORDS under the military, Director of Central Intelligence Richard Helms had warned him that success in South Vietnam depended on a "motivated population, not merely an administered one."[43] Others made similar arguments in the Nixon administration. Recognizing the link between the GVN's political base and negotiations, Lake advised that the key factor would be how many areas of the country were "*loyal* to the GVN—not those militarily occupied or undergoing pacification." Lake warned that GVN "control" of areas of the country where the population was not loyal would prove ephemeral, especially when the GVN could no longer benefit from U.S. troops and resources and had to spread itself more thinly. Instead he suggested that the GVN carry out local political reforms, to include province and district elections, in areas where support for it was already the deepest. The development of a true political base for the GVN "puts the most meaningful kind of pressure on Hanoi . . . since it threatens their future prospects in a way that current casualty levels cannot."[44]

As Johnson had brushed Helms's concern aside, so Kissinger did with Lake's. While Lake's focus on priority areas may have seemed to chime with Kissinger's preference for "100 percent control over 60 percent of the country," it also rested on a fundamentally different concept of what constituted "control." For the purposes of the negotiations, which were Kissinger's hope of ending the war without the risks of mere unilateral withdrawal, the GVN's ability to claim control of the rural population was more important than whether it had gained their "loyalty." Kissinger focused on the GVN's institutions of control rather than on whether it had developed ties of mutual obligation with its population. Another reason to minimize the role of loyalty was that it was difficult to measure. A Special National Intelligence Estimate released just before Nixon's inauguration had warned that it was "almost impossible to measure" the GVN's progress in "gaining the allegiance of the people."[45] This was a stark admission of the limited manner in which U.S. nation builders, even those with a wider conception of their task, had managed to penetrate and understand South Vietnamese rural society.

Like the reports of a decline in enemy morale that Laird and Nixon had questioned in their first NSC meeting, an assessment of loyalty to the GVN was bound to be impressionistic and vague. Kissinger's interests in what he sometimes called "the control war" were more concrete.[46]

This became apparent as the VSSG developed, under his tutelage, the most sophisticated analysis of the situation in the South Vietnamese countryside that had yet graced the White House. The analysis reflected both the administration's focus on what could be tangibly and reliably measured and its interest in the extent of GVN control of the rural population. An early VSSG study defined control as "the ability of one side or the other to possess resources—people and their production—for its own purposes and to deny the use of such resources to the enemy."[47] This was a narrow conception of nation building that concentrated on population control rather than active political loyalty. This physical control of the countryside was thought to be "closely related" to the overall strength of the GVN, as "the GVN must achieve dominate [*sic*] control over the countryside, if it is to survive."[48] Control was defined as the permanent presence in any given hamlet of both local GVN officials and local security forces to the complete exclusion of their equivalents from the NLF, the hamlet infrastructure, and local guerrillas. Conversely, a hamlet was said to be under enemy control if the latter two existed to the complete exclusion of the GVN equivalents. In between these two poles lay a large gray area of hamlets said to be "influenced by both sides."[49] Those under GVN control, meanwhile, had to be subject to its predominant influence both day and night.

Within the study, the concept of control was explicitly differentiated from the concepts of "security" and of "support." While security was said to exist where the population was safe from enemy-initiated violence, this was seen as a mere prerequisite for control and not in itself indicative. An area may be secure simply because the enemy had made a decision not to challenge security at that time, perhaps to carry out other tasks of military significance such as recruiting or political activity. This meant that areas of apparent security always exceeded areas of GVN control in size, a situation that the authors of the study felt had given a misleading impression of the GVN's strength in the past. The situation with regard to the concept of support was different. The authors considered positive endorsement of one side or the other by the population to be of "only limited relevance" to the situation in South Vietnam, as well as being difficult to measure.[50] Within this framework, neither USAID's materialist approach or the cadre programs designed by Chau and the CIA had any significance. As Kissinger pointed out in a meeting to discuss the paper, social and economic assistance programs did not necessarily have implications for control, as the enemy could simply be choosing not to contest these programs.[51] As critics of the Tigers had pointed out in the past, nor was it the case that support for the GVN could necessarily be inferred from a program's existence. The VSSG concluded that popular support was more likely to follow than lead control gains, and that social and economic reform was not necessarily relevant to control, as the NLF could welcome such improvements without any lessening of control. Reforms "may even be credited to the Viet Cong if Viet Cong presence is viewed as the only guarantee that the GVN will continue to perform on behalf of the rural inhabitant."[52]

Using this framework, the VSSG set about analyzing recent shifts in the "control war" and what had brought them about. Writing in late 1969, the group concluded that the GVN had improved its position markedly since the enemy offensives of 1968. Prior to the offensives, a situation that the report labeled a "control stalemate" had existed, with the GVN in control of around 20 percent of the population compared with the NLF's 35 percent, and the rest under the influence of both sides. CORDS hence seems to have had little impact. But while the GVN position had then suffered markedly as a result of the Tet Offensive, the decimation of the NLF's infrastructure and personnel during the offensive had prepared the way for impressive GVN control gains afterward. By September 1969, the VSSG concluded that the GVN controlled 54.7 percent of the rural population to the NLF's 6.7 percent, with 38.6 percent under the influence of both sides.[53] However encouraging these figures sounded, an analysis of the factors that had brought them about was less so. The study was based on an in-depth analysis of the situation in five provinces, and in four of them it was found that it was principally aggressive action by U.S. forces that had created the environment in which the control gains were possible. So even though the proximate cause of the increase was a vast expansion of the GVN apparatus and local security forces, this had taken place behind a shield of U.S. forces. It had also been helped by the damage that had been dealt to the enemy infrastructure during the 1968 offensives.[54]

A trip to South Vietnam by Lynn and the NSC staffer Robert Sansom in January 1970 "to make a first hand evaluation of the situation in the countryside and of the extent and durability of recent improvements in GVN control over the rural population" only reinforced these impressions. The two found that the momentum of GVN control gains seemed to be slowing rapidly and that it was "far more likely that the GVN will lose control than it is they will significantly increase it" during the period of American troop withdrawals.[55] Even though Sansom was an expert on the social and economic situation in South Vietnam who would soon publish a book titled *The Economics of Insurgency in the Mekong Delta of Vietnam*, he and Lynn made little comment on such matters in their report, instead focusing narrowly on population control.[56] They agreed that popular support tended to follow rather than lead control, placing the emphasis on "pacification."[57] As they likewise attributed control gains to aggressive actions by the very U.S. forces that were now being withdrawn, it followed that the loss of control likely to follow would be significant.

Kissinger wrote in his memoirs that the conclusions of the VSSG studies were "moderately encouraging, but we also knew that North Vietnam's confidence was unbroken."[58] He put his finger here on the central weakness of the GVN position. As the VSSG analysis had recognized, recent control gains were attributable to the two factors that the United States and the GVN were least able to control in the future. The first was the presence of American forces, which provided the shield behind which GVN control had been consolidated, and the second was the damage done to the Communist movement in 1968. If the Communist movement could capitalize on its "unbroken" confidence to challenge the GVN again, Saigon would be in trouble. As U.S. forces continued to be withdrawn, it was not clear if ARVN local security forces would be able to meet this challenge in the long term. None of the VSSG studies indicated that Vietnamization was proceeding quickly enough to allow the ARVN to take over from the United States militarily. Moreover, the conclusion that measures leading to increased popular support had only a marginal impact on control indicated that there was also little opportunity for the GVN to improve or maintain its position through reforming local governance.

Boasting about the studies to the British counterinsurgency expert Sir Robert Thompson in a way that also revealed his doubts about the underlying reality in South Vietnam, Kissinger said: "There never before had been a government consensus on what was actually happening, and we were trying now to reach such a consensus—perhaps five years too late."[59] Both parts of this statement were significant. It was certainly true that the VSSG allowed for a sober and clear-eyed view of the "control war," even if narrowly defined, in a way that the Johnson administration had never managed. Nixon thought the resultant analysis "excellent."[60] But the VSSG studies illustrated just how fragile those "control" gains could be, especially in the face of exogenous shocks like Communist offensives. They also took a pessimistic view of future trends, and dismissed the idea that nation building as it was understood by many Americans on the ground in South Vietnam—as encouraging the emergence of a rural GVN administration that was considered legitimate by its citizens—could have a meaningful impact on the future course of the war.

The analysis, pointing as it did toward the weakness of the GVN in the event of U.S. withdrawal, can only have hardened Kissinger's desire for a negotiated settlement that would not amount to a unilateral withdrawal but rather would win concessions from North Vietnam to relieve pressure on the South and allow it to weather the storm of withdrawal. The incursions into Cambodia and Laos also appeared logical within the VSSG framework. They allowed diminishing U.S. forces to be leveraged to maximum effect to disrupt enemy lines of communications and supply caches in a way that further relieved pressure on the GVN and allowed it to consolidate its control gains. The operations also increased the pressure on North Vietnam to negotiate. Thus Nixon's chief of staff, H. R. Haldeman, recorded Kissinger saying that the Laos operation in 1971 "would in effect end the war because it would totally demolish the enemy's capability."[61] If Haldeman recorded this remark accurately, it was a brief moment of ebullience that soon passed.

The Fragility of Control

According to the VSSG's "control indicator," GVN control did indeed expand steadily, standing at 76 percent of the rural population of the country in December 1971.[62] But then came the Easter Offensive of March 1972, which dealt just the sort of setback to GVN control that the VSSG had warned of. Although the offensive was eventually beaten back, the damage to GVN control of the rural population was extensive, and only during the declining pace of hostilities following the signing of the Paris Peace Accords did the GVN manage to achieve 74 percent control, still below the level of a year earlier.[63] The fragility of GVN control in the face of major enemy offensives had hence been established, especially as the Easter Offensive had been contained only by the extensive deployment of U.S. air and naval assets. This clearly threatened the long-term survival of the GVN, but it was not a surprising situation—indeed, Kissinger had worried about this scenario all along, and it was one reason he had set up the VSSG to provide a comprehensive analysis of the situation in the countryside and the progress of nation building. Thus although the analysis proved prescient, the question remains as to whether it was too narrow and whether the decision to slight the importance of social, economic, and political reform and to regard it as marginal to the GVN's ability to withstand military attack led to deficiencies in the understanding of the situation in South Vietnam or in Washington's ability to influence it.

This question arises because of the paradox of the Nixon administration's Vietnam War policy, which was that even though none of the main policy-making triumvirate—Nixon, Kissinger, and Laird—showed much interest in the reform of South Vietnam, by the time they came into office the role had already been institutionalized under CORDS. As we saw in this chapter, while Kissinger brought in outside experts and set up a sophisticated system for understanding the progress of "the control war," he did little to intervene in the way it was being run. As we shall see in the next chapter, CORDS had a great deal of autonomy in deciding how to approach nation building in South Vietnam. That this was so is apparent from the fact that CORDS stressed the very reformist measures Kissinger and Nixon underplayed in their approach to the problem of nation building in South Vietnam. Kissinger and the VSSG recognized that the GVN had to expand its control of the rural population and to generate the manpower and revenues necessary to defend South Vietnam from the Vietnamese Communist movement, but did not believe that reform measures aimed at actively generating support for the GVN were particularly consequential. They hence stressed only one part of the equation of mutual obligation between the GVN and its citizens, which Helms had referred to when he called for creating a "motivated population, not merely an administered one." This was an idea that Colby and other CORDS officials had taken to heart, even if Nixon and Kissinger had not. Using the autonomy they had gained under Johnson, CORDS officials were able to implement their ideas in the latter years of the war. Even though Kissinger and Nixon remained uninterested and even largely unaware of it, Americans in South Vietnam were attempting a nation-building effort of ambitious scope. The question that remained was whether they would be successful and could prove the skepticism of their superiors in the White House to be invalid.

6

CORDS AND THE VILLAGE SYSTEM

Back on the ground in South Vietnam, the sun rose over a changed war on January 31, the anniversary of the beginning of the 1968 offensives. Unable to summon anything like their effort a year earlier, the Communist movement stepped up artillery strikes and terror attacks on urban centers. Five rockets landed in Hue, and bombs killed two girls near a school in Saigon. About fifty miles northwest of the city, near the Cambodian border, the U.S. First Cavalry Division were busy operating in a Communist base area that they had previously been unable to penetrate. After driving off the rear-echelon forces who were left to guard it, they discovered a tunnel complex covering four square miles and containing a three-thousand-bed hospital. Large formations of NVA had been forced to disperse under the American pressure, and a counterattack they launched on a nearby First Cav firebase was easily repulsed. Meanwhile, deep in the Mekong Delta near the town of Can Tho, American B-52 bombers unloaded one thousand tons of explosives on "suspected enemy troop concentrations," bringing terror to the countryside.[1]

These events presented a microcosm of the war over the next several years. Recovering their poise in late 1968 and taking advantage of the failure of Hanoi's offensives, U.S. and ARVN forces had swept out into the countryside like never before, drastically expanding the GVN-controlled area. Reeling from their losses in the 1968 offensives, the Communist movement was forced to break down its large units into smaller and smaller pieces in order to avoid American sweeps. Lacking the freedom of movement they had enjoyed for years and with even their base areas under pressure, they risked becoming targets for devastating displays of American firepower when they massed for assaults. They were increasingly unable to deter the allies from operating in the former "liberated areas," leaving the NLF's local and regional guerrillas and cadres vulnerable. At the same time, U.S. and ARVN counteroffensives were saturating parts of the country with a tremendous amount of firepower, causing civilian casualties on a scale hitherto unknown in some populated areas. In one well-documented case, the U.S. Ninth Division, which became the first U.S. unit of its size to operate in the delta during the entire war, claimed 10,889 enemy killed in one operation, but recovered only 748 weapons, suggesting there were a large number of civilians among the dead. Attempting to escape this indiscriminate bombardment of Communist-controlled zones, a sizable number of civilians relocated to areas dominated by the GVN, further depriving the revolutionary movement of manpower and resources.

These military operations rapidly increased the number of civilians who were living in areas that were secure in the narrow sense defined by the VSSG studies of the Nixon administration. The attrition of the Communist movement's political as well as its military apparatus, along with population movements occasioned by allied firepower, loosened the movement's grip on the population in much of the delta to its lowest ebb of the entire conflict. In its traditional strongholds on the central coast, the movement was stronger, but still on the defensive in a manner it had not been prior to the military debacle of 1968.

These shifts in the dynamics of the war coincided with the emergence of a new CORDS leadership determined to take advantage of the situation, along with Thieu's consolidation of power, to translate temporary security gains into a genuine long-term strengthening of the GVN. Headed by William Colby, the group had all been sharply critical of the way the war was fought prior to 1968. They favored a new strategy that would minimize the role of the military's firepower and divisions and stress nation building in the rural villages, just as the Communist movement did. Though these individuals often found themselves working at cross-purposes to the military units providing the security shield on which their efforts depended, the final years of the war presented them the most favorable conditions in which to attempt their approach. Their ideas came to dominate CORDS and determine the shape of U.S. nation-building efforts.

CORDS's Strategy for Rural Reform, 1969–1972

Since CORDS's formation by Komer, its officials had believed that the absence of large enemy units was a vital prerequisite to nation building. The Communist movement's travails after the 1968 offensives created the most permissive environment for U.S. forces to operate in since 1965 and made it much easier to keep

NLF and NVA units away from populated areas. Colby told the Senate in 1970 that it had been "amply proven" that CORDS's programs could not be effective "unless hostile regiments and divisions are kept away." But he added: "At the same time, however, we have found that their absence does not thereby produce peace nor offer political fulfilment to the people." Representing the "CIA school" of nation building that had been present in South Vietnam since the early 1960s but marginalized when CORDS was headed by Komer, Colby had definite ideas about how to offer "political fulfilment" of a sort that he hoped would allow the GVN to build a base of support comparable to that of the Communists.[2]

Prior to becoming the head of CORDS, Colby had spent decades in the CIA, including a term as chief of station in Saigon in the early 1960s. He had believed that neither the military's focus on training the ARVN to fight an offensive war nor the State Department's concern with liberalizing the Diem regime held the key to the conflict. A conventionally oriented ARVN would struggle against guerrillas, and a liberalization of the Diem regime to include other nationalist factions meant little to villagers who rarely left their own district. The key to the conflict, he thought, "would be found only in the villages, not in political circles in Saigon or in General Staff Headquarters."[3] Colby was not in a policy-making role in the early years of American involvement, and he later spoke with deep regret about how the correct "counter to revolutionary war" was developed by CORDS only long after the war had already been Americanized.[4] He had watched the escalation of the conflict under Johnson with alarm, and continued to believe that true victory lay in the GVN involving South Vietnam's rural population in a collaborative effort against the Communists—that is, in nation building. He was concerned like many of his agency colleagues that the militarization of nation building under CORDS would undermine the need for "some degree of engagement by the population as shown by a willingness to contribute to intelligence, local security and community development." He further warned of an "impatient desire on our part to impose 'pacification' and security on the population rather than engaging in a common effort."[5]

Although concerned about nation building being placed under military leadership, Colby eventually came to see how CORDS could be turned to his advantage—provided it was kept under operational civilian control. After going to Saigon to become Komer's deputy in 1967, he saw how CORDS's sandwich structure of management in fact allowed for wide discretion in the running of the organization by its civilian head. He even came to appreciate Komer. "Komer knew that if you put pacification under the military it would be lost, because the military would go out and shoot everybody," Colby explained to Chau. "But Komer also understood that the military would never accept anything but unity of command. Therefore the only way to make it work was to put pacification under the military, in civilian hands. He had the genius to see that."[6]

CORDS was now in Colby's very own hands, and, as he put it in the memoirs, he finally "had the chance to try out my idea that political development from the ground up was really the central part of winning a people's war, and not just a supplement to the military and territorial-force part."[7] Colby's tenure also saw the ascendancy of a certain faction of other like-minded officials who shared his approach to the war. This group, including Colby's deputy George Jacobson, John Paul Vann—who under Colby served as head of CORDS in the delta and later the top American adviser in II Corps—and his policy chief Clay McManaway, made a sizable imprint on the war effort. Theirs was a collaborative effort that built on what they had learned during their many years in Vietnam. An internal CORDS assessment written in June 1969 put it this way: "The 1969 pacification plan represents the culmination to date of progressive developments in the techniques of attaining Vietnamese popular identification with the Government of Vietnam and a concurrent increase in control of the government over its population."[8] But this was an understatement. Rather than just being an incremental progression of what had come before, Colby's focus on building mutual ties of obligation between the GVN and its citizens transformed the character of U.S. nation-building efforts after 1968.

Since the early 1960s, Colby believed the key to the war was building up the civil institutions of the GVN at the lowest level rather than militarily defeating the Communist movement. The inspiration for his schemes came not from American modernization theorists, of whom he seldom if ever talked, but rather from what he understood of the practice of the Vietnamese Communist movement. Colby's interest in the techniques of the Communist movement dated back at least to his time as chief of station in Saigon in the early 1960s, when he spent long hours discussing revolutionary warfare with former president Diem's brother Ngo Dinh Nhu, who shared the fascination.[9]

As Colby told a military audience in 1971, he believed that the basis of "revolutionary war" as fought by the Vietnamese Communists was "the organization of the people and the use of the people."[10] Colby believed that the success of the Vietnamese Communist movement depended on their superior ability to motivate and organize the rural population in support of their movement, and that the GVN had to replicate this success to survive. The Vietnamese Communist movement engaged in what he called "political development from the ground up," mobilizing the rural population into functional groups focused on discrete tasks such as intelligence gathering, land reform, women's affairs, and youth activities.[11] Colby understood that Communist rule was a participatory experience for the villagers, creating a sense of political identification between them and the movement for which they worked, against their shared enemy in the Saigon regime. This not only provided a means for the NLF to control the population; it also created a sense of joint enterprise. Colby wanted the GVN to organize the population in a similar way, believing that successfully replicating this Communist practice was key to the war effort. Vann had likewise come to believe in the importance of the "organization of the population" through his long association with Chau, and became an enthusiastic backer of Colby's ideas.[12]

The approach to nation building that CORDS advanced during Colby's tenure reflected this, although Colby favored the word "participation" (of the people) over the term "use." "The war cannot be won," he repeatedly said, "unless the people participate."[13] Rejecting the attempt to impose nation building from the top down, Colby instead wanted to build a nation from the bottom up by focusing on what he called the "three selfs"—"self-development, self-government and self-defense."[14] From the Accelerated Pacification Campaign (APC) onward, CORDS sought to actively involve the country's rural citizens in the running of their own affairs under the auspices of local GVN authorities. This did not require the construction of a sense of South Vietnamese nationhood and patriotism, which had thus far proven elusive. Instead, like the Communist movement, CORDS aimed to engage with the rural population not as citizens of a wider entity called South Vietnam but instead as citizens of their home village. Like the NLF, they would stress concrete reforms and social empowerment that had an immediate and tangible impact on villagers' lives within their own sphere of interest in the village. Doing so would give rural citizens a stake in defending the new village order, in paying their taxes promptly and volunteering for service in the local militia. This focus on the village also chimed with Vietnamese tradition. As a GVN strategic plan for 1970 observed, the village was "the traditional community in Vietnamese society."[15] The village had indeed been the central unit of Vietnamese rural life since the time of the Chinese conquest, and since Viet colonizers had first moved onto the central plains and Mekong Delta centuries afterward. As with the Communists who had based their own system of administration and mobilization on the village, the new strategy would require a blend of "relevant tradition and necessary innovation."[16] Appropriately enough, the Americans called their innovation "the village system."

This approach was one that Jeffrey Race, in his classic analysis of the Vietnamese Communist movement, called "communalism." The movement's effort, he said, was "communal in the sense that it took place within the framework of the peasant's span of interests, largely limited to issues within his own community." The loyalty of the population to the movement was based on its ability to "resolve concrete local issues . . . [such as] land, taxation, protection from impressment into the national army, or a personally satisfying role in the activities of the community." Race found in his extensive research in the province of Long An that nationalism as such was rarely a motivating theme for villagers. Rather, it was defense of the local order in their village, plus the direction of Communist leadership cadres whose job was to ensure the village acted in the strategic interests of the movement, that led peasants to give service to the NLF. This was the beginning of the conveyor belt that allowed the movement to mobilize the population and transmit taxes, food, and manpower to the higher levels. Race criticized GVN efforts to mobilize the rural population for focusing on nationalism and a "diffuse anticommunism," for which peasants were unwilling to make sacrifices in their personal interests.[17] While a strident and highly centralized South Vietnamese nationalism did indeed mark Diem's nation-building efforts, after 1968 CORDS attempted to work with the GVN to foster something different. The village system was based on a vision of rural communities that was remarkably similar to the bottom-up approach pursued by the Communists. "Rather than considering it the lowest of a series of bureaucratic levels through which authority descends from the Palace to the people," Colby claimed in 1970, "it became the first assemblage of the population to conduct its own affairs."[18]

In its broad outlines, the village system drew on a wider discourse of colonial counterinsurgency among Westerners who had fought movements similar to the NLF in Malaya, Algeria, and colonial Indochina. All of these theorists believed that conventional military operations were useless or downright harmful in such conflicts, and that the organization and motivation of the population was the key to victory. Sir Robert Thompson was the most prominent. He had earned his reputation in Malaya as, according to the British magazine the *New Statesman*, "the world's leading counter-insurgency expert."[19] Although he could sometimes be blind to the differences between the situation in Vietnam and that which had pertained in Malaya, Thompson drew some lessons from his earlier career that chimed with Colby's thinking. Like Colby, Thompson was critical of the role played by the U.S. military in South Vietnam after the Americanization of the conflict, believing that its heavy use of firepower alienated the population. Meanwhile, the United States had shortchanged the only thing that could ultimately give them an exit strategy from the conflict: nation building. In a book published in 1969, Thompson wrote that "the problem in Vietnam was, and still is, that of government in its broadest sense and of organization, both in the military and civilian administrative structure." It was a problem, he claimed, that the Americans had hitherto "refrained from tackling."[20] Thompson viewed the Revolutionary Development program and its parapolitics as a "pathetic" gimmick that ignored the need to reform the regular GVN bureaucracy.[21] Although he had an authoritarian streak, Thompson agreed with the necessity of involving the rural population in the effort rather than simply imposing outside solutions on them. During his time in Malaya, Thompson had believed that a nation-building effort had "to involve the people" as well as government institutions.[22] Similarly, in Vietnam, he believed that only the South Vietnamese villagers themselves could bring about victory. But an administrative "machine" had to be created in the villages to discipline their efforts and lead them there, just as the Communists created their own organizational machine to both mobilize and control the population.[23]

In Thompson's view, there were three main components to the U.S. effort in Vietnam. The most important was "nation building," which was the "offensive constructive programme" that strengthened the GVN and eventually set the conditions in which U.S. withdrawal could take place. Military operations, the second component, were defensive in nature and designed to hold off the military forces of the Communist movement while nation building proceeded. "The programme which linked these two together was pacification," he remarked, "because on the one hand it was designed to restore governmental control throughout the country and to establish a permanent link between the central government and the villages and, on the other hand, to destroy the hold which the Vietcong's political underground organization had on the population."[24] Pacification—the third component—allowed for the clearing away of the organizational infrastructure of the Vietnamese Communists. It also brought the GVN into contact with the rural population. But pacification alone was not enough. Nation building meant building permanent links between the GVN and its citizens. The strengthening of village governments, local militias, and village police would allow the GVN to organize and control the population and preclude the Vietnamese Communist movement from doing the same. Thompson believed that it was this nation-building element that the Americans had given short shrift, as they had been too focused on the mere territorial control implied by "pacification."[25]

Other European writers agreed with Thompson, particularly veterans of France's war in Indochina.[26] Bernard Fall was a prominent French war correspondent and academic who had arrived in French Indochina in 1953 to carry out research into the war there. Fall likewise saw a stark difference between "pacification" and the establishment of durable ties between the central government and the rural population. Noting that "to the last breath a government will try to collect taxes," Fall had checked village tax rolls in areas of the Red River Delta that the French claimed were pacified and found that most of the population of the delta was not paying taxes. He similarly discovered that although village schoolteachers were supposedly assigned by the central government, there were large areas in which they were not present. Even though the entire area was inside a large French military cordon, he concluded that the central government could not be said to have an administrative presence in about 70 percent of the delta. This lack of administrative and political links between the central government and the villages was what allowed the Viet Minh "to take over a country under our feet" by bringing the rural population under its own administration. As he wrote in a U.S. military journal in 1965, Fall believed that "when a country is being subverted it is not being outfought; it is being out-administered." If the Americans were going to avoid losing in Vietnam, they would have to avoid the same fate. "The question in my mind is this," wrote Fall. "Can we in Viet-Nam, or anywhere else, save (or improve) the administrative or governmental structure?" Only by extending government administration into the villages, where the bulk of the population resided, could the Americans win the war.[27]

Fall in turn drew on the works of Roger Trinquier, a veteran of the French wars in both Indochina and Algeria. In 1962, Trinquier published his book *Modern Warfare*, in which he synthesized the experiences he and many other French officers had drawn from these two conflicts. Like Colby, Thompson, and Fall—who wrote the introduction to an English translation of *Modern Warfare*—Trinquier was critical of the traditional military establishment. He wrote that "our military machine reminds one of a pile driver attempting to crush a fly, indefatigably persisting in repeating its efforts." The key to winning what he termed modern wars—by which he meant counter-guerrilla campaigns that required nation building—was not firepower but the organization of the populace. It was not necessary, he held, to have "the sympathy of the majority of the population in order to rule them. The right organization can turn the trick." He believed that groups like the NLF derived their success from a "specially adapted organization" that allowed them to mobilize the population to provide them with manpower, supplies, and intelligence. Neither Thompson nor Trinquier was myopic enough to totally dismiss the fact that groups like the NLF enjoyed popular support. But they believed that a more salient factor was that the government had ceded control of village organization and administration to the insurgents.[28] Like Thompson, Fall and Trinquier advocated spreading central government control over rural areas, uprooting the local infrastructure of the Vietnamese Communist movement, and then building up a pro-government infrastructure from below. They referred to this process by the French term *quadrillage*, or "gridding."[29] Only by dismantling the enemy's political and administrative infrastructure and constructing a "similar organization" on the government side could the GVN hope to triumph.[30] This required the establishment of a governmental presence in the villages and the mobilization of the population into pro-government militias and political organizations.

This all implied a renewed focus on the village itself. South Vietnam was a unitary state whose constitution provided that power was vested in the villages in a manner of the central state's choosing. The village was the lowest rung of the GVN that was allowed to make a budget, levy taxes, and own property, and was therefore considered by the GVN to be "the basic echelon of rural administration."[31]

This legal standing made it able to become the basis for a lasting devolution and decentralization of power.[32] As the GVN's 1969 pacification plan explained, this would "ensure lasting success."[33] The cornerstone of the village system was "a decentralization of some degree of power to the population in order to stimulate them and invite them into . . . participation."[34] In turn, this was based on the idea of the "three selfs." Through "self-government," villagers would be able to elect their own village leaders. "Self-development" entailed the provision of central government material aid to the village administrations so that they could, at least in theory, respond to the need of their constituents. "Self-defense" programs aimed to raise local militia who would defend the village against small Communist units and free up the ARVN to take the place of departing American forces. The village system tied together numerous strands of American nation-building thinking—the materialist, the security-oriented, and the participative.

The focus, though, was definitely on the latter. The self-government, self-defense, and self-development programs were designed to create a mesh of organizations in each village that would structure and direct the energies of the population in the service of the GVN and against the NLF. In 1969, Thompson had critiqued the nation-building effort to date for allowing the GVN's "administrative organization . . . to decay while the corresponding Vietcong asset was allowed to flourish." This had allowed the Vietnamese Communist movement greater success at "harvesting the surplus energy, manpower and production of the South Vietnamese people."[35] The village system was designed to change that. Just as Thompson, Fall, and Trinquier recommended, the pro-government administrative structure at village level would match and—it was hoped—ultimately displace the NLF's own structure. Summing up the new American nation-building thrust in 1969, McManaway wrote that "the PSDF [People's Self-Defense Force], village self development, and village administration programs are directly aimed at building an organizational structure within which political activity can flourish. Our 'rural political strategy' . . . is to get as many people as possible affiliated in *some* kind of organization—whether para-military, economic, social, youth, or political—using self-interest as the incentive."[36] Just as CORDS used the GVN's own self-interest in mobilizing rural resources to persuade Saigon to adopt reforms, so the reforms themselves aimed to use the decentralization of power to villagers to convince them that their own self-interest lay with the Saigon government.

Building up the capacities of the GVN in the villages also meant progress on another issue on which Colby and the European theorists were in agreement: the importance of reducing the military's role. From the vantage point of a memoir written decades later, Thompson would criticize the United States and the GVN for a tendency to militarize civil functions, and contrast the situation unfavorably with Malaya. "In Malaya the army supported the civil power during an 'emer-gency,'" he wrote, "but in Vietnam the civil power, where it existed, supported the army in a war."[37] Trinquier, Fall, and Colby also believed that large-unit sweeps and heavy firepower were counterproductive. Instead, the village system was designed to eventually allow the burden of the war to be shifted onto locally raised militias and village governments. As Vann explained, overreliance on the military led to what was effectively an "occupation" of rural areas by a GVN and ARVN administration imposed from the outside. This was not only unlikely to elicit the active support of the population, but also inevitably allowed the NLF to reemerge when government forces moved on.[38] "Without an overt commitment from the population in favor of GVN objectives," read policy guidance written in 1971, "pacification is hardly distinguishable from military occupation."[39]

Though the military occupation of rural areas and the driving out of large Communist units constituted a first step, the village system was designed to translate these short-term gains at pacification into durable nation building. According to Vann, "the willing cooperation of the people with their government because they believe it will be in their own self-interest," along with the rejection of the NLF, would allow the GVN to withdraw its military forces from an area sometime after the initial "occupation." This was a vital facet of the village system at a time when Vietnamization was reducing the number of U.S. forces who were able to provide a security shield behind which nation building could take place, meaning that the ARVN would have more tasks to accomplish with declining resources. By contrast, the active participation of the population meant that "a relatively smaller number of armed men, more centrally located, can respond to the warnings or 'intelligence' given by a watchful loyal population."[40]

The opportunity to implement the village system arose in part because declin-ing violence across South Vietnam between 1968 and the Easter Offensive led to a vast improvement in the country's refugee situation. The number of internally displaced persons recorded in official statistics in South Vietnam peaked in early 1969 at nearly 1.5 million before declining thereafter. In 1969, just over half a million of these refugees returned to their original homes, and another 586,388 were paid resettlement allowances by the GVN to allow them to move some-where else.[41] At the same time, the practice of forcibly relocating civilians during military operations was increasingly discouraged by both the United States and Thieu. In January 1968, Westmoreland had noted that the allies had two basic options to isolate the civilian population from the NLF. "Either the communists and their political control must be driven from the populated areas and secu-rity provided to keep them out," he wrote, "or the people must be relocated into areas that will facilitate security and prevent communist control apparatus from re-entering the community." While the first course of action was "preferred," it was also "time-consuming and expensive."[42] Civilians had therefore often been forcibly moved to areas of GVN control from the time of the Strategic Hamlet Program under Diem. The resentment and disruption this caused undermined attempts by the GVN to build a positive relationship with its rural citizens. Recognizing this, from 1969 onward Thieu and Colby repeated the mantra that security should be brought to the people rather than the people to security.[43] As GVN territorial control spread and the pace of military operations in populated areas declined, huge numbers of rural citizens returned to their villages. This made it possible for the village system to be implemented on a scale that would have been impossible during the chaotic and fluid environment before the 1968 offensives.

In the context of wider U.S. policy under Nixon, the village system represented the civil side of Vietnamization. In fact, as one briefer noted in 1971, CORDS had been involved in a process of Vietnamization ever since its creation in 1967.[44] Official policy guidance on Vietnamization sent out by Colby and General Creighton Abrams in 1971 asserted that "the nub of the policy is assistance and support of the Vietnamese constitutional structure to build the strength necessary to sustain itself in the future against the external and internal problems it will face."[45] Vietnamization also placed new pressures on the GVN. The U.S. involvement in South Vietnam was now time-limited, subject to political pressures in the United States. GVN leaders likewise realized that they would increasingly have to rely on their own resources to run South Vietnam and keep the Communists at bay as American forces and monetary assistance were withdrawn. As an American government economist who studied South Vietnam intensively for USAID argued, since 1965 the GVN had pursued a policy of relying on foreign resources to fight the Communists rather than mobilizing domestic assets.[46] Both the American combat troops fighting for Saigon and the American aid dollars flowing into its coffers attested to this. With the onset of Vietnamization, Thieu and his allies in Saigon realized that there was a need for their government not only to spread its control of the rural population but also to harness the assets of rural South Vietnam—its manpower and economic resources—to bolster itself for a time when it would have to rely much more on its own resources.

The GVN and the Village System

The village system represented a blending of American and Vietnamese thinking on political organization and revolutionary war in South Vietnam. But the Vietnamese figures whom Americans like Colby and Vann had learned from were not mainstream ARVN province chiefs or GVN politicians, but mavericks and outsiders like Chau. In turn, Chau had based his thinking on the example of the

Vietnamese Communist movement and his own time in the Viet Minh. Much of what he taught went against the entrenched interests and worldview of the urban class who staffed the ARVN officer corps and served as provincial and district officials. CORDS advisers who tried to bring about the implementation of the village system were hence always working with and simultaneously against the GVN.

The fate of Chau and Major (later Colonel) Nguyen Be, his successor as head of the Vung Tau center, illustrated the problem. Both were eventually jailed by Thieu, who disliked their independent streaks, opposition to the GVN hierarchy, and closeness to the Americans. A former Viet Minh battalion commander like Chau, Be shared his distaste for the typical province chiefs who were distant from the rural population. Be once told a visiting Vice President Hubert Humphrey that the majority of district chiefs in South Vietnam were corrupt, raising eyebrows from Washington to Saigon.[47] Training GVN cadres at Vung Tau, he preached about the evils of landlordism and official corruption in the Vietnamese countryside, as well as the danger of the Communist movement. As can be imagined, these views did not endear him to his fellow officers who staffed the lower levels of the government bureaucracy. Be believed in creating a genuine village democracy, but feared that his program would be diluted or destroyed by entrenched interests in rural government. Thieu was wary of Be, and remarked on at least one occasion that "better educated and more patriotic people—Army people" ought to be put in charge of the RD cadre program that Be was now running.[48] Only the fact he was highly regarded by the Americans protected Be from Thieu's wrath, and Bunker had to head off at least one attempt to fire him.[49] Criticizing his own countrymen while enjoying the protection of the Americans placed Be in a tricky position. When American advisers had all left following the Paris Peace Accords, Be was promptly accused of embezzlement, fired, and replaced by a Thieu loyalist.[50] Chau, meanwhile, had entered politics as a legislator and become highly critical of Thieu. After being accused of making contact with his brother who was serving in the NLF—hardly an unusual act, given how political loyalties had fractured families across South Vietnam—Chau was imprisoned following a controversial trial.[51] Neither example encouraged the emergence of other crusading reformers from within the ARVN or the GVN.

CORDS's activities in the final years of the conflict involved a complex dance of negotiation and compromise with the GVN at all levels, from Thieu and his ministers in Saigon down to the province and district chiefs with whom field advisers worked. Colby and his lieutenants in Saigon were successful at persuading Thieu and officials in the Ministry of Rural Development to adopt the tenets of the village system, at least in principle. A series of decrees promulgated by the GVN, including a major circular on the reorganization of village government in

April 1969, laid the groundwork for the village system.[52] Each year afterward until the American withdrawal, ministries in Saigon promulgated large strategic plans that provided instructions for priority rural reforms and the implementation of the village system over the coming year. These documents reflected CORDS's priorities well, not least because CORDS officials had a heavy hand in writing them.

These plans continued to run into problems when passed to local officials for implementation, reflecting the entrenched difficulty of bringing about reforms at the local level. Some Vietnamese officials such as "Anh" were in sympathy with the aims of the village system and its de-emphasis of the military role. As early as 1967, Anh complained about the pattern of occupation followed by withdrawal that typified "pacification." Military units would move in, order the people to cooperate with government forces, then "before the village is strong enough they move to another place because they are understrength . . . leaving the village to the VC again. After such an experience, you can never expect to be successful if you come back the second time."[53] But while NIA-trained officials like Anh were more likely to support the village system, the military-trained province and district officials and corps commanders who held most sway in the countryside would ultimately decide whether implementation of it would be successful. Anh and most civilians like him never rose to the position of province chief, which remained mostly a military prerogative. There was only so far Thieu was able—or wanted—to go in imposing the village system on the military officers who still staffed most of the GVN. Thieu had consolidated his position following the 1968 offensives and had been able to replace a sizable proportion of local leadership. But it was very tricky for him to carry out what amounted to a revolution in local governance while relying on the very officials whose power the revolution would undermine to both carry it out and to keep fighting the war. In the paraphrased words of an American officer, Thieu did not have the luxury of destroying the GVN in order to save it. Nor, as his treatment of Be and Chau showed, was he in total sympathy with the aims of the reformers.

From the 1969 plan onward, the GVN stressed the need to capitalize on the improved security environment to carry out reforms. "We are now stronger than we have ever been, and the enemy is at his weakest period," exulted the 1969 plan. "Presently, our resources ready to be used in the Pacification Program are larger than ever before." In rhetoric that echoed Colby's words about the need for correct technique, it warned that "we may repeat the same mistakes of the past if we do not learn and apply the important Principle of the Community Spirit." This principle, which recurred frequently in GVN discourse on nation building, called for "cooperation among the people, cooperation between the people and the Government, and cooperation among Government organizations."[54]

Although the Community Spirit Principle was compatible with the American concept of the "three selfs," it tended to stress the responsibility of citizens toward the GVN more than the reverse. In private remarks, top GVN officials also consistently placed more emphasis than CORDS on the fact that the bargain between people and government did not just involve resources and rights flowing downward to the people, but also demanded that they actively assist the GVN. "The important factor here is to instill in the people a sense of responsibility for their community for it is the people themselves who must actively combat the Communists," Thieu explained in early 1969. "The people must participate in all activities to defend and develop themselves."[55] Along with the Americans, Thieu felt that "the people must be held under GVN control from a political and ideological point of view, not just administrative."[56] Yet it is interesting that he talked of ideological and political control rather than democracy and participation, as the Americans did. According to his aide Nguyen Tien Hung, Thieu and his close advisers believed that Vietnam was not ready for democracy and went along with liberalizing ideas only to maintain American support.[57] This made him unwilling to risk too much of his support from the military for the sake of ideas of whose usefulness he was not convinced. Nghiem Dang, the head of the NIA, also placed a greater accent on the control of the population rather than seeking spontaneous commitment. "Whether interest groups are spontaneous or co-ordinated or whether they are organized for the purpose of public control or for population regimentation," he wrote, "the very fact of their existence shows the extent to which citizens participate in administrative activities."[58] Prime Minister Huong likewise stressed the responsibility of citizens, saying that "the guiding principle of the program was that the people would do more for themselves and that the government would support them."[59] The 1970 plan also took up his theme, stressing on its first page: "All people must understand their mission, their private responsibility, and support the government."[60] As Vietnamization advanced, this point remained pertinent. In fact, it amounted to a matter of the GVN insisting that the burden of Vietnamization would fall on the country's rural citizenry. With the withdrawal of U.S. military forces, the need for the GVN to enlist the cooperation of its local citizens in national defense only grew stronger. The result was that, as the 1971 plan explained, "a greater share of the burden of defense must be borne locally, by the villagers themselves."[61]

On the other hand, Thieu realized that the reforms CORDS pushed were a logical response to Vietnamization because they helped enlist the GVN's citizens in the common defense. He also appreciated the value of keeping the Americans onside for as long as possible. As Colby explained, Thieu had a particular way of dealing with his American advisers, realizing that "to handle their enthusiasm it was not appropriate to challenge them directly . . . but it was sensible to accept their ideas rather than reject them and then try to adjust them to make them more practical." In this way he channeled CORDS's ideas "to what could practically be accomplished in the real world of Vietnam."[62] Of particular relevance to Thieu was that the village system chimed with his own need to expand the coercive reach of the GVN throughout the South Vietnamese countryside. Thieu and his principal subordinates could see the benefits of enacting reforms in local government to enable them to enlist South Vietnamese citizens in militias and police forces that would help with this goal. Their priorities for the implementation of the village system reflected this. After the war, ARVN chief of staff Cao Van Vien remembered CORDS's role in raising local militias and police as "by far the most important and outstanding among US contributions" to what he called "pacification."[63] Thieu and many other generals could see the benefits of changes to rural governance that promoted pacification.[64] But this did not necessarily mean they had embraced a vision of participative nation building.

Nor did it mean Thieu had become a mere puppet of the Americans. Thieu and his principal allies in the GVN might see the benefit in the broad outlines of the village system, but they were by no means prepared to go along with a clean sweep of rural administration. Like every South Vietnamese leader since Diem who had stacked the localities with his own allies, Thieu's consolidation of power gave him an interest in protecting the structure he had established. By 1970, he was becoming less susceptible to American advice about the hiring and firing of province chiefs.[65] Frank Scotton, who during these years was working for Colby on the case files of officials suspected of corruption, could not remember one case, from 1970 to 1972, of the United States managing to have a senior official removed.[66] Thieu's growing distrust and paranoia as the war wound down made him seem increasingly distant in the final years of the American presence. On Kissinger's first visit to South Vietnam, he met with opposition leaders as well as making a trip to the Presidential Palace, which Thieu took as a disturbing indication that Washington was still keeping eggs in more than one basket. According to Hung, he even put forces on alert against a possible coup. Thieu also suggested that Americans whipped up debates against his regime, claiming, "Any time the American ambassador came to see me and asked me to do something and I refused, you could count two weeks before the demonstrations erupted."[67]

Yet it was clearly out of the question for Thieu to break with the Americans, and he sought to pursue what he called a "long haul / low cost" strategy to keep the United States engaged as long as possible.[68] In different ways, Vietnamization and the village system both allowed for the GVN to reduce the cost of U.S. involvement in the conflict, thus allowing the United States to engage for a longer period. The support of CORDS, which had aimed from the beginning to build the capacities of the GVN to the point that it could exist independently of American support, was naturally vital to this process. Thieu's goals were to squeeze as much support out of the Americans as possible while keeping one eye on the time when the Americans would be gone and he would have to rely on his own political base to stand up to the Communist movement. "I know that you are going to go, but before you go, you have to leave something for us as friends," he told Nixon at Midway. "Leave something to help me out."[69]

From Pacification to Nation Building?

The first major post-Tet initiative undertaken by CORDS was the Accelerated Pacification Program (APC). As Komer later explained, the APC was a "highly simplified" program whose purpose was to get GVN forces back out into the countryside to reestablish a minimal government presence. The aim was to organize pro-GVN militias, install a GVN hamlet government—preferably by election, but by appointment if the security situation did not permit it—and to carry out one local development project in each target hamlet. Over thirteen hundred hamlets were eventually targeted.[70] The APC benefited from close coordination with large U.S. military units and their heavy firepower, which operated to screen target hamlets from overt attack and separate cadres and guerrillas from villagers. At Colby's insistence, the APC focused on the Mekong Delta, where some six million South Vietnamese lived. It was also the area where MACV believed that the NLF was still at its strongest, an anomaly given that 70 percent of the enemy's combat and combat support strength in South Vietnam was assessed as being NVA by early 1969.[71]

CORDS officials conceived of the APC as the first step before they could move to implement the village system. It was the necessary pacification, or "occupation," element of establishing control over the countryside before genuine nation building could be attempted. Vann, now head of CORDS in the delta, saw the APC as a process of a "fast and thin" expansion of GVN control aimed at "unwrapping the GVN from around the province and district flagpoles they had clustered to during the 1968 Tet offensive."[72] Colonel Robert M. Montague, Komer's military aide, later described the APC as a "once-over-lightly" whose goal was "to show the government's flag."[73] CORDS officials also hoped that the APC would focus the minds of GVN local government on the problem of expanding control of the rural population. Under the plan, district chiefs were required to visit target hamlets once a week, and village chiefs were required to visit them three times a week.[74] Furthermore, in Colby's words, "the arrival of government force and authority was accompanied by some immediate impact project such as a school." Although in the past these material projects had usually been assessed as having little impact on villager loyalty or motivation (a fact Colby did not mention, but was aware of), it was hoped they would "give an immediate visible indication of government presence, benevolence, and intention to stay."[75]

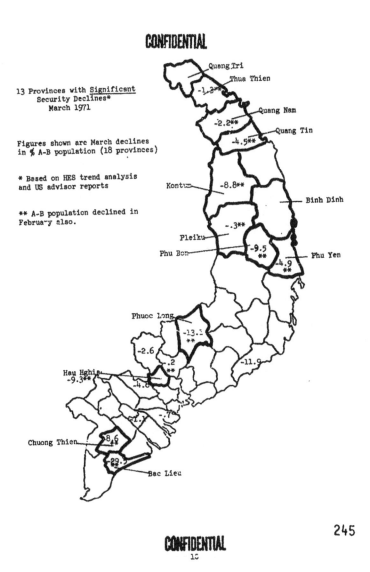

FIGURE 8.   Deterioration in pacification in eight provinces as measured by HES, August 1970–August 1971. Thomas C. Thayer, ed., *A Systems Analysis View of the Vietnam War, 1965–1972*, vol. 9, *Population Security* (Washington, DC: OASD(SA)RP Southeast Asia Intelligence Division, 1975), 251.

Measuring the impact of such intangibles was difficult, but the APC inaugurated a period of almost uninterrupted gains in government control of the countryside, which lasted until the Easter Offensive of 1972. According to Hamlet Evaluation System (HES) figures, some 1.6 million more Vietnamese were living in rural areas classified as secure when the APC came to an end at the beginning of February.[76] Elections were held in 41 percent of the targeted hamlets, and 170,000 weapons were distributed to local militia.[77] While the number of weapons distributed was easy to measure, CORDS officials were more cautious about the other figures. Given pressures to succeed and the subjective nature of the HES figures, Colby was careful not to read too much into them. "Some of the statistics . . . we thought were fairly soft, to put it mildly," Colby later wrote. He considered reports of 1.1 million recruited to the People's Self-Defense Force, with four hundred thousand trained, to be particularly risible.[78] Bunker cabled Washington that while the HES numbers were "sometimes questioned," their value lay in giving a "definite reflection of the trend."[79] One reason to believe that the figures were at least useful for establishing a trend was that HES ratings had tracked sharply downward following the Tet Offensive, showing that the system also measured setbacks.[80] The HES system also continued to measure localized setbacks despite the broad pattern of increasingly positive results between 1968 and 1972. By the summer of 1971, the HES system was showing some 77 percent of South Vietnam's population were living under government control, but also showed that a sharp deterioration had taken place in eight provinces since the previous summer. This deterioration, depicted in figure 8, vindicated HES's usefulness as a tool that measured setbacks as well as trumpeted victories, but also carried an underlying warning about the fragility of apparent gains in the face of increased enemy activity.[81] Top CORDS officials such as Colby were aware of this, and therefore treated the overall HES trends (shown in table 3) with skepticism. In the words of Willard E. Chambers, a high-ranking CORDS official in Saigon, South Vietnam in late 1971 was "pockmarked with areas where both advisors and their counterparts are suffering from a euphoria which the VC could negate overnight."[82]

TABLE 3. Percentage of population living in hamlets with security rated "A" or "B" by HES, 1968–1971

	DEC. 1969 (%)	DEC. 1970 (%)	DEC. 1971 (%)	TOTAL CHANGE (% POINTS)
I Corps	63.3	76.5	84.4	+21.1
II Corps	63.2	63.1	71.7	+8.5
III Corps	86.8	89	94.7	+7.9
IV Corps	60.1	68	81.6	+21.5

pp. 157, 266

Even if the impressive HES figures in table 3 are taken at face value, Colby and his team knew they did not necessarily represent a success at the more intangible task of nation building. This was clear even in the immediate aftermath of the APC. In September 1969, CORDS's Pacification Studies Group (PSG) carried out an assessment of security in a village in Phu Yen Province whose HES ratings indicated it was secure. They found that the RD cadre and territorial forces who were supposed to be keeping the village free of enemy influence were in fact "submissively cowed to the point where contact is avoided when possible." The lack of security incidents in the village was due to the fact that the enemy forces who dominated it did not want to draw attention to the village and have their freedom of movement disrupted.[83] Vann had warned earlier in the year that large areas of the Mekong Delta may have appeared more secure than they were because the NLF was quietly governing areas and harnessing their resources in ways that fell below the GVN and U.S. radar.[84] As we saw in the last chapter, the Nixon White House had reached similar conclusions about the limited optimism that could be derived about the true progress of nation building from a mere absence of violence. For Colby, the Phu Yen report reinforced what he had long known. "When we started the APC we said that our objective was to expand government authority 'thin and fast,'" he wrote in response. "It is quite apparent that that is exactly what occurred. The government presence in this area is a thin veneer indeed."[85] It was clear that establishing a governmental presence in the countryside under the APC was only the beginning of nation building; establishing mutual bonds of obligation between the GVN and the people, and thus transitioning from "occupation" to true nation building, was longer and more nebulous work. As MACV believed that the lack of serious enemy opposition had been the main reason the APC has been successful, nation building would also be reliant on continued cooperation by the enemy.[86] The serious deterioration that took place in Phu Yen shortly afterward (see figure 8) showed what could occur when such cooperation was not forthcoming.

As GVN control of the rural population spread, CORDS advisers and higher officials in Saigon began to grapple with the much thornier problem of implementing the village system. As one of Vann's subordinates in the Mekong Delta argued in a think piece he wrote for his boss, now that the GVN was in "direct contact with the six million people of the Delta" it was time to capitalize on the "momentum in military security" and "parallel that effort with a political effort."[87] This political effort was intended to move beyond the mere "occupation" of rural South Vietnam and instead to implement the "three selfs." This proved a far more difficult task. The shift from quantitative targets based on improving security to qualitative ones based on political development raised a host of problems that advisers had to struggle with. In a candid assessment for

Bunker in July 1970, Colby said that "the novelty and excitement of expanding into new territories" had been "followed by the comparative drudgery and inconclusiveness of improving performance, remaining alert, and wrestling with fundamental economic and social problems."[88] These thorny problems would consume the efforts of American nation builders until the end of U.S. involvement in South Vietnam.

7

IMPLEMENTING THE VILLAGE SYSTEM

The strength of the GVN in the final years before American withdrawal in 1973 has long been in dispute. Some contemporary observers believed that the Communist movement in South Vietnam had been fatally undermined during these years. People who could remember the insecurity and destruction of the first phase of the war were particularly bewitched by the apparent calm that had spread over the countryside. "The most dramatic event taking place thus far in the 1970s is the increase in security in the South Vietnam countryside," wrote Allan E. Goodman, a seasoned observer of the South Vietnamese scene, in 1971. "For most of the 1960s the debate over security centered on how to measure the little that existed." By the early 1970s, the amount of security achieved was "no longer a subject of official debate."[1]

Many other observers were similarly bullish. Sir Robert Thompson later wrote that by 1970 the fruits of pacification and Vietnamization were "unassailable." The Brit had shifted from leveling stark criticisms of the U.S. effort during the Johnson administration to now warning that the main threat under Nixon was a "comprehensibility gap." The public simply did not understand how well the war in South Vietnam was now going.[2] William Colby has likewise stated that "we had won the guerrilla war" by the time of the Easter Offensive in 1972.[3] John Vann—never one to shrink from telling truth to power—gave his own upbeat assessment of the security situation to the Senate Foreign Relations Committee in 1970. Vann by this point headed CORDS in the entire Mekong Delta, the most populous area of South Vietnam. The area saw a "rather tremendous improvement in security" over 1969, he claimed, and it was now possible to drive safely to any provincial capital during the daytime.[4] Cao Van Vien remembered after the war that "conditions in the countryside radically improved and prospects for the future were never so bright" as in the years after 1969.[5]

Even officials in the British Embassy in Saigon, who had often been skeptical of American claims of progress, felt change blowing in the wind. In May 1969, the British defense attaché reported that the military position of the Communists in the Mekong Delta was "weak," allowing pacification "to continue its progress."[6] A review of events in South Vietnam during 1971 prepared by the British Embassy noted that at year's end the two southern military regions—which contained Saigon and the Mekong Delta—"were, broadly speaking, secure." The report concluded that for South Vietnam, 1971 was a "good year" in which "a tolerable level of security" had been achieved.[7] A reply sent back from London gave South Vietnam "a sporting chance" of survival.[8] All of this seems to lend some credence to Lewis Sorley's claim that the war "was won" at some point in "late 1970."[9]

But in guerrilla warfare and nation building, surface appearances can be deceiving. As Goodman noted as early as 1971, the debate over the extent to which apparent security had been achieved in South Vietnam gave way to another debate: what exactly this appearance of security meant, and whether it was significant.[10] The question rested on the distinction between pacification and nation building that Thompson, Vann, and others had noted in their criticisms of the war effort in earlier times. Pacification could bring apparent security through a military occupation of the rural areas by South Vietnamese and American forces, but nation building was much more nebulous. While many contemporary observers and subsequent historians have focused on the apparent calm that spread across South Vietnam during these years, this chapter instead probes the extent to which the GVN put down durable roots among its population.

Crucial evidence of the GVN's failure to do so comes not only from American observers but also Vietnamese. During the final years of the war, a branch of GVN inspectors produced "pacification research reports" based on surveys of dozens or hundreds of rural villagers on a particular issue. Vietnamese inspectors would enter hamlets and villagers incognito, unaccompanied by any American, and question the locals about their views toward issues such as taxation, the draft, and corruption. They were often able to elicit a great deal of criticism toward the GVN, which was more revealing of rural attitudes in the final years of the war than the surface calm that pervaded South Vietnam. Taken with other evidence, these surveys call into question any claim that the GVN had carried out successful nation building in the latter years of the war.

After the 1968 offensives, the GVN's control and administration of the countryside via a network of province and district chiefs were much more secure than they had been during the period of high-intensity warfare from 1965 to 1968. Yet the failure to engender enthusiasm toward the GVN throughout the villages of South Vietnam called into question whether CORDS's nation-building strategy could work even in the absence of large-scale violence or enemy activity. CORDS officials had hoped that they would be able to foster what they called a "friendly infrastructure" in each village that, much like the NLF's infrastructure, would act as GVN partisans and oppose the Vietnamese Communist movement actively without the need for an "occupation" by the ARVN. But on the eve of the Easter Offensive, by which time CORDS had nearly been dissolved and the U.S. presence in South Vietnam was in its final months, this dream still seemed far away.

Theory and Practice

Before the creation of CORDS, training for American nation builders had been limited or nonexistent. Some of the Tigers had picked up at least some Vietnamese language ability from previous service in the country, whether it was with an NGO or in the military. But Fraleigh and Phillips had placed more emphasis on a can-do attitude than on local knowledge, and they had frequently sent recruits into the field essentially unprepared. One American was dispatched to Kien Hoa after only one hour of language training.[11] Fraleigh and Phillips had hence sent the Tigers off with a broad remit to improve the social, economic, and political life of the rural population by making GVN local government more effective and responsive to popular needs, but without extensive formal training. The lack of training not only meant that the Tigers would have difficulty understanding either Vietnamese rural society or their counterpart, but also meant that they had a wide degree of autonomy and were not working according to some centralized plan or program.

As a large bureaucracy that prized central direction and unity of purpose, CORDS had more intensive training needs. In April 1967 the Vietnam Training Center (VTC) had been inaugurated in Washington to provide a standardized education to Americans from various agencies who would soon become part of CORDS. Some two thousand Americans passed through the VTC during the course of its existence.[12] As part of the Foreign Service Institute, the VTC provided courses up to ten months long in which future province and district advisers took classes in Vietnamese language, history, and culture, the theory and practice of countering revolutionary war, and their role within CORDS. It was a testament to the scale and significance of the American nation-building effort in South Vietnam that an educational institution dedicated to understanding this one country was founded. Nothing of its kind has existed before or since in the American foreign policy establishment.

The purpose of the VTC was to equip trainees to understand Vietnamese rural society, the Vietnamese Communist movement, and the government they would be aiming to shape. Course attendees read texts on the culture and history of South Vietnam and received lectures from luminaries such as Thompson and Fraleigh.[13] In theory, trainees could also learn about the province to which they would be assigned by talking to personnel who previously served there and reading province-specific literature. In reality, however, trainees often did not find out their assignment until they arrived in-country, making this aspect of the course of dubious use. "I believe it is a basic mistake to regard Vietnam as an homogenous area for which detailed directives and procedures can be established at central level and stipulated to be applicable throughout," remarked James Megellas, leader of CORDS in II Corps in 1970. "Even within any specific CTZ [Corps Tactical Zone] the individual provinces have enough differences to preclude this type of direction being feasible at regional level, much less on a country-wide basis."[14] If the new advisers were lucky, they might overlap with their predecessor long enough to pick up information on the local situation from him, but this was not always the case. Given the differences between provinces in terms of their social and economic condition, the quality of the local GVN government, and the disposition of the local NLF organization, there was a steep learning curve for advisers. Yet during their training, advisers often had no idea whether they were going to be deployed to an almost entirely peaceful province like An Giang or a raging war zone adjacent to North Vietnam.

Reactions to the course were mixed. Although language training was a large part of the course, few advisers were able to engage in much more than small talk when they arrived in South Vietnam. Many province chiefs spoke English or French, but advisers without facility in the Vietnamese language were unable to speak with the ordinary villagers whom they were supposedly there to understand and help.[15] Nor was the language training always in the appropriate dialect. "Johnny" described the "shock" he had arriving in Quang Tri Province in 1965 and discovering that the locals spoke "such a rude rural central dialect." General Thi's regionalist uprising that broke out in early 1966 must only have heightened his discomfort at speaking the dialect of the capital.[16] Given that it was technically possible for advisers to get by speaking to their counterparts in English or French, it was rarely possible for them to be spared from their jobs long enough to develop fluency in the Vietnamese language. Even the legendary John Paul Vann requested to take leave to develop his poor Vietnamese language skills in 1971—and had his request denied.[17]

In the view of "Brad," a USAID official who was embedded directly in the staff of a GVN agency in 1966 and thus saw the relationship from the other side, the poor standard of English spoken by GVN officials often led their American advisers to view them as intellectually inferior.[18] One Saigon-based adviser who traveled many provinces as a program auditor reported being "terrifically" impressed in the mid-1960s that "you could go to practically any province and you found people who spoke English." While urbane GVN officials like Nguyen Duc Thang were accorded respect for their linguistic skills, those Vietnamese who could not match them were looked down upon.[19] This naturally piqued their South Vietnamese counterparts, for whom speaking good English had little obvious connection to their aptitude at navigating their own country. "The Americans tended to have greater confidence in those of us who spoke good English," remarked Tran Van Don, adding that this was "hardly a qualification for military command or denoting special ability, courage, or integrity."[20] Even the language with which Americans were trying to influence their Vietnamese counterparts was thus politicized and charged. Thomas Barnes, the head of CORDS in the populous Mekong Delta in 1971, even felt it necessary to issue a directive banning advisers from speaking in pseudo-English "baby talk" to their counterparts because it demeaned the relationship.[21]

Another problem was the fact that being unable to speak Vietnamese meant that the range of local perspectives advisers were exposed to was limited to those of English-speaking or perhaps French-speaking Vietnamese, who tended to be highly educated and from urban backgrounds. With rare exceptions, this meant that the ease with which advisers could converse with the Vietnamese was inversely proportional to the degree of connection of their interlocutor to rural society. Vien believed that all province and district advisers "should have been required to speak the language too, because this was the only means of obtaining the insight in the local problems of pacification and developing the kind of rapport with the local people that was conducive to success."[22]

Although the Vietnamese language element of a VTC education was wanting, some trainees emerged believing themselves to be fluent in the language of revolutionary warfare. A rural development adviser who attended the course in 1967 remembered it as his first introduction to the idea that insurgencies had political causes and needed political solutions. Despite his recent introduction to the topic, he felt that "if a person took any interest in the course at all that it became clear to him fairly soon what causes an insurgency and how you must deal with it."[23] Others found arriving in province for the first time to be hugely discombobulating and soon had a more modest view of their capabilities. One PSA who served on the central coast in 1968 found that he had not really been able to imagine the reality of "what you're going to be doing in Asia" from the comfort of a classroom.[24] An assistant province adviser who had received six months of training, including five months working on the language, remembered: "When you first get out to a province you are bewildered, you don't know what on earth you're going to do. You really haven't been told, except in a general sort of way, exactly what it is you're supposed to do."[25] Some advisers complained of more quotidian experiences of culture shock of the sort that American travelers abroad have long voiced. "Felix," a naturalized Filipino American, found he could not distinguish between the various provinces of South Vietnam upon arrival "since they all seemed to have similar names." He also complained of being serviced by "shoeshine boys" and obliged to pay them whether he wanted to or not.[26] Although Felix felt that his previous experience of living in the Philippines had helped cushion him from the culture shock of arriving in South Vietnam, most American recruits had not had similar preparation.

Some of the Tigers had worked in the same province for years and gained an understanding of Vietnamese language, culture, and history. CORDS instead operated on the principle that older individuals with no experience of Vietnam could be taught the necessary minimum. "Johnny," the adviser who only discovered he spoke the wrong dialect upon arriving in Quang Tri, replaced a Tiger who had been in the province for three and a half years.[27] Fraleigh had believed that young minds were the most adaptable to new cultures and less prone to be prescriptive and rigid in their view of what was to be done to aid GVN local governments. By contrast, many of the inductees to the VTC were already experienced professionals whose worldviews were more difficult to mold through several months of training. For instance, although experts in "cross-cultural communication" were retained in teaching positions, many course attendees believed they had little to be taught in this area.[28]

An example can be found in the VTC's attempts to mold trainees' view of the Vietnamese peasantry. During training, advisers read a document titled "The Vietnamese Peasant: His Value System." The document was full of sweeping generalizations such as the supposed fact that "the peasant . . . likes war movies, perhaps because he can identify with them." Given the suffering and dislocation that the war had inflicted on many parts of rural South Vietnam, this statement served only to illustrate the distance between the authors of the document and their subject. The overall thrust of the document was that peasants lived in a harmonious if primitive society before the advent of the Communist movement, and even since then they were uninterested in any ideological commitment or higher concern than their own physical safety and prosperity. It reflected USOM's materialist view of peasant motivations, perhaps unsurprisingly, given the VTC was operated by USAID. Trainees were told that "the greatest majority of people will go to whichever side they believe will give them a better deal." The idea that peasants might make a positive commitment to the ideals of the Communist movement—or even its front organizations—was disregarded. The document encouraged trainees to view peasant grievances as manufactured by the Communist movement, as "normally there is little friction between the peasant and the landlord," a statement that reflected the idealistic and ignorant view of rural society taken by many urban South Vietnamese.[29] Even had the document avoided inaccurate generalizations, its usefulness would have been limited, as can be seen by imagining an analogous document titled "The American Town Dweller: His Value System."

While some advisers seemed to internalize this stock portrait of the Vietnamese peasant, others proved resistant.[30] This was not necessarily an advantage, as many advisers seemed to believe that no special knowledge of Vietnamese culture or history was needed to understand its people. One took comfort by assuring himself that the Vietnamese farmer "probably wants the same thing that the farmer in Georgia or Alabama wants."[31] Another adviser thought it fruitful to consider that the Vietnamese were akin to "American Jews" rather than the "Negro or Mexican sub-cultures" because the Vietnamese were merit oriented.[32] Such analogies between Vietnamese society and the American society that advisers were more familiar with often became absurd. An assistant province adviser not fluent in Vietnamese even went so far as to claim that because America was a "basically democratic society" without class distinctions, there was a wider gap between Vietnamese villagers and GVN officials than there was between U.S. advisers and those same villagers.[33]

It was certainly convenient for Americans to believe they understood the villagers without the need for communication, given that the vast majority of advisers could not speak Vietnamese. Still others drew more realistic conclusions, and developed a healthy appreciation of the limits of their own knowledge. One U.S. Army officer with three years of experience as a PSA by 1971 rejected easy generalizations about the Vietnamese and felt that true wisdom lay in knowing what you did not know. "Show me a person who says he understands the Vietnamese," he commented, "and I'll show you a person who only thinks he does."[34] "Earl," a trainee who held less-than-progressive views on race relations in the United States, espoused careful sensitivity to the worldview of the Vietnamese. "I haven't had any cross-cultural problems myself. I realize that the Vietnamese act and react differently than we do," he explained. "If you go from Mississippi to Indiana you will find people act and react differently. I think if your idea is to go over there and help these people and you're really interested in people, you're not going to have these problems."[35]

Some advisers avoided the generalizations that lumped all villagers together either as simple farmers akin to their American cousins or as devious and selfish egotists, instead gaining an appreciation of the complex social and political structure of the villages and provinces in which they worked. The most sophisticated of all realized that this complex structure often had no overlap with the official GVN power structures with which they interacted. In 1970, a deputy PSA in Phu Yen lamented that "there are many undercurrents and back room politics that brew within the Province that no American really knows about or understands." He considered it difficult to know what the people really thought of the GVN, because all he saw was "what the Vietnamese wants us to see."[36] Edward Lansdale, who served in various roles in South Vietnam between 1954 and 1968, believed that most American advisers did not have a sufficient understanding of the "rather highly organized" informal political structure that existed in each district and village. While Americans tended to interact with GVN officials more than anyone else, there was often little overlap between the formal structures of GVN power and the traditional community leaders in the village.[37]

Lansdale had spent many years in South Vietnam to develop this understanding, but the short tour of the typical adviser provided little scope in which to do so. South Vietnamese officials themselves complained that the tours of American advisers were far too short to gain a comprehensive understanding of the country and its problems. According to Vien, "not only was Vietnam a totally alien country, the nature of the war being fought was also unfamiliar to American military experience." One year was not long enough for advisers to acquire the experience necessary to operate at maximum usefulness, and Vien would have preferred they came back for multiple tours—preferably in the same area.[38] But with problems attracting and retaining personnel, CORDS was never able to institute such a system.

When combined with the problems, explored in previous chapters, of influencing their counterparts, the difficulty of understanding rural South Vietnam meant the typical CORDS advisory tour was confusing, confounding, and short. Advisers faced innumerable problems both in understanding their environment and influencing it. The learning curves involved in communicating with the Vietnamese, learning about the local area, and building a rapport with their counterparts often meant advisers were never able to become even minimally effective in a one-year tour. Given CORDS's need for relatively large amounts of personnel and the limited time available in which to train them, there was only so much the VTC could do to alleviate these problems. In attempting to implement the village system in the final years of the war, the limitations of what individual American nation builders could accomplish became obvious.

Self-Government

The first of the "three selfs" that advisers were supposed to implement in rural South Vietnam was self-government. In line with the general thrust of CORDS and GVN policy between the Tet and Easter offensives, the push for self-government involved not just a decentralization of power from the central GVN but also a mobilization of people and resources from below. A village government with an elected chief was, in theory, at the center of these reforms. Under Colby, CORDS sought to persuade the GVN to carry out a broad democratization of the village level of government while simultaneously investing more power in it. This meant institutionalizing the "village system" whereby villages would raise more taxes, direct their own local security operations, and carry out development projects. CORDS's view was that the new breed of village governments should be given latitude to make mistakes, and that if they did, then their constituents could vote them out. The emergence of village governments with a mandate from their people would allow popular aspirations to be met and finally, it was hoped, allow the people to identify with at least one organ of GVN governance.

Such a sweeping change did not go unchallenged. Province and district officials who were used to controlling the security forces and resources that were now to be devolved to village chiefs did not always give up such control gracefully, and the central GVN in Saigon likewise had doubts about some aspects of CORDS's passion for decentralization. And while CORDS and the GVN organized an industrial-scale training effort for hamlet and village officials, several years was clearly too short a time in which to revolutionize previous patterns of governance in rural South Vietnam. By the time the Easter Offensive struck in 1972, causing a significant backsliding in the name of security needs, the results of the push for self-government were fragile.

U.S. officials had long seen the GVN's weakness at village level as a key impediment to nation building. Although the ravages of war—along with the economic opportunities the war bought to the cities—had created an unprecedented degree of mobility among the rural population, most villagers had little experience of any political unit larger than their home village. The province and even the district were remote, alien institutions—and Saigon much more so. As a handbook for CORDS advisers explained, "It is the village/hamlet official, not a faraway district or province chief, who personifies the Government of Vietnam to the rural citizens."[39] What experience most villagers had of the direct hand of Saigon was limited to marauding bands of security forces controlled either by the province chief or the local ARVN division commander, and against whom local village and hamlet officials had little redress. Empowering these local officials would allow them to respond to local needs and give them a voice that might be levied against the ARVN and higher levels of the GVN in response to villagers' needs.[40] CORDS accordingly wanted to use the village level of government as a vital intermediary between the rural people and Saigon.[41] "We should sort of complete the circuit between some form of Vietnamese government and the people it serves as well as governs," one adviser explained. "Until we provide some evidence that the government's concerned about its constituents, I think we'll just have an open circuit. So we're trying to plug this in and make it a flow of information, a flow of loyalty."[42]

Vann hoped that the new hamlet and village authorities would stand up for the interests of villagers and in so doing come into conflict with the central GVN, forcing it to "mend its ways."[43] As we saw in the last chapter, this focus on constructing a pro-government village administrative structure as an intermediary between the people and the central government accorded with the thinking of many European theorists. As Thompson described in 1969, the "needs of the people" should come up through the village administrative machine "while the benefits went down."[44] GVN documents likewise talked of the need to free the rural people from "venal and tyrannical officials" by restoring "the vital forces and prestige of the villages and hamlets through the democratic activities carried out by the local people."[45]

These were the views that individuals like Chau and Nguyen Be had been advocating within the GVN for some time, and under the village system they saw them come closest to implementation. On April 1, 1969, Thieu rearranged village government by issuing Decree 45. Village and hamlet governance had previously been governed by a decree set forth in late 1966 that provided for a significant degree of higher-level control over village affairs. Villages could not make loans, spend money on development projects, set tax rates, or control any security forces within the village. The village council could not even move its office without the permission of a ministry in Saigon.[46] On the basis of this earlier structure, elections were held in 939 villages and 5,450 hamlets in South Vietnam during the spring of 1967, constituting less than half of those in the country.[47] NLF terrorism and the 1968 offensives subsequently killed many officials or drove them to seek refuge in the government-controlled cities. Before the APC, only sporadic replacement elections were held. The expansion of security and government control from late 1968 onward was followed both by the reform of village powers in Decree 45 and a renewed push to hold elections. By early 1970, 95 percent of villages in the country had elected administrations, and by January 1972 there were only sixty-six villages out of 2,162 that did not have an elected government in residence.[48] Decree 45 also gave village administrations new powers in the realm of security and development.[49]

These measures—especially the control of security forces and access to development resources—were an unprecedented grant of authority to villages. Village councils would face the judgment of the electorate every three years on whether they had used this authority wisely. Copying the Communist movement's practice of "communalism," the GVN also sought to educate and shape its community leaders to serve its own ends, while staying in touch with their own people. An intensive training course was set up at the National Training Center (NTC) at Vung Tau, still run by Nguyen Be. Village and hamlet officials took their place at the center alongside other "GVN infrastructure cadre" for a course that included both technical and political education.[50] Copying the language of the Communist movement, Colby described this as the process by which the GVN's cadres were "indoctrinated."[51] Over four weeks, officials were trained in leadership, paramilitary organization, and self-defense and given an overview of a variety of technical topics such as rural electrification, how to run post offices, and how to organize the village budget. Political education covered such topics as "what is democracy?" "the role of the Allies in the RVN struggle," and "Communist plots regarding the cease-fire, peace-talks and counter-measures to be taken."[52] Some 31,000 officials and cadres received training at the NTC during 1969, and a further 37,322 in 1970.[53] They then returned to their home villages and hamlets to become the backbone of the GVN "friendly infrastructure."

Yet from the time of the promulgation of Decree 45, the GVN proved unwilling to push this policy of decentralization too far. Nor was it easy to force province and district chiefs to give up their prerogatives. While the village chief's power and prestige appeared strong under the new system, in reality he was hemmed in by powerful deputies who were appointed by the province chief. The village chief's command of the local militia ran through both a deputy for security and a military commissioner, and he did not have a free hand in appointing either. While the village chief nominated an individual for the position of deputy for security, in reality he served at the pleasure of the province chief.[54] Meanwhile, implementing instructions sent to province chiefs some time after the promulgation of Decree 45 and without CORDS input mandated that the village chief had to appoint the senior militia platoon leader as military commissioner. These old hands, who had close ties to the district and province chiefs who had formerly appointed and commanded them, retained operational control of their units while serving as commissioners. "In summary," a CORDS report complained, "this arrangement seems likely to change the outward appearance while preserving the status quo."[55] Two months after Decree 45 was promulgated in 1969, the head of the Pacification Studies Group warned that village control of local security forces remained "mythical."[56]

Nor did the GVN's implementing instructions extol the virtues of decentralization. Instead they pointed out to province chiefs that villages had already "enjoyed a liberal grant of authority" under earlier decrees and now needed only to be made "more effective."[57] By making the issue the effectiveness of local administration rather than portraying decentralization as an inherent good, the GVN left a substantial leeway for province and district officials to rationalize their own continued involvement in village and hamlet government. Colby remembered how one village chief whom he met at the National Training Center listened "with near disbelief" to the idea, expounded by Nguyen Be, that a village chief should have the authority to decide on the expenditure of development funds. "The idea," Colby wrote solemnly, "brought tears to his eyes."[58] Yet in reality, district and province chiefs often did not give up their powers so easily. Many retained the paternalistic view of villagers typical of their class—and also, as we have seen, typical of American training documents—and refused to decentralize power. Conversely, a more centralized system was certainly effective for at least one group of people—namely, the province and district officials who were able to benefit from the corruption that it enabled. This gave them another disincentive to enthusiastically pursue the implementation of the "village system."

Corruption remained endemic throughout South Vietnam, even at the height of CORDS's influence. While it is impossible to determine its exact scale, especially insofar as it was carried out in petty ways at province level and below, there is reason to suspect it was very widespread indeed. Measures against petty corruption were less than impressive, and most CORDS advisers did not consider it a proper subject of their attention. "The American attitude seems to be based on the assumption that corrupt practices are part of their way of life and must be accepted," stated one long-serving official, "Frank," in 1967. "Objections are based not upon kind but degree. A certain level is permissable [sic], but more than this calls for corrective action. I subscribe to this view myself."[59] Frank saw 10 percent of cash or 25 percent of construction materials as an unacceptable level of corruption, whereas others saw 10 percent cash as acceptable.[60] Such views were widespread, and advisers routinely normalized corruption. A handbook for advisers noted in 1971 that corruption was the "pervasive vice" of Vietnamese administration and was not to be dealt with through "denunciations and counter-denunciations."[61]

Vann, a key architect of the village system, differentiated between "good corruption" and "dirty corruption."[62] Many other American advisers drew a distinction between "necessary" corruption and that which aimed at making individuals conspicuously wealthy.[63] This distinction underlay the words of a USAID employee in 1968, who stated that corruption was a "cancer" but also "the lubricant by which everything moves." Remove the lubricant, he warned, and it "would be like removing all of the grease from a machine."[64] Several structural factors encouraged this view. The first was the extremely low level of salaries for GVN officials, combined with the high rate of inflation that afflicted South Vietnam during the war years. A 1968 study found that the average province chief had a monthly deficit equivalent to 18 percent of expenses, while for district chiefs the figure was nearly 29 percent. Thieu had himself explained corruption as a result of low salaries, providing a justification from the top for officials to engage in it.[65] This gave rise to a second structural cause of corruption, which came in the form of demands placed on officials lower down the GVN food chain to supplement the income of their superiors. Recalling the period of U.S. escalation, one former province representative said: "The District Chief was like a little god in these districts and they were not above lining their pockets at anybody's expense."[66] Playing god was not an easy habit to get out of, and village and hamlet officials who attended the training course at Vung Tau frequently complained that district chiefs demanded money out of their budgets. This, in turn, required that the village officials engage in corruption of their own, for instance by charging for the issuance of documents that were supposed to be free.[67]

Vietnamese officials, even the honest ones, often bristled at sweeping accusations of corruption that implied it was somehow an ingrained Vietnamese trait. Instead, they pointed to the structural factors that made it unavoidable for many officials. They also blamed the Americans for having a corrupting influence on Vietnamese society and government. "What creates corruption?" asked "Anh," the NIA-trained official. "The Americans," he answered. Anh pointed to the twin impacts of high inflation caused by the U.S. presence and the "new demands" for luxuries like air conditioning that the Americans had brought with them to the country. Vietnamese officials, he said, are "underpaid" and had to "steal somewhere to survive and to raise their families." On the other hand, there were also those—mainly high-ranking officials—who "steal to live very luxuriously," which in turn made "average people ambitious or jealous and want to be equal." Only systemic reforms could stop corruption, and in the meantime Americans had to be aware of its causes and stop casting aspersions on the average Vietnamese official. "What we cannot accept is the distance and the distrust," he complained. "I cannot. Many of my friends cannot."[68]

Yet as inflation continued to run rampant in South Vietnam, this source of distrust remained, and it was still common in 1971 for province and district officials to demand money from village budgets to meet their own costs—legitimate and otherwise.[69] Advisers who were aware of factors such as these tended to see corruption as a practical rather than a moral issue. Yet the money to keep the system of official corruption oiled had to come from somewhere, and it was the rural population who eventually bore the costs via myriad forms of petty graft. As inflation continued to run rampant throughout the final years of the war without commensurate salary increases, the problem remained. Given these factors and the limited options that American advisers had to respond to instances of corruption, it is little wonder that one of the last CORDS advisers to leave the country in 1973 warned that corruption was still a problem across the delta. There had been only "lip service" paid to corruption, he complained, and now he wanted to see "heads roll."[70] Yet with CORDS closing down imminently, the chances of the United States providing the pressure that would fulfil his wishes seemed remote.

Pacification research reports produced by GVN surveyors underlined the pervasiveness of corruption even after years of efforts by CORDS advisers and attempted reforms of the village system. In the wake of the Easter Offensive, opportunities for corruption increased as villagers attempted to escape renewed draft calls. A report in the province of Chau Doc in 1972 found that security agencies would falsely certify villagers as undercover agents so they could avoid the draft, or simply take money from draft dodgers to look the other way. The GVN surveyor concluded that the corruption situation in the province was "grave" and added: "The people feel the present government is bad, since all district or province authorities are more or less corrupt." Because the proceeds of corruption were shared equally between low and high officials, who were "tightly organized," the system seemed impossible to break. According to the surveyor, central government inspectors sent to address the situation would only have their heads turned by "wine, nice girls or expensive gifts."[71] Another survey in Bac Lieu after the Easter Offensive noted that many respondents believed that corruption was still driving villagers into the arms of the NLF, especially those who could not afford draft deferments.[72]

The persistence of corruption was one example of how CORDS had not been able to fundamentally transform the attitudes of individuals at all levels of local government. The structural changes that had been introduced with the "village system" worked only if they were observed in the localities, which they often were not. The problem of "interference in village affairs by higher echelons of government" remained in 1970, with precious little time left to tackle it.[73] The effort to indoctrinate hamlet and village officials in their new duties and powers also began to lose steam after an initial push in 1969. Despite a U.S. preference that ever-increasing numbers of local officials attend the Vung Tau training center, nearly 50 percent of those picked to attend in 1971 chose not to go. Many saw their positions as community leaders imperiled by spending a long period away from the village. Local loyalty came above the duty owed to the GVN, which still seemed an alien and faraway institution. By carrying out its recruitment, training, and indoctrination locally, the Communist movement was hence not only at a practical but also a symbolic advantage. Village and hamlet chiefs from Annam, much of which was a stronghold of the Communist movement and where regionalist suspicion of Saigon was widespread, had particularly poor attendance records at Vung Tau.[74] The areas that had long had the worst record of integration with the GVN and high levels of Communist support remained the most untouched by the self-government program.

In such circumstances, it was not clear that CORDS's post-Tet programs had produced anything more than surface change in either the quality of local government or its responsiveness to the people. It was difficult for advisers, few of whom were equipped to truly understand the political situation in the villages in their area of remit, to even tell. Lansdale believed that most American advisers did not have a sufficient understanding of the "rather highly organized" informal political structure that existed in each district and village. While Americans tended to interact with GVN officials more than anyone else, there was often little overlap between the formal structures of GVN power and the traditional community leaders in the village.[75] Lansdale made his comments in 1968, before village and hamlet elections had been held in most areas. Yet given that district chiefs retained tight control over who was eligible to stand in these elections, in many areas the informal and formal power structures continued to have little crossover. In the most insecure areas, such as Binh Dinh Province, local government was still little more than the facade Colby had considered it shortly after the APC. "Underneath this smattering of government," noted CORDS officials who spent ninety days evaluating the situation in Binh Dinh in mid-1971, "is a society basically in enemy hands."[76]

Even where security was better, high-level CORDS officials did not think that the GVN's "friendly infrastructure" had genuinely won over the rural populace. In 1970, a deputy PSA in Phu Yen noted that it was difficult to know what the people really thought of the GVN because all he saw was "what the Vietnamese wants us to see."[77] This meant that American advisers were reliant for information on the implementation of the village concept from the very same GVN officials at district level and above whose own prerogatives were threatened by it. This only became more of a problem as American eyes and ears were withdrawn from the provinces. In late 1971, a briefer from CORDS told a committee that had gathered to consider the organization's future that the GVN was still not "stuck together" at village, hamlet, and province level. Whether it ever would be "depends on how fast the GVN moves." CORDS officials who worked on local government believed they needed to remain into the post-hostilities period.[78] But with CORDS quickly being wound down, the organization had already passed the peak of its influence.

Consequently CORDS's success in implementing self-government was spotty at best. District and province chiefs who were drawn from the ranks of ARVN officers and appointed to areas they knew nothing about continued to retain a great deal of control over village and hamlet affairs. The idea of introducing elected province chiefs was opposed by Thieu, and American officials also took the view that placing these local jobs in the hands of civilians could drastically weaken security and the effectiveness of the government at lower levels.[79] Hence even elected village and hamlet officials were hemmed in by military men from a vastly different social class appointed to positions above them. Unlike in the Communist system, the careers of these village officials were sharply delimited, and they were unable to rise above the position of village chief. Rather than being seen as the most important rung on a ladder from which power flowed from the bottom up, they remained essentially the local tools of a top-down, distant regime. For as long as ARVN officers with little experience of civil affairs but a great deal of experience in benefiting from corruption retained such power at district and province level, this situation was not likely to change, as efforts to implement the other two parts of the village system—self-defense and self-development—showed.

Self-Defense

One of the ways in which self-government was supposed to be actualized was through the idea of local self-defense. As seen by CORDS, the program had two main goals. The first was to spread security throughout rural South Vietnam at a time when regular military resources in the country were declining rapidly with the withdrawal of U.S. forces. By enlisting South Vietnamese citizens in the defense of their own provinces and villages, the self-defense program freed up the ARVN to take on the mobile offensive role in which the United States had previously taken the lead. The second goal of the program was political. It aimed to strengthen the ties of commitment between the people and the regime by enlisting the former in a national effort. The military training and equipment the regime gave the people symbolized its trust in them. Taken together, these political and military goals aimed "to confront and supplant the enemy's political/military organization in every village with a deadly rival—a 'friendly infrastructure.'"[80]

The value of this infrastructure would lay in its overt commitment to the GVN and equally overt rejection of the NLF. As a CORDS study noted of the People's Self-Defense Force (PSDF) in 1969, "the political value of the program stems from the degree of commitment represented by the PSDF member at the time he chooses to join the PSDF for his self-defense."[81] Vann also agreed that the primary purpose of enlisting villagers in the PSDF program was not "for the expectation of having them fight the enemy," but to have them "overtly committed to the side of the government." The organization of a pro-GVN militia in a village symbolized the overt rejection of the NLF and made it more difficult for the latter to gain control, not least because they might have to shed the blood of a grassroots organization, as opposed to the ARVN, to do so.[82]

FIGURE 9. Female "volunteers" of the People's Self-Defense Forces patrol Kien Dien, a hamlet fifty kilometers from Saigon. Some PSDF participation was more voluntary than others.

National Archives identifier 541865, Miscellaneous Vietnam Photographs, Record Group 306, National Archives II at College Park, Maryland.

The organization was also intended to have a transformative impact on its participants. As Colby explained to a military audience: "They were pretty poor soldiers. They lost a few of the weapons and didn't fight very hard, but they began to participate. They took that gun as a symbol that somehow the government both trusted them and looked to them to use the weapon in their own defense and not just to carry out the directives of the local authorities."[83] Once again, Colby's words sounded rather like they could have come from Thompson's mouth. The Brit had likewise felt during the Malayan Emergency that armed opposition to the Malayan Communists could not be left solely to the military and police, but also had to involve the people. He had been a key proponent of efforts to arm the Chinese population in Malaya, noting that the point was "not that these units would make a great military contribution to the defeat" of the guerrillas "but that the readiness of the Chinese to commit themselves to an armed role and the Government's trust in them would be a major factor" in the guerrillas' "political defeat."[84] Roger Trinquier likewise had written that "for the inhabitant to elude the threats of the enemy, to cease to be an isolated target that no police force can protect, we must have him participate in his own defence."[85]

Thompson and Trinquier were not the only ones to agree. Of all the nation-building programs that CORDS encouraged Saigon to embark upon, the expansion of territorial forces was the one in which GVN officials could see the clearest benefits. While they were concerned about inadvertently arming and training individuals who would eventually turn their guns on the GVN, the government stood to gain a much-bolstered security position from the program. The GVN's preference for this aspect of nation building above all others was a natural result of its preference for measures that increased its control of the rural population. For CORDS too, it was logical to place great emphasis on measures that promoted security, which had been proven to be a prerequisite for reform measures. The self-defense program seemed to promise a way to provide security while avoiding the "occupation" of rural areas by outside forces that the architects of CORDS saw as the hallmark of previous pacification efforts. Now, the people themselves would provide security against the NLF's local guerrillas, freeing main-force units to battle the enemy's own large formations, preferably far from population centers.

The task of self-defense fell primarily on the shoulders of three separate forces in South Vietnam. Two of them—the Regional Forces (RF) and Popular Forces (PF)—were formed in 1964 to replace the Diem-era forces known as the Civil Guard and Self-Defense Corps. However, it was only in the changed conditions after 1968 that they began to make a sizable contribution to the war effort. The third force, the PSDF, sprang up informally on a small scale during the Tet Offensive and then was formalized with the GVN's Mobilization Law of June 1968.

The three forces had different roles and missions, but they shared certain characteristics. First, they were recruited from the areas in which they served. As well as increasing the morale and motivation of the forces, this was designed to bolster the GVN's nation-building goals. Local forces were considered less likely to perpetrate abuses against the civilian population, and they also had less firepower and therefore were not as prone to causing collateral damage. Shifting the provision of security for population centers to territorial forces was designed to minimize the harm that came from the deployment of ARVN and U.S. forces in such roles. If this did not actively encourage people to identify with the GVN, it could at least avoid having them alienated by large combat operations. On the other hand, serving in the territorial forces was supposed to represent a positive commitment to the GVN on the part of those serving, bonding them to the government in a relationship that was both transactional and ideological. From a transactional perspective, they received payment in both cash and in kind for doing their jobs, and they received weapons with which they could defend their local communities. Those serving also received ideological indoctrination designed, in the spirit of "communalism," to create a mental link between their service to their local communities and the greater national cause. Conversely, the GVN demonstrated its trust in rural citizens by arming them. The territorial forces were under the command of officials in the GVN's civil chain of command, running from the province chief down to the district chief and, in theory, to the village chief. This meant that they supposedly would act in ways more attuned to the needs of the rural population than would either ARVN or U.S. main-force units.

For many years, the RF and the PF had been outgunned by the local NLF forces they were supposed to contend with. The territorial forces remained outmatched by the NLF during the 1968 offensives, with only 53 percent of RFs and 44 percent of PFs having firepower equal to or greater than the enemy units they faced in the second quarter of 1968.[86] The parlous security situation and their own poor state of readiness inculcated a cautious mentality in the territorial forces from 1965 until the 1968 offensives, at which point many units were withdrawn from the countryside entirely to defend urban areas. Following this nadir, the United States embarked on a major program of modernization to increase both the equipment and training of the RFs and PFs. By mid-1969, 84 percent of RFs and 77 percent of PFs had equivalent or greater firepower than their local antagonists.[87]

Local security was also augmented by the new force created during 1968, the PSDF. The PSDF were civilians who were enlisted in the direct defense of their own hamlet, mainly by acting as lookouts and to deter the surreptitious movement of small groups of guerrillas at night. They received only the slightest training and were armed with the obsolete weapons that the RF and PF were in the process of swapping out for more modern armaments. Colby, who had been involved in running a similar program during the Diem era, had long favored the distribution of weapons to local militias in this manner, as had Vann.[88] The opportunity to urge this program on the GVN came during the 1968 offensives, when groups of citizens—primarily but not entirely in the cities—began to request that the GVN arm them so that they could defend themselves against attack by the Communists. Many high-ranking GVN officials—led by Prime Minister Huong—were opposed to the large-scale distribution of weapons to citizens, believing that they would not be employed effectively and might fall into the hands of the enemy. Colby and Komer managed to overcome this resistance by pointing out that the NLF already had far superior weapons to the arms that they were proposing to give to the militia, and by focusing on the essentially political aspect of the program. They agreed with Huong that the militia would not be effective enough to battle the NLF, but that was not the point. As a CORDS document later explained, the point of the program was for both citizen and government "to make a public commitment to the other."[89]

This commitment, however, was not necessarily to be voluntary, as the GVN's law implementing the program made clear. Huong having been won over, in June 1968 the GVN passed a Mobilization Law mandating that all citizens ages sixteen to seventeen and thirty-nine to fifty were to be enlisted into what became known as the PSDF.[90] By 1972, some 3.5 million people—both men and women— were registered in the PSDF, of whom one million were classed as "combat PSDF." The remaining 2.5 million "support PSDF" were trained in first aid, firefighting, and similar functions. Of the combat PSDF, only about half were armed.[91]

The mandatory nature of this mobilization already undermined the political goals that CORDS had envisaged for the program. For the GVN, the rapid expansion of territorial forces was mainly about meeting a pressing security need, given U.S. troop withdrawals. From 1969 onward, the ARVN had to shoulder a greater part of the main-force war because of the progressive withdrawal of U.S. forces. In addition, as the GVN expanded its presence throughout South Vietnam between late 1968 and 1972, it was faced with the task of controlling and defending a larger population than ever before. In an environment of decreasing U.S. resources, the GVN would not have been able to establish an armed presence throughout all the country without enlisting greater manpower. A reliance on territorial forces was therefore central to the GVN's security planning from 1969 onward. As Thieu explained in late 1970, the idea was that "local communities will care for themselves against local threats."[92] Within a limited zone around populated areas, RFs conducted offensive operations or assisted in static security, according to the wishes of the province chief. The PFs had a more static role, focusing on the security of their own villages while also contributing to defending important roads, waterways, and bridges. Finally, the PSDF remained within secure zones, where they acted as the eyes and ears of the other units. If confronted by an overwhelming force, they hid their weapons and acted like normal civilians, just as the NLF cadres would do.[93]

Judged against their first goal of generating more manpower to secure rural South Vietnam and allowing the ARVN to replace departing U.S. forces, the "self-defense" forces performed admirably. Territorial force strength exceeded that of the ARVN by an average of just below 19 percent from 1970 to 1972.[94] Casualty figures indicate that the territorials were bearing an even heavier share of the war than the ARVN in these years, with the combined losses of the RFs and PFs between 1968 and 1972 standing at 69,291, versus 36,932 for ARVN regulars.[95] These figures reflect the Communist movement's decision to place an emphasis on attacking the emerging grassroots infrastructure of the GVN, and also their success in doing so. Reflecting their own understanding of the way that political power was built from the bottom up and was most effective when rooted in rural communities, the movement had long placed a great emphasis on stopping the GVN from building its own "friendly infrastructure." As one cadre told his captor after Tet: "If the GVN loses a province chief, it will appoint another to replace him. If it loses the Seventh Division, it will send in another one. At the grass-roots level, the hamlet chiefs, the interfamily group chiefs, and the security agents should all be swept away, and replaced by the Front's own base-level organizations in order to gain the initiative." As the historian David Elliott notes in citing this quote, this illustrates the view that grassroots officials and organizations rooted in a local community were both more valuable to the government and dangerous to the movement.[96]

The enlistment of so many rural citizens into pro-GVN paramilitaries and militias had concrete results in terms of making it much harder for the NLF to operate in some areas, and in freeing up the ARVN to replace U.S. forces. One of the main successes of the self-defense program was in getting large units of ARVN and U.S. forces away from populated areas and thus preventing them from alienating the population through their actions. This accorded with CORDS's general goal of attempting to shift away from a situation in which the GVN was viewed as an occupying military force. As the GVN's nation-building plan for 1970 stated, "The Vietnamese villager fears military forces of both sides, since their operations constitute a threat to the safety of him and his family."[97] This recognized that for many villagers, "security" did not consist of the absence of the forces of the Communist movement but a general protection from physical harm.

The military campaign in support of the APC in 1969 had brought some of the most sustained violence of the war to populated rural areas. One example was Operation Speedy Express, which was launched by the U.S. Ninth Division in the Mekong Delta in late 1968 and early 1969. The Ninth Division was commanded by Major General Julian Ewell, who relentlessly pressured his subordinates to achieve a high body count.[98] During the operation, the division claimed

10,889 enemy killed while recovering only 748 weapons. It also achieved a highly unlikely kill ratio of 45:1. After the war, Ewell published a book titled *Sharpening the Combat Edge*, which explained that his division had operated on what he called the "constant pressure concept." Small units engaged in relentless patrols accounted for 80–90 percent of the division's kills, and many of them came during airborne operations. Many also occurred at night. Given the ease with which small units of NLF or NVA could conceal themselves or their weapons and thus avoid contact, this mode of operations gives further reason to suspect that many of the dead were civilians.[99] Vann, who took over as DepCORDS in IV Corps in April 1969, estimated that twice as many civilians were being killed and wounded from air and artillery operations than were members of the NLF. The "relaxed" rules of engagement operating in the Mekong Delta had turned "very large areas of the country" into "free fire zones, whether or not announced as such," he added. When it was time for the Ninth Division to withdraw from the delta, Vann was "absolutely delighted."[100] By 1970, RFs and PFs made up 80 percent of total allied strength in IV Corps, meaning main-force units had largely withdrawn from the delta.[101] The result, according to Vann, was that civilian casualties were a "fraction" of what they had been during the intense fighting of mid-1968.[102] It was only the recruitment of territorial forces on a large scale that made this possible, and which largely—although by no means entirely—reduced the threat to villagers from allied firepower.

The territorial forces helped to make this transition away from "occupation" possible. Although the dramatically reduced tempo of combat in populated areas certainly made life safer for the majority of the country's population, it is less clear that the goal of actively stimulating pro-GVN sentiment was achieved. Nor was Colby's vision of autonomous self-governing villages that ran their own affairs, including security, much more than a pipe dream. Few village chiefs welcomed the responsibility of commanding the disparate militias, recognizing that they lacked the military experience and that diluting the civilian character of their role might make them the target of NLF assassination or abduction. According to the ARVN general who first commanded IV Corps and then had overall responsibility for territorial force development, the contribution of village chiefs to local defense was in fact "marginal."[103] Both U.S. and GVN officials believed that the continued effectiveness of the territorials depended on their being commanded by leaders with military experience of their own, which meant in reality they continued to be directed by the district chiefs. When the ideal of self-government conflicted with the best possible security arrangements, the latter retained priority.

Thus, although the territorial forces might not maraud around villages or call in air strikes on populated areas in the manner of U.S. and ARVN main forces, they were still controlled by outsiders. This was especially so in the case of the RF. As Vietnamization continued, and manpower was in even greater demand to conduct large operations aimed at countering the NVA's own big units, the RFs increasingly morphed into regular infantry who were deployed farther and farther from home. They were in this way deprived of their local character as Vietnamization proceeded.[104] As early as May 1969, only 25 percent of them operated in or adjacent to their home village. While the figure for PFs was 80 percent, they were still often viewed as outsiders, because they answered to the district chief and not the village authorities.[105] By 1971, PFs were also increasingly serving farther away from home. The sense of detachment of villagers from territorial forces that this could encourage was apparent by an incident investigated by the United States in Kien Hoa in May 1970. Following an audacious attack by up to two battalions of NLF—rare at this point in the war—a battle ensued in which twenty civilians and various ARVN and territorial forces were killed. Although the district chief and two PFs perished, they were "not considered as local losses" by the villagers—they were outsiders.[106] In this case and many others like it, the GVN and its representatives continued to be seen as part of a system imposed by the regime from the top down and not a bottom-up expression of the community.

Even in the case of organized units of PFs and PSDFs serving in their home village, support for the GVN was often much lower than it appeared on paper by looking merely at the size of these forces. After the GVN's Mobilization Law, eligible individuals in GVN-controlled villages faced the choice of serving either in the ARVN or the territorials. Volunteering for the latter would mean they stayed closer to home. "What we're really doing is recruiting, by god, the local VC squad," General George Jacobson explained to a skeptical Abrams in October 1969, as the force was undergoing rapid expansion. "And they want to stay home so bad that they'll join the . . . PF to do it."[107] Bumgardner said as late as October 1971 that "there are a great many PSDF that are the enemy's forces."[108] A Communist Party province leader in the delta confirmed this, telling his superiors that "over half the posts in the zone had secret contact with us, and the remainder, except for a few cruel tyrants, were passive and watched over the bricks [of their post] while drawing a salary."[109] That joining the GVN's territorial forces was seen as an alternative to both the ARVN and the NLF can be seen by the example of Bac Lieu Province, where villagers who could not afford to bribe their corrupt local officials to avoid the ARVN draft and join the territorials instead fled to join the guerrillas.[110] Where territorial forces were not simply just enemy forces incognito, apathy in the ranks was often the order of the day. In late 1971, the head of CORDS's Territorial Security Directorate reported that the rapid expansion of territorial forces had led to a problem with motivation, especially the need for territorials to "identify" with the GVN if the program was to be deemed

FIGURE 10:   A Popular Forces militia member stands guard at the village gate in 1968. Such flimsy defenses were easy for the NLF to infiltrate.

National Archives identifier 532459, General Photograph File of the U.S. Marine Corps, Record Group 172, National Archives at College Park, Maryland.

successful.[111] The lack of such a feeling of identification suggested that although the self-defense program had helped to bolster security across South Vietnam, it had not succeeded in its political aims.

Another factor that made the large number of territorial forces less impressive than it appeared was that, as Truong noted, many villagers were "induced" to join the territorial forces.[112] In areas where this happened—often meaning that former NLF members or sympathizers were dragooned into service—they could not be relied upon. One such chief in Binh Dinh said that only 30 percent of the local PF could be counted on to fight, and the PSDF could not be trusted at all because of their "close relationships" with the NLF.[113] Although the extent of such accommodation cannot be reconstructed, it is indicative that throughout 1968 and 1969, only about half of PF platoons were considered by CORDS advisers as sufficiently aggressive in engaging the enemy.[114] One Pacification Studies Group officer who spent a yearlong tour traveling the country assessing the performance of territorial forces concluded in February 1970 that the RF and PF remained "self oriented" and "extremely reluctant to engage the enemy." The PSDF were even worse, especially considering their essentially political purpose. "If the intent of the program is to produce large rosters and represent these people to be supporters of the Government, then the program is a success," he noted. "If, on the other hand, the intent is as avowed, then the program is a failure. There is very little commitment to the Government in the program and all too frequently resentment is the case."[115]

In an attempt to strengthen the political aspects of the program through indoctrination, training courses were established for senior officers and cadres in the territorial forces. Abrams had joked that "if they're just recruiting the local VC squad then maybe you don't need to send them to the training center at all."[116] But as with other individuals whom the GVN aimed to make part of its "friendly infrastructure," this training was much more political than it was tactical. PSDF leaders, for instance, received seven hours of training on village development, and six hours on "Communist plots during peace-talks and cease-fire and coun- ter-measures to be taken." By contrast, only two hours were spent on the subject of patrolling.[117]

Yet as with the course for village and hamlet leaders, there was a limit to how much an individual's outlook could be changed in a training course that averaged four to six weeks in length. Truong conceded that despite indoctrination, most RFs and PFs "lived far removed from central authority and were seldom conscious of the national cause," but claimed that "being simple soldiers with rural origins" they were "easy to influence." Yet even he believed that in the last analysis, most territorials fought "not for any political philosophy but for the practical reason that they did not want anyone to harm their wives, their children, their parents, or violate the properties that they had helped build over the years."[118] He could have added that often this harm came from ARVN forces—forces that might stay away from the villages after militia were established, providing another incen- tive for villagers to join. If this assessment by a high-ranking GVN general who oversaw the territorial forces is accurate, then it suggests that the political aims of the territorial force program went unrealized. Villagers who joined because they were forced to do so by local officials or because of a desire to be left alone with their families were not likely to be made into ardent supporters of the GVN by a short visit to a training center. Many PSDF leaders, supposedly standard-bearers for the GVN in their communities, refused to attend the training center at all.[119]

Pacification research reports carried out by Vietnamese personnel confirmed that the self-defense program had failed in its political goals. As late as July 1972, a survey of An Giang Province found that the vast majority of respondents did not consider it their duty to join the ARVN and instead sought out positions in territorial units so they could stay close to their families. Corrupt local officials helped draft dodgers become PSDF members for a price, and those who could not afford it went into hiding. Given that An Giang Province was considered a showcase of pacification with a weak Communist organization, this lack of willingness to serve the government and success at evading military service even here was a sign of how far the GVN still had to go in achieving genuine nation building. Only police operations, much resented by the local population, were successful at hoovering up recruits for the ARVN, a sign that the GVN was still relying on force rather than cooperation to achieve its aims.[120] A survey of sixty-eight respondents in Ba Xuyen in the same month found that only fifteen were willing to either join the ARVN or have family members do so. Many villagers saw an inherent tension between serving their families and the GVN, which would require them to travel far from home and abandon their local responsibilities. The PSDF by contrast was seen as a way to "serve both the country and family," meaning members opted for the most limited form of support for the GVN that was compatible with being left alone by draft enforcement officers.[121] Numerous GVN surveys attested to a large increase in corruption as a result of renewed attempts at manpower mobilization after the Easter Offensive. This represented a double blow. As well as illustrating that the GVN had not been successful in moving to a paradigm of willing cooperation between the rural population and the government, it showed that the need to squeeze more manpower and resources out of the villages as American assets were withdrawn would only drive a larger wedge between the government and its citizens. While those who could afford it could buy their way out of their obligations to the government, the poor were forced to unwillingly shoulder them—or to flee to join the NLF.

Truong believed that the motivation of most members of the PSDF came from the fact they were simple villagers who were "adverse to anyone who disturbed the comfort of their natural surroundings."[122] But given the Communist movement's method of building political power from the ground up, the GVN remained much more of an outsider in most villagers than the NLF was, as illustrated by the GVN's continued difficulties at mobilizing manpower. Although the GVN had managed to gain physical control of much of the countryside, it had done little to move beyond the paradigm of "occupation" as the architects of the village system intended. This would have required both a great popular upswell of pro-GVN sentiment and a genuine system of local control of security forces. Neither of these occurred. Villagers knew it was wise to join the territorial units to avoid getting drafted into the ARVN, especially if the creation of PF and PSDF units kept friendly firepower away from their villages. Yet even Truong only claimed that "hundreds of thousands" of people had actively volunteered for the PSDF as opposed to being dragooned into service. In light of the fact that most U.S. advisers considered the total number of people the GVN claimed to have enrolled in the PSDF to be highly inflated, even this was a dubious assertion.[123] Exactly what it meant to volunteer in a situation where service was known to be mandatory is also questionable. Widespread cases of PF and PSDF units refusing to engage the enemy, or reaching accommodations with them, attest to this. In areas known for their long allegiance to the NLF, the GVN's territorial forces simply became a way for guerrillas and cadres to bide their time while drawing a government salary. All of this helped to bring quiet and security to the countryside in the period between the 1968 offensives and the Easter Offensive. What it did not do was amount to genuine rural nation building.

Self-Development

The Village Self-Development Program (VSD) was, along with territorial security, the flagship of the CORDS nation-building effort between 1969 and 1972. Both were designed to be the means by which self-government was actualized, and to have benefits that went beyond their surface security and economic benefits. The VSD offered monetary assistance to villages to conduct small development projects if they could match the funds offered with contributions of their own. The contributions could come in the form of either cash, goods in kind, or labor, the latter being all that many of the poorest peasants who were thought to be the most open to NLF inducements possessed.

The projects included agricultural, fishery, and animal husbandry improvements through to the construction of schoolrooms, dispensaries, roads, bridges, and housing. But as far as CORDS and the central GVN were concerned, what mattered much more than the projects embarked upon was the process by which villagers planned and implemented them. For the ultimate goal of the VSD was to teach Vietnamese villagers what Alexis de Tocqueville called "the art of associating together."[124] At the start of every year, groups of villagers were encouraged to form pressure groups in favor of certain projects and make a case for how it would benefit the village. They then put their cases to the elected village council, which would ultimately decide which projects to pursue. Yet the purpose of the program was not the delivery of the aid projects per se, but rather to build a political connection between village governments and their constituents. The program was based on the idea that the peasantry was naturally apathetic and lethargic and had to be prodded by outsiders into bettering themselves. The VSD was designed as a "pump-priming" intervention in village affairs, necessary "since spontaneous local development is rare in developing countries and external stimulus plays a major part in the process."[125] Once the villagers got used to the idea that they could band together to solve economic and social problems with the help of their government, the process would repeat itself naturally.[126]

Giving village governments the resources with which to respond to the demands of their constituents was equally as important a process as seeing that these demands were expressed in the first place. Colby claimed that "to be given an actual right to determine how money would be used in the local community was quite startling and quite effective with the local population."[127] As with the PSDF program, the aim was to advance the GVN's "Community Spirit principle" and foster ties of mutual obligation between the people and the government. "The primary purpose of self help is to involve the rural Vietnamese population and the Government of Vietnam in a joint effort which will create an associative identity of the people with the government," explained one CORDS document. Development projects were merely the "medium" through which this occurred.[128] According to another document written by U.S. planners in Saigon, the program aimed at nothing less than "creating and developing in the rural population . . . a new set of attitudes, awareness, and responses that eventually will lead to a class that is democratically and politically active." This would be in contrast to how the authors of this document viewed the workings of a "traditional" village, in which the interests of individuals and groups were "not effectively articulated" because of the "pressure of custom and conformity."[129] While such "traditional" villages were controlled by local notables who did not take account of the aspirations of most villagers, the "village concept" called for a different type of leadership. "Projects provided a means for local officials to be made visible, as GVN representatives, to the general populace," said a CORDS retrospective on the program. "People could literally see their government at work where previously, in many cases, there had been a void."[130]

Such a program was highly ambitious and, at least in theory, had the potential to undermine the authority of traditional rural power brokers. The GVN's centralized bureaucracy had tightly controlled development spending prior to the VSD. If a province wanted to construct even a single new village schoolroom, it needed Saigon's approval, and there was little to no chance for even village or hamlet chiefs to have any input into development spending. The idea that mere villagers might know what was best for themselves was an alien one to most province chiefs. Even where province and district chiefs could be convinced by this process that the villagers had legitimate desires that government had to meet, they did not appreciate losing control over the opportunities for graft and kickbacks that accompanied the management of development funds. When coupled with the fact that the formation of pressure groups and the process by which projects were decided upon were usually completely opaque to American advisers who neither spoke Vietnamese nor understood the intricacies of village life, the results of the VSD were much less revolutionary than had been intended.

The program's negligible economic impact was not of primary concern to central CORDS officials, who stressed time and again that the purpose of the program was political. Yet while the economic impact was easy to quantify, measuring the impact of VSD on nation building was much more difficult, as CORDS officials acknowledged.[131] Given the goals of the program, the two key variables for measuring its success were the extent to which the VSD encouraged genuine responsiveness to local needs by village governments and the extent to which it encouraged local people to identify with the GVN and see it as the protector of their interests. These two factors of effectiveness and legitimacy were central to the idea of nation building. The VSD was in fact, as one CORDS document said, "the *primary* instrument of decentralization of government authority to the village level."[132] Evidence on whether the program met these goals was necessarily partial and anecdotal, especially given the difficulty that advisers had comprehending the inner workings of village life and the GVN.

Yet CORDS assessments continually found that although the VSD was successful in generating development projects, the political goals of the program were rarely met. Rather than causing whole new classes of villagers to emerge and line up behind a GVN that could finally promote their interests, the program was instead adapted to existing modes of village governance. As they had with other CORDS programs, lower levels of the GVN warped the program and implemented it their own way, often with outcomes very different from those that CORDS had intended. As advisers lacked a detailed understanding of village political dynamics, they tended to focus instead on the quantitative goal of establishing as many projects as possible without being able to understand or influence the underlying political dynamics.[133] These political dynamics therefore remained largely unchanged.

One of the most glaring flaws in the VSD was that it required village officials themselves to educate the people in their village about the program and to oversee its implementation. Given that a large part of the intent of the program was to encourage villagers to challenge their own government in perhaps uncomfortable ways—and then to vote it out of office if their demands were not met—this seemed unlikely to be achieved if the entire process was under the control of that same government. Central to the VSD was the idea that citizens would form together into project groups to lobby the village government to spend development funds in a certain way. The groups, a document for CORDS advisers said, "could be defined simply as that group of individuals who having the same occupations, interests or problems are united together to lobby for and carry out a desired project."[134] Yet the reality was far different. U.S. evaluators found that the process of citizens forming into groups was rarely spontaneous and was instead usually overseen by village and hamlet officials, who would come up with projects and then corral citizens into groups who ostensibly supported them for the purposes of acquiring funds.

A team of U.S. and Vietnamese evaluators who visited four provinces to assess the VSD in mid-1970 found that the "popular groups" were in fact "largely paper exercises" and "neither active nor spontaneous." Projects were "often selected by village and hamlet or other officials rather than by the people."[135] Surveys of villagers elsewhere in 1969 and 1970 backed up these findings. When the 1969 program was coming to its end in December of that year, a survey found that a third of respondents still did not believe or know that VSD funds had been made available to their hamlet. Surveys in the last three months of the 1969 program in III and IV Corps found that on average only 19.5 percent of respondents felt they had "enough opportunity" to participate in decisions about the spending of VSD funds. Only just over 14 percent felt it was "the people of the hamlet" who decided what projects would go ahead, as opposed to village, hamlet, or district authorities.[136] In September 1970, another survey across the whole country found that only 29.6 percent of respondents who were in a project group reported that the group had been created spontaneously. That many villagers were excluded from these meetings and not allowed to participate in groups can be seen by the reasons given for nonparticipation in the same survey. Even though the VSD allowed contributions of labor in lieu of cash from villagers in an express attempt to extend the program to the poorest, 20.8 percent reported that they were too "poor" to join. An additional 23.8 percent said membership was "limited to small groups of people." Only 4 percent of respondents felt that it was the people themselves who were supposed to decide which projects their groups would request approval for.[137]

The VSD was a subject of particular interest for the surveyors who produced pacification research reports, and dozens of assessments were made of it in the early 1970s. Few of them found the program operating as intended. One GVN survey found that "proper regard is not being given to the ideas of the villagers in the selection of projects," with local authorities instead mandating what projects would be carried out.[138] A survey in Quang Ngai found that only 20 percent of respondents were aware of the program, and that local officials simply decided how to spend the extra money themselves without organizing popular groups or involving villagers in "any decision making processes related to the projects." The surveyor suggested that the provincial government intervene to explain the program to the villagers—but given the involvement of provincial officials in profiting from corruption associated with the program, this was unlikely to happen.[139]

None of this suggests a program that was successful in either organizing the population into effective decision-making groups as the NLF did, or at creating pressure on local governments to respond to the desires of their citizens.

Rather than making village government responsive to the people, the program was warped to fit into the traditional rural GVN mold of making the people responsive to the government. While many villagers undoubtedly benefited from the economic aspects of the program, GVN officials continued to use it primarily to further their own ends and not to further nation building. This included novel methods of corruption. In Quang Tri Province, 9.47 percent of the money sent from Saigon for the 1969 program somehow disappeared en route to the province treasury.[140] District chiefs often lurked in the background, pressuring village chiefs to select certain projects and then employ certain contractors so they could earn kickbacks or profit from padded contracts.[141] The fact that most villagers learned about the program from the same local officials who benefited from manipulating it for their own profit made this possible, as the GVN minister responsible for the program noted in late 1970.[142] Although the exact scale of corruption in the VSD is impossible to determine, its existence meant that projects were not always benefiting their ostensible recipients. For if villagers were corralled into project groups by officials and then forced to contribute cash and labor to complete them, the program in fact became a means of extracting resources from villagers in the name of "self-development." Some American advisers were aware of this problem, such as a PSA from Khanh Hoa who reported in 1971 that "many hamlet people are forced to involve themselves against their will; they do not like or understand that." It had been official policy since the start of the program that the groups be truly voluntary, but the practice of forced involvement continued until its end.[143]

The ability of CORDS advisers to remedy these problems was limited. Many viewed corruption as a natural part of South Vietnamese society, so long as it was kept below a certain level. The funds that went missing from Quang Tri, for instance, were eerily just short of the 10 percent threshold commonly cited by advisers as an unacceptable level of corruption. Yet corruption in the case of the VSD was about more than the skimming off funds—it cut right to the core of why it remained in the interests of GVN officials to maintain their control over the VSD program rather than encouraging the emergence of a genuinely democratic system of deciding how the funds were spent.

In fact, it cut to the core of why lower echelons of the GVN had an interest in sabotaging the entire village system. Those advisers who did attempt to involve themselves in the formation of project groups faced chastisement for going against the spirit of the program, which aimed merely at creating the "proper environment" for project groups and responsive village governments to flourish.[144] Here, as in so many cases, CORDS officials ran up against the problem of leverage—they ultimately could not achieve their aims if they sharply diverged from those of their GVN counterparts. Advisers were told never to work around the existing government structure, because this could only weaken and not strengthen it. With the program's ability to promote the reform of the GVN so limited, it is little wonder that even villagers who benefited from it saw it primarily as an economic giveaway rather than understanding and appreciating the VSD's political intent.[145]

Although it was the flagship development program from 1969 until its termination in 1972, the VSD was not the only one. From 1970 onward, several other programs were also launched in an attempt to bring socioeconomic reform to the villages. The first was the Land to the Tiller (LTTT) initiative, which was signed into law by President Thieu in March 1970 after years of wrangling between South Vietnamese and USAID officials. The post-Tet pacification drive had already been accompanied by some reforms in land policy in areas newly (re) occupied by the GVN. In late 1968 and early 1969, the GVN had announced that peasants living in such areas would not have their land confiscated and returned to its original owner, as had happened in the past. The government also froze rents, first in newly pacified areas and then across the whole country. In many cases, this meant that the Saigon regime was acknowledging that NLF land distribution was a fait accompli. Nevertheless, such a policy was hard to enforce at the local level where the landlords actually lived. It also placed the GVN in the position of recognizing the legitimacy of NLF redistribution without having any positive program of its own to offer.[146]

The entry into force of LTTT was designed to change this. The law mandated that ownership of land had to pass from landlords to those who farmed it. Families in the Mekong Delta would receive plots up to a maximum of three hectares (7.4 acres), and those in the Central Lowlands one hectare. Landlords, who could keep only fifteen hectares for direct cultivation, were to be compensated by the government in a mixture of cash and bonds for the land they lost as a result of the law. The internal GVN politics that led to the passage of the GVN law are murky, but it is clear that Thieu pushed it through the legislature against significant opposition from landlords and with the enthusiastic backing of many Americans. Shortly after the law was passed, the *New York Times* lauded LTTT as "probably the most ambitious and progressive non-Communist land reform of the twentieth century".[147]

Although LTTT was not an integral part of CORDS's village system, its fate intersected with it. As with so many other GVN initiatives, implementation at the local level became the key sticking point. This was particularly the case in northern parts of the country and the Central Lowlands, where it was common for village officials to also be landlords themselves and hence to resist implementing the program. Officials and tenants feared that if they initiated a claim under the law, they would face the wrath of powerful local landlords. This was a particularly acute problem given that both the compensation of landlords and the distribution of land titles became the subject of massive delays, increasing the time in which "irate landlords, including a few gun-toting Military officers" might take out their frustration on their tenants. Peasants in northern areas of the country were said by American observers to have little faith that the GVN could protect them against such retaliation.[148]

In the Mekong Delta, where only 10 percent of village officials were estimated to also be landlords, the program proceeded more effectively.[149] This was important, because most of the land eligible for redistribution lay in this region. By the end of 1971, land titles had been legally awarded to 375,250 individuals nationwide, for a total of 1.14 million acres of land, with 73 percent of these titles actually having been distributed by the GVN bureaucracy.[150] The lack of a reliable cadastral survey makes it hard to estimate the percentage of tenant farmers affected, but a 1970 estimate placed the number of tenant families in South Vietnam at six hundred thousand and the area of land they worked at 3.2 million acres.[151] Even allowing for an overstatement in the official figures compared to the land reform actually achieved in practice, the impact of LTTT on reducing tenancy was significant. By July 1974, the U.S. Embassy in South Vietnam claimed that tenancy in the country had been "virtually eliminated," although by this point U.S. officials were not present in sufficient numbers to verify that such claims corresponded to the reality on the ground.[152] Nevertheless, surveys of villagers in areas of the Mekong Delta that had benefited from LTTT in the early 1970s reported widespread awareness of the program and appreciation of its benefits.[153] The implementation of the program in the delta was particularly impressive because it was administered at the local level by village officials, whose autonomy and effectiveness had been so limited in the other areas discussed in this chapter.

The LTTT law was the most impressive rural reform that the GVN carried out, both in its impact on the ground and the fact it showed the Saigon regime's rural apparatus to be capable of driving through major social change. But it was also too little, too late. The law responded to a social reality in the delta that the NLF had largely created, first through its own land reform and second by forcing landlords to flee the insecurity of the countryside to the cities. Once there, many had become cut off from their land and involved in more profitable ventures, meaning they lacked the ability or interest to contest the law's implementation. This dilution of the power of the landlords and NLF achievement of land reform, which it would have been politically disastrous for the GVN to reverse, explains why LTTT was politically possible at this time rather than earlier in the war. Its implementation was also reliant on the decision of the Communist movement to shift to preparing for the major offensives of 1972 and subsequently 1975 at the expense of contesting territorial control in the delta. Perhaps if it had come earlier, LTTT would have done more to prepare the Saigon regime to meet this challenge, which depended on the ability to mobilize fiscal and manpower resources as the Americans withdrew. But the frustrated progress of other aspects of the village system demonstrated that LTTT did not do enough in these final years to change the apathetic or hostile attitude of a sufficient portion of South Vietnamese villagers toward their government. It was a reform that had been wrung out of the government by the NLF, rather than representing a fundamental change in the dynamics of GVN rule. As one American skeptic put it in 1972, "Land reform is nice icing, but it will not help if the cake is rotten."[154]

The aptness of this comment becomes apparent if we consider the final major plank of rural government reform in the latter years of the war: an attempt to improve village fiscal autonomy known as the Local Revenue Improvement Program (LRIP). The LRIP focused on mobilizing resources via taxation at the village level. Although villages had tax-raising powers under the 1967 constitution, before 1969 these powers were sharply circumscribed. In late 1967, revenues from agricultural land taxes had been assigned to the village budget, potentially giving villages the opportunity to tax up to one-half of South Vietnam's private national income.[155] With the spread of territorial security during and after the APC, a stable environment was created to finally collect it. Recognizing this, Decree 45 provided for a village tax commissioner charged with increasing revenue. As well as improving security, another factor driving change was that the South Vietnamese national budget felt the pressure of Vietnamization strongly. As a USAID paper stated, Vietnamization "carries the clear indication that government administration, at both central and local levels, must prepare to shift for itself without extensive external assistance."[156]

With U.S. aid set to decline in the future, Saigon finally began to look seriously at how to finance its own expenditures. This was vital, given that other aspects of the GVN's strategy of rural reform such as VSD and the LTTT cost rather than generated revenue. In particular, LTTT had undercut the fiscal viability and autonomy of villages by mandating the transfer of communal lands that had previously allowed villages to generate rent. In response, the LRIP merged the goals of encouraging overall GVN fiscal sustainability and maintaining local autonomy. Colby saw measures to increase village tax collections as both a way of tapping the resources of the rural population to support the GVN and a way of strengthening the "village system" of autonomous village governments. As with other aspects of the village system, this extra grant of government authority also came with the expectation that it would encourage rural South Vietnamese to share the burden of defeating the insurgency. "At this time of national crisis," a paper presented to the GVN by CORDS stated, "when the need for sacrifice is paramount, local government is failing to obtain an adequate share of local wealth for the common effort."[157] The central GVN had paid the salaries of village officials since 1967, constituting a significant burden on its finances. If villages could improve local tax receipts to cover even just this item, it would remove a significant cost from the national budget. An improvement in local revenue collection would also allow local development activities to continue after the termination of U.S. funding for the VSD, putting local development on a sustainable and democratic local basis. Hence the LRIP served two purposes—advancing the cause of decentralization, and decreasing the GVN's overall reliance on the United States as part of Vietnamization.

As in so many areas of the American nation-building effort in South Vietnam, the LRIP achieved some apparent progress but fell far short of expectations and failed to achieve its political objective. It was an effort that was particularly difficult for American advisers to involve themselves in, given both the political sensitivities involved in raising taxes and the arcane nature of tax administration. By the beginning of 1972, a CORDS progress report found that U.S. influence on the improvement of tax collection had been "almost negligible."[158] As USAID had warned, the LRIP demanded "knowledge of how to collect taxes from people who voluntarily won't pay taxes."[159] Even had CORDS advisers possessed the technical knowledge, they did not have the necessary knowledge of village life and economics. Their numbers were anyhow dwindling. This meant that the impetus for the program would have to come from the GVN. Yet the GVN also lacked personnel trained in local tax administration and faced enormous political obstacles in increasing revenues from a population that was still highly resistant to paying GVN taxes. The LTTT had been accompanied by a substantial tax holiday because the GVN had feared that villagers would resist applying for land titles if they believed it would lead to an increased financial burden.[160] This had been necessary to encourage peasants to apply for the legal rights to land they had in many cases received de facto rights to from the NLF without having to pay GVN taxes. Saigon's lack of political will or ability to make higher fiscal demands on its population took on a tragicomic hue when the GVN refused to pay the relatively small salaries of technical cadres who were supposed to travel around villages helping them improve their tax administration. Rather than shouldering the costs itself, the GVN felt the United States should pay for the cadres. As USAID noted, this was hardly an encouraging start to a program aimed at making the GVN self-sufficient.[161] On the eve of the Paris Peace Accords, around 25 percent of villages were reported to be at least 95 percent self-sufficient in terms of operating expenses. This figure was also difficult to verify, since the few American advisers remaining still lacked access to budget data.[162] Even more significantly, the fact that 75 percent of villages could not even cover their own operating expenses meant that when the VSD terminated, these villages would have no funds for development projects. Of the total funds being expended in the localities in 1971, only a sixth was locally raised—and the half of the remainder made up by U.S. development support was about to be terminated.[163] This placed the future of the village system in a perilous condition, as its cornerstone was the availability of local assets to respond to local needs. If village governments had to squeeze their populations even just to cover their own operating expenses, they seemed to face an uphill struggle in the broader battle to establish constructive links with the population. As the last CORDS advisers left the country, this contradiction remained unresolved.

All of this suggested that the GVN had failed to establish ties of mutual obligation with its own citizens at the village level, which would vastly complicate its attempts to continue to battle the Vietnamese Communist movement. This was the case whether Hanoi stuck to a strategy of conventional attacks or moved to reenergize its guerrilla campaign. Despite successes in a hugely belated land reform program, the GVN's failure to move from what Vann and Colby considered a form of occupation to a paradigm of joint effort between the government and its citizens was symbolized by the failure of the LRIP. Lacking the legitimacy and administrative prowess to raise taxes to a level that would allow even for the self-sufficiency of village governments, much less to pay for the huge national military and other institutions necessary to combat the Communist movement, Saigon instead allowed resources to continue to be embezzled and coerced from the rural population as part of a pervasive and abusive system of corruption. The corps commander system had ultimately not been broken, and it seemed that an even greater level of exploitation would be needed as U.S. aid declined further after the Paris Peace Accords. Faced with all this evidence of the GVN's failure to put down durable and sustainable roots despite enjoying years of relative calm in the villages, it is hard to disagree with the claim by Douglas Blaufarb, a former CIA official in South Vietnam, that GVN control might best be likened to Mark Twain's description of the River Platte: "an inch deep and a mile wide."[164]

HUMILITY AND NATION BUILDING

The Communist offensive of 1972—known in the West as the Easter Offensive—was the beginning of the end for South Vietnam. Since the failure of the 1968 offensives, the Communist movement had carefully husbanded its armed strength and avoided provocations that might have slowed the U.S. withdrawal or led to a widening of the war. In 1972, hundreds of thousands of NVA soldiers with Chinese equipment and armored vehicles surged across the DMZ and the South Vietnamese borders with Laos and Cambodia. In the midst of the supposedly highly "pacified" Mekong Delta, the Communists managed to seize the provincial capital of Ben Tre. Just as Nixon and Kissinger's Vietnam Special Studies Group had predicted, the reentry of NVA divisions of regiments into the war swiftly changed the balance of forces, and the GVN was unable to respond effectively. The ARVN grimly held on, supported by an enormous wave of U.S. airpower. But it would not be able to rely on the saviors in the sky much longer. Meanwhile, the Communist movement took advantage of its momentum to reconstitute its administrative and political apparatus in the populated areas, especially the Mekong Delta. Assailed from all sides, the GVN was forced to cannibalize territorial units to make up the losses in its main forces, only weakening its grip on the rural areas further. Just as its inability to mobilize the resources and manpower to combat the Communists had led to American escalation ten years earlier, the GVN again lacked the effectiveness or legitimacy to organize an effective resistance. Nation building had failed.

CORDS had reached the peak of its influence between 1968 and 1971. Barely had a generation of advisers begun to grapple with nation building before they began to be withdrawn from 1971 onward. Many had begun to take a more hands-off approach to their job in the final years anyway. "The day is past when advisors walk hand-in-hand with counterparts across the ride paddies and through the weeds," said one adviser who served in 1971. "We should not be required to bolster courage and leadership at the small unit level. That day is past. If we haven't imparted those techniques as yet, we never will."[1] By October 1971, Everett Bumgardner, executive assistant to the head of CORDS, said that "most" province chiefs no longer looked to their counterparts for advice.[2] Some fought back against the withdrawal. After serving on a task force in 1971 that eventually decided—against his wishes—to scale back and ultimately dissolve CORDS, former I and II Corps official Willard E. Chambers quit in disgust in November 1972, issuing a parting blast at "the leadership and philosophy being applied" to the nation-building effort.[3] Far from believing the war was "won" or that nation-building was complete, many CORDS advisers believed they needed five to ten more years. But with public support for the war in the United States exhausted, the clock had run out.

CORDS had failed despite its attempt in the latter years of the war to emulate the successes of the Vietnamese Communist movement through the village system. While this was only the latest in a series of efforts to do so, it was certainly the most comprehensive. Through the village system, CORDS had abandoned the attempt to build rural support on the basis of an imagined community of the South Vietnamese nation, and instead had shifted to the idea of "communalism," which the Communists had used so successfully. By attempting to tap into the village autonomy and identity, which had been the building block of Vietnamese rural life for centuries, they had moved far beyond the crude focus on physical control that had characterized earlier "pacification" efforts. Despite nation building being taken over by the military, the approach favored by many civilians—foremost among them Colby—had won out.

But it was precisely the political content of CORDS's programs, and its attempts to forge a network of pro-GVN village communities, that failed. The GVN never managed to become effective enough at mobilizing rural support or legitimate enough to demand the sacrifices needed to win the struggle against the Communist movement. The "friendly infrastructure" that CORDS had hoped to nourish was unreliable and uncommitted until the end. The village system offered limited local empowerment and some sense of belonging and advancement to pro-GVN militiamen and officials. But its architects never managed to replicate the true keys to the success of the Communist movement—its deep and organic local roots, its offer of fundamental social and economic change, and the prospect of advancement through a political structure that stretched from the remotest village to the Politburo in Hanoi. Never able to truly understand or trust its rural citizens, the GVN could not deliver the decentralization, empowerment, and ideological vision that might have made the village system meaningful. As outsiders both in understanding and in influence, American nation builders could hardly do so either.

Nor could the Americans, or their forward-thinking allies among the South Vietnamese, bring about wholesale reform of the GVN in a way that might have made its rural nation-building efforts more likely to succeed. There was ultimately only so far the GVN could be pushed. Time and again—from Robert Komer's decision to work within the existing corps commander system in 1966, to the rejection of Major Nguyen Duc Thang's proposals to reform it in 1967, and the quiet shelving of Operation Shock in early 1968—U.S. officials opted for evolution over revolution. Historians such as James McAllister have suggested they should have acted more forcefully.[4] Yet this book has shown that U.S. freedom of action was always constrained by its desire not to unleash chaos of the sort that had followed the coup against Diem. Nor could the Americans ignore nationalist sensitivities. The key assumption underlying Operation Shock had been that as Saigon was unable to claim all the attributes of sovereignty without American assistance, it was reasonable for the Americans to ask for that sovereignty to be conditioned and limited according to American demands for reform. Yet fearing a complete collapse in the Saigon regime's legitimacy if it was seen to be taking orders from the Americans, CORDS continued to attempt to operate behind the scenes and indirectly. The result was, for the Americans, the worst of both worlds: the influence of American advisers was sharply limited, but their very presence continued to provide the Communist movement with a propaganda boon.

Their evolutionary approach meant that the reforms favored by those Americans most concerned with nation building were very slow to be implemented. The tardiness was on the U.S. side as well as the Vietnamese. Even though the military and civilian agencies like the CIA and USOM had been attempting to strengthen the GVN for nearly a decade by the time of the Americanization of the war in 1965, it took two years from the arrival of the first U.S. combat units to the creation of CORDS. A semblance of political stability in the GVN arrived only in late 1966, whereas Thieu managed to consolidate power and put an end to factional squabbles at the top of the GVN only during 1968. As the VSSG studies produced in the Nixon White House had pointed out, the surface stability and security that allowed for the attempted implementation of the village system from 1969 onward was itself dependent on the Communist movement's decision to lie low and engage in an economy-of-forces strategy while the U.S. withdrawal continued. The limits of American leverage and its dependence on events over which the United States had no control meant that even if American nation builders had possessed a perfect understanding of South Vietnam and a clear vision for how to achieve nation building, the conditions in which they operated made it impossible to do so. In reality, they possessed neither of these things anyway.

Despite the questionable wisdom of their efforts, the American experience of attempted nation building recounted in this volume does challenge claims by some historians that the Americans were totally indifferent to the existing state of South Vietnamese politics and society or that their approach was dominated by assumptions from modernization theory.[5] On the contrary, this book has shown that some American nation builders from Saigon down to the villages were keenly interested in understanding and influencing the intricacies of South Vietnamese rural life. They also devoted attention to studying the successes of the Vietnamese Communist movement and attempting to replicate them, learning heavily from former Viet Minh fighters such as Tran Ngoc Chau and Nguyen Be. Nation-building efforts from the RD program through to the village system showed their heavy imprint. Recognizing that they were faced with the same tasks of political organization and mobilization that the Communist movement had carried out so effectively, Americans and South Vietnamese attempted to replicate the very movement they were attempting to save South Vietnam from. Their efforts were also in accord with the conventional wisdom of contemporary theorists of revolutionary and colonial warfare. American nation building in South Vietnam was shaped by many influences.

By providing an analysis of how these ideas played out in practice, this book has presented the most detailed account yet of the failure of U.S. nation building in the latter years of the war. It has moved beyond orthodox accounts of U.S. nation building in Vietnam that focus on structural reasons for its failure while neglecting the evolution of U.S. nation-building policy or the agency of the actors involved, especially in the later years of the war. By coloring between the historical lines laid down by these accounts, this book has aimed to deprive revisionists of the space in which to make claims about the successes of U.S. nation building in the later years of the war. This book has shown that there is little evidence the GVN had built a base among its own people that would have justified continued U.S. support in 1974–1975 and afterward. The eerie peace that settled over much of South Vietnam in the early 1970s might have been testament to successful pacification, but it certainly did not amount to nation building. It also took place in a security environment that was permissive largely because of a change in Hanoi's strategy. Had the U.S. militarily intervened to defend South Vietnam in 1975 when Hanoi again took the offensive, the GVN may have stumbled on for several more years, but it would have been no closer to overcoming the legacies of ineffectiveness and illegitimacy that dated back to 1954. Nation building in South Vietnam had produced a regime highly dependent on American support and unable to survive without it. That support was now gone. "Having given us the needles," as the Vietnamese American novelist Viet Thanh Nguyen has the protagonist of his novel *The Sympathizer* remark, "they now perversely no longer supplied the dope."[6] Nor was the Saigon regime showing any serious signs of getting over its addiction to American largesse. No counterfactual "what if" can escape the fact that by the time of Hanoi's final offensives, nation building had not been achieved and did not look likely to be achieved anytime soon, despite twenty years of American and South Vietnamese efforts. Meanwhile, the U.S. public's appetite for continuing to support Saigon had run out. A strategy reliant on a level of public support that evaporates before victory can be achieved can hardly be considered a winning one. Hearts and minds at home matter, too. This was not a "lost victory."[7] It was simply a defeat.

The American experience of nation building in South Vietnam hence ought to be a humbling and sobering lesson for would-be nation builders. Too many adherents of nation building, and indeed of counterinsurgency, focus on technical issues of implementation rather than acknowledging the immense structural barriers in the way of their goals. One example is the concept of "unity of command," the idea that ever-closer coordination between the military, other agencies, and their equivalents among the host government is the key to success. Sherard Cowper-Coles, a former British ambassador to Afghanistan, described this idea as "snake oil."[8] CORDS had the greatest unity of command of any U.S. attempt at nation building in history, and yet still it failed. When we consider the immense time and effort required from the presidential level down to assure that this unified, if ultimately futile, effort was established in the first place, we begin to see the magnitude of the challenge facing would-be nation builders. CORDS boasted thousands of personnel, unity of command, a sophisticated operating concept based on an understanding of its main antagonist, theoretically close integration with the host government, and even a training institute dedicated to producing personnel skilled in understanding the country in which it operated. Still it failed. No doubt in the future there will be those who say they can succeed in its stead, but they ought to have to reckon with its failure all the same.

The story told in this book also has much to teach us about the relationship between pacification, which is now often called counterinsurgency, and true nation building. While counterinsurgency doctrine has progressed since the time of the Vietnam War, it still suffers from an unclear relationship to strategic victory. Just as the endless churn of pacification operations in Vietnam did little to address the fundamental weaknesses of the GVN and the rural sociopolitical structure, so today's "population-centric" counterinsurgency often fails to address the root causes of a conflict.[9] This has led one contemporary critic to deride counterinsurgency as a "strategy of tactics," an echo of Colonel

Harry Summer's famous labeling of U.S. strategy in the Vietnam War as a "kind of grand tactics" because it provided no route to strategic victory.[10] But as the relationship between pacification and attempts at more sophisticated forms of nation building in Vietnam shows, the link between counterinsurgency and strategic victory—at least in theory—is nation building. In practice, without achieving true nation building, the gains of pacification are likely to prove ephemeral, and counterinsurgency is indeed doomed to be little more than a "kind of grand tactics." By demonstrating the difficulty of carrying out the sort of deep political and socioeconomic change called for by nation building in South Vietnam, the site of the most ambitious and energetic attempt by the United States to date, this book ought to give pause to those who in the future see in nation building the key to strategic victory. A clear-eyed understanding of the failure of U.S. nation building in South Vietnam is more useful than fantasies of a "lost victory."

This study also teaches us to be wary of the metaphor of "nation building." Policy makers who embark their countries on such ventures should be aware of how little control they will have over either the finer details of implementation or the prerequisites for success. Once the process has begun, high-level policy makers are only able to intervene with broad brushstrokes rather than with regard to the finer detail. Leveraging reform from an allied government whose officials have also to look out for their own political interests is highly challenging, however cleverly the scaffolding of influence is constructed. While the metaphor of "nation building" seems to promise tractability and predictability, in reality the process is influenced by myriad actors with divergent agendas, of whom the intervenor is but one. Nation building is ultimately an activity that privileges local knowledge and action and is hostile to grand designs.

The temptation to go chasing after grand designs is an expression of what Hannah Arendt, writing just as the anti-Diem popular uprising was about to burst forth in South Vietnam in the late 1950s, called the gravest political sin—that of hubris.[11] Many of the Americans who worked against the odds to strengthen the Saigon regime and ensure its survival in the face of the Vietnamese Communist movement were guilty of it. But even more so were the policy makers in Washington who embarked on a war that was dependent on such an improbable task being accomplished. Nation building was an unavoidable condition of victory for the United States in the Vietnam War. It was also, given the legacies of Vietnamese history and the unfolding course of the war, almost certainly preordained to be impossible to achieve. Thus does U.S. strategy in the Vietnam War stand guilty of the sin of hubris, and thus did it fail.

Abbreviations

CDD	Community Development Directorate
CF	Country File: Vietnam
CORDS	Office of Civil Operations and Revolutionary Development Support
FCO	Foreign and Commonwealth Office
FRUS	*Foreign Relations of the United States*
GP	Allan E. Goodman Papers
HIA	Hoover Institution Archives, Palo Alto, CA
JFKL	John F. Kennedy Library, Boston
K-L	Komer-Leonhart Subject Files
LBJL	Lyndon Baines Johnson Library, Austin, TX
LOC	Library of Congress, Washington, DC
LTTT	Land to the Tiller
MACV	Military Assistance Command, Vietnam
memcon	memorandum of conversation
NARA II	National Archives II at College Park, MD
NPL	Richard Nixon Presidential Library, Yorba Linda, CA
NSC Files	National Security Council Institutional Files
NSF	National Security Files
NSSM	National Security Study Memorandum
PPP	Plans, Programs and Policies Directorate
PRO	Public Records Office
RG	Record Group
RHP	Roger Hilsman Papers
RKF	Robert W. Komer Files
RKP	Robert W. Komer Papers
telcon	telephone conversation
TNA	The National Archives (UK), Richmond, Surrey
TTVA	Texas Tech Virtual Vietnam Archive
VCF	Vietnam Country Files
VSF	Vietnam Subject Files

Notes

INTRODUCTION

1. Arnold R. Isaacs, *Without Honor: Defeat in Vietnam and Cambodia* (Baltimore: Johns Hopkins University Press, 1983), 482.

2. Tran Ngoc Chau, *The American Syndrome: An Interview with the BBC* (1991), folder 1, box 62, Neil Sheehan Papers, Library of Congress, Washington, DC (hereafter LOC), 9.

3. Jeffrey T. Clarke, *Advice and Support: The Final Years, 1965–1973* (Washington, DC: Government Printing Office, 1998), 497

4. Quoted in Frank L. Jones, "Blowtorch: Robert Komer and the Making of Vietnam Pacification Policy," *Parameters* 35 (Autumn 2005): 104.

5. It has been over twenty years since a monograph last addressed this topic, the semi-official account contained in Richard A. Hunt, *Pacification: The American Struggle for Vietnam's Hearts and Minds* (Boulder, CO: Westview, 1995). Much of the archival material used in the present volume was not available to Hunt.

6. Among the new sources drawn on in this book are a collection of oral debriefings with Americans and South Vietnamese who were involved in the nation building in South Vietnam, housed in the Allan E. Goodman Papers in the Hoover Institution Archives. Some of these interviews are also available in the National Archives facility at College Park, Maryland. The extensive collection in the Goodman Papers has not, to my knowledge, previously been cited by researchers. Some 112 interviews, which have an average length of twenty-two pages, were reviewed in the preparation of this book. Because of a restriction imposed by Goodman's deed of gift to the Hoover Institution, which bans the identification of any person still living, it is not always possible to name the individuals whose words are being cited or to give precise details of when and where they served in South Vietnam. Instead, broader descriptions such as "a province senior adviser who served in the delta just after the Americanization of the war" are used in this book. For extended discussions of individuals, pseudonyms such as "Mike," initially in quotation marks, are assigned in addition to these descriptions. As printing the folder titles themselves would in some cases violate this deed of gift, interviews are instead cited by number and box, which is sufficient for any researcher to locate the cited material with ease.

7. William S. Turley, "Urban Transformation in South Vietnam," *Pacific Affairs* 49, no. 4 (1976/77): 607–24; Allan E. Goodman and Lawrence M. Franks, "The Dynamics of Migration to Saigon, 1964–1972," *Pacific Affairs* 48, no. 2 (1975): 199–214.

8. On Diem see Philip E. Catton, *Diem's Final Failure: Prelude to America's War in Vietnam* (Lawrence: University of Kansas Press, 2003); Edward Miller, *Misalliance: Ngo Dinh Diem, the United States, and the Fate of South Vietnam* (Cambridge, MA: Harvard University Press, 2013); Jessica Chapman, *Cauldron of Resistance: Ngo Dinh Diem, the United States, and 1950s Southern Vietnam* (Ithaca, NY: Cornell University Press, 2013); Geoffrey Stewart, *Vietnam's Lost Revolution: Ngo Dinh Diem's Failure to Build an Independent Nation, 1955–1963* (Cambridge: Cambridge University Press, 2017); Jessica Elkind, *Aid under Fire: Nation Building and the Vietnam War* (Lexington: University Press of Kentucky, 2016). On the period up to 1968 see James M. Carter, *Inventing Vietnam: The United States and State Building, 1954–1958* (Cambridge: Cambridge University Press, 2008).

9. The best-known and most influential of these authors is Lewis Sorley. See his *Westmoreland: The General Who Lost Vietnam* (New York: Harcourt, 2011) and *A Better War: The Unexamined Victories and Final Tragedy of America's Last Years in Vietnam* (New York: Harcourt, 1999).

10. Mark Atwood Lawrence has written that the "respectful reception" of the revisionist thesis has been influenced by the fact that "most scholars of the Vietnam War are less comfortable with" the historical facts of the later period of the war. The present monograph aims to increase their comfort levels. See Mark Lawrence Atwood, "Too Late or Too Soon? Debating the Withdrawal from Vietnam in the Age of Iraq," *Diplomatic History* 34, no. 4 (2010): 589–600.

11. Thomas R. Hietala, *Manifest Design: Anxious Aggrandizement in Late Jacksonian America* (Ithaca, NY: Cornell University Press, 1985), 177–78.

12. Quoted in Philip Weeks, *Farewell, My Nation: The American Indian and the United States, 1820–1890* (Arlington Heights, IL: Harlan Davidson, 1990), 288.

13. Quoted in Ralph H. Gabriel, "American Experience with Military Government," *American Political Science Review* 37, no. 3 (1943): 419.

14. Quoted in Robert W. Johannsen, *To the Halls of the Montezumas: The Mexican War in the American Imagination* (Oxford: Oxford University Press, 1985), 172.

15. Paul A. Kramer, *The Blood of Government: Race, Empire, the United States, and the Philippines* (Chapel Hill: University of North Carolina Press, 2006), 162.

16. Kramer, 157.

17. Kramer, 29.

18. On this parallel see Richard Drinnon, *Facing West: The Metaphysics of Indian-Hating and Empire-Building* (New York: Meridian, 1980), 448.

19. Frank Ninkovich, *The Global Republic: America's Inadvertent Rise to World Power* (Chicago: University of Chicago Press, 2014), 67–78. This is not to deny that security-oriented considerations, or at least justifications, played a part in the spread of the American empire.

20. James D. Fearon and David D. Laitin, "Neotrusteeship and the Problem of Weak States," *International Security* 28, no. 4 (2004): 12. The authors refer to such interventions as "postmodern imperialism."

21. For instance see Francis Fukuyama, ed., *Nation-Building: Beyond Afghanistan and Iraq* (Baltimore: Johns Hopkins University Press, 2006); James Dobbins, Seth G. Jones, et al., eds., *The UN's Role in Nation-Building: From the Congo to Iraq* (Santa Monica, CA: RAND, 2005); Peter Sercombe and Ruanni Tupas, eds., *Language, Education and Nation-Building: Assimilation and Shift in Southeast Asia* (Basingstoke, UK: Palgrave, 2014).

22. For an example of a single work that expands the definition of "nation building" to encompass extremely diverse policy practices see Jeremi Suri, *Liberty's Surest Guardian: Rebuilding Nations after War from the Founders to Obama* (New York: Free Press, 2012).

23. I draw here on Hannah Arendt's distinction between "work," the shaping of physical objects, and the realm of political "action." See Arendt, *The Human Condition* (Chicago: University of Chicago Press, 1957), pts. 3 and 4.

24. Henry Kissinger, *Diplomacy* (New York: Simon & Schuster, 1994), 648–49.

25. Around the same time, policy makers were embracing "modernization theory" as an all-embracing way of understanding—and influencing—these non-Western political processes. See Michael E. Latham, *The Right Kind of Revolution: Modernization, Development, and U.S. Foreign Policy from the Cold War to the Present* (Ithaca, NY: Cornell University Press, 2011).

26. Karl W. Deutsch and William J. Foltz, eds., *Nation-Building* (New York: Atherton, 1963).

27. Miller, *Misalliance*, 17.

28. Michael Rear, *Intervention, Ethnic Conflict and State-Building in Iraq* (New York: Routledge, 2008), 139.

29. For two examples see James Dobbins, Seth G. Jones, et al., eds., *The Beginner's Guide to Nation-Building* (Santa Monica, CA: RAND, 2007); Paul D. Miller, *Armed State-Building: Confronting State Failure, 1898–2012* (Ithaca, NY: Cornell University Press, 2013).

30. Roger Hilsman, "A Strategic Concept for South Vietnam," 2 February 1962, folder "Vietnam strategic concept for South Vietnam 2/2/62," box 3, Roger Hilsman Papers (hereafter RHP), John F. Kennedy Library, Boston (hereafter JFKL) 3, 9.

31. A fact that has not prevented many historians appropriately applying the term to a range of American activities in the conflict.

32. For usages of the term see Robert Komer oral history interview, no. 2, 18 August 1970, Lyndon Baines Johnson Library, Austin, TX (hereafter LBJL), 25; Austin Long, *On "Other War": Lessons from Five Decades of RAND Counterinsurgency Research* (Santa Monica, CA: RAND, 2002).

33. Frank Scotton, *Uphill Battle: Reflections on Viet Nam Counterinsurgency* (Lubbock: Texas Tech University Press, 2014), 54.

34. Latham, *Right Kind of Revolution*, 142; David Ekbladh, *The Great American Mission: Modernization and the Construction of an American World Order* (Princeton, NJ: Princeton University Press, 2011); David C. Engerman, Nils Gilman, Mark H. Haefele, and Michael E. Latham, eds., *Staging Growth: Modernization, Development, and the Global Cold War* (Amherst: University of Massachusetts Press, 2003).

35. "Diary of an Infiltrator," December 1966, *Vietnam Document and Research Notes Series: Translation and Analysis of Significant Viet Cong / North Vietnamese Documents* (Bethesda, MD: University Publications of America, 1991), 16.

36. North Vietnam also benefited from the rotating presence of hundreds of thousands of Chinese engineering and antiaircraft artillery units in North Vietnam, freeing up the NVA to carry the war to South Vietnam. But, unlike the GVN, the Hanoi regime never relied on foreigners to fight for it. Chinese troops were withdrawn from North Vietnam in 1969–1970 following a breakdown in relations between Hanoi and Beijing, and yet North Vietnam was still able to win its war. An analogous withdrawal of U.S. forces from South Vietnam would have led to the South's immediate collapse.

37. Ernest Gellner, *Nations and Nationalism* (Oxford: Blackwell, 1983).

38. Benedict Anderson, *Imagined Communities: Reflections on the Origins and Spread of Nationalism* (New York: Verso, 1982).

39. Jeffrey Race, *War Comes to Long An: Revolutionary Conflict in a Vietnamese Province* (Berkeley: University of California Press, 2010), 179.

1. THE DIEM YEARS

1. Nghiem Dang, *Viet-Nam: Politics and Public Administration* (Honolulu: East-West, 1966), 329; David G. Marr, *Vietnamese Tradition on Trial, 1920–1925* (Berkeley: University of California Press, 1971), 5.

2. Li Tana, *Nguyen Cochinchina: Southern Vietnam in the Seventeenth and Eighteenth Centuries* (Ithaca, NY: Cornell University Press, 1998), 99.

3. Pierre Brocheux, *The Mekong Delta: Ecology, Economy, and Revolution, 1860–1960* (Madison: University of Wisconsin–Madison, 1995), 2. See also David Biggs, *Quagmire: Nation-Building and Nature in the Mekong Delta* (Seattle: University of Washington Press, 2010).

4. Guy H. Fox and Charles A. Joiner, "Perceptions of the Vietnamese Public Administration System," *Administrative Science Quarterly* 8, no. 4 (1964): 448.

5. Alexander Woodside, *Vietnam and the Chinese Model: A Comparative Study of Vietnamese and Chinese Government in the First Half of the Nineteenth Century* (Cambridge, MA: Harvard University Press, 1971), 125.

6. Thomas Lionel Hodgkin, *Vietnam: The Revolutionary Path* (New York: Palgrave, 1981), 103, 150–53.

7. Ton Tho Tuong and Phan Van Tri, "Collaboration vs. Resistance," in *Patterns of Vietnamese Response to Foreign Intervention: 1858–1900*, ed. Truong Buu Lam (New Haven, CT: Yale Southeast Asia Studies, 1967), 81–86.

8. Quoted in Hodgkin, *Vietnam*, 176.

9. Roy Jumper, "Mandarin Bureaucracy and Politics in South Viet Nam," *Pacific Affairs* 30, no. 1 (1957): 47.

10. Quoted in Philip E. Catton, *Diem's Final Failure: Prelude to America's War in Vietnam* (Lawrence: University of Kansas Press, 2003), 33.

11. Dang, *Viet-Nam*, 187; Fox and Joiner, "Perceptions of the Vietnamese Public Administration System," 449.

12. Duong Van Mai Elliott, *The Sacred Willow: Four Generations of Life in a Vietnamese Family* (Oxford: Oxford University Press, 1999), 47.

13. Alexis de Tocqueville, *The Old Regime and the French Revolution* (1856; Mineola, NY: Dover, 2010), 83.

14. Kennedy and Thuan, memorandum of conversation, 14 June 1961, folder "Vietnam, general, 6/3/61–6/18/61," box 193A, National Security Files (hereafter NSF): Countries, JFKL.

15. Quoted in Catton, *Diem's Final Failure*, 56; Geoffrey C. Stewart, "Hearts, Minds and Cong Dan Vu: The Special Commissariat for Civic Action and Nation-Building in Ngo Dinh Diem's South Vietnam, 1955–1957," *Journal of Vietnamese Studies* 6, no. 3 (2011): 48.

16. Marr, *Vietnamese Tradition on Trial*, 3.

17. Ngo Vinh Long, *Before the Revolution: The Vietnamese Peasants under the French* (Cambridge, MA: MIT Press, 1973), 48.

18. David Anderson, *Trapped by Success: The Eisenhower Administration and Vietnam* (New York: Columbia University Press, 1991), 140.

19. Long, *Before the Revolution*, 69–70.

20. Marr, *Vietnamese Tradition on Trial*, 4.

21. There is a debate among scholars over the extent to which this social division predated the colonial period or was a product of it. Nevertheless, by the time of the events discussed in this work, it certainly existed. See Samuel L. Popkin, *The Rational Peasant: The Political Economy of Rural Society in Vietnam* (Berkeley: University of California Press, 1979); James C. Scott, *The Moral Economy of the Peasant: Rebellion and Subsistence in Southeast Asia* (New Haven, CT: Yale University Press, 1976).

22. Nguyen Thi Thu-Lam, *Fallen Leaves: Memoirs of a Vietnamese Woman from 1940 to 1975* (New Haven, CT: Yale University Press, 1989), 7–8; Nguyen Thi Tuyet Mai, *The Rubber Tree: Memoir of a Vietnamese Woman Who Was an Anti-French Guerrilla, a Publisher and a Peace Activist* (Jefferson, NC: McFarland, 1994), 9–10.

23. Huynh Kim Khanh, *Vietnamese Communism: 1925–1945* (Ithaca, NY: Cornell University Press, 1982), 82.

24. On the role of the famine in the August Revolution see Fredrik Logevall, *Embers of War: The Fall of an Empire and the Making of America's Vietnam* (New York: Random House, 2012), 93–94.

25. David W. P. Elliott, *The Vietnamese War: Revolution and Social Change in the Mekong Delta, 1930–1975* (London: Sharpe, 2003), 1:80–84, 122–27.

26. Popkin, *Rational Peasant*, 83.

27. Jeffrey Race, *War Comes to Long An: Revolutionary Conflict in a Vietnamese Province* (Berkeley: University of California Press, 2010), 9.

28. Race, 179.

29. Truong Chinh, *Primer for Revolt: The Communist Takeover in Viet-Nam* (New York: Praeger, 1963), 98.

30. Edgar O'Ballance, *The Indochina War, 1945–54: A Study in Guerilla Warfare* (London: Faber, 1964), 81.

31. Quoted in Robert K. Brigham, *Guerrilla Diplomacy: The NLF's Foreign Relations and the Viet Nam War* (Ithaca, NY: Cornell University Press, 1999), 12.

32. On this "preemptive" social strategy see Race, *War Comes to Long An*, chap. 4.

33. Race, 161.

34. Race, 128.

35. Edward Miller, *Misalliance: Ngo Dinh Diem, the United States, and the Fate of South Vietnam* (Cambridge, MA: Harvard University Press, 2013), 88.

36. Bernard Fall, *The Viet Minh Regime: Government and Administration in the Democratic Republic of Vietnam* (New York: Institute of Pacific Relations, 1956), 81.

37. Lien-Hang T. Nguyen, *Hanoi's War: An International History of the War for Peace in Vietnam* (Chapel Hill: University of North Carolina Press, 2012), 31; Pierre Asselin, *Hanoi's Road to the Vietnam War, 1954–1965* (Berkeley: University of California Press, 2013), 18–19.

38. Tuong Vu, *Vietnam's Communist Revolution: The Power and Limits of Ideology* (Cambridge: Cambridge University Press, 2017), 132.

39. Miller, *Misalliance*, 6–7.

40. Catton, *Diem's Final Failure*; Miller, *Misalliance*; Jessica Chapman, *Cauldron of Resistance: Ngo Dinh Diem, the United States, and 1950s Southern Vietnam* (Ithaca, NY: Cornell University Press, 2013); Geoffrey Stewart, *Vietnam's Lost Revolution: Ngo Dinh Diem's Failure to Build an Independent Nation, 1955–1963* (Cambridge: Cambridge University Press, 2017).

41. Christopher Goscha, *Vietnam: A New History* (New York: Basic Books, 2016), chap. 4.

42. William J. Duiker, "Phan Boi Chau: Asian Revolutionary in a Changing World," *Journal of Asian Studies* 31, no. 1 (1971): 80.

43. Miller, *Misalliance*, 19–51.

44. For more on Mounier see John Hellman, *Emmanuel Mounier and the New Catholic Left, 1930–1950* (Toronto: University of Toronto Press, 1981). On Nhu see Miller, *Misalliance*, 41–48.

45. Dang, *Viet-Nam*, 124.

46. Quoted in Stewart, "Hearts, Minds and Cong Dan Vu," 48.

47. Hai B. Pho, *Vietnamese Public Management in Transition: South Vietnam Public Administration, 1955–1975* (Lanham, MD: University Press, 1990), 59.

48. Dang, *Viet-Nam*, 140–41.

49. Tana, *Nguyen Cochinchina*.

50. Fox and Joiner, "Perceptions of the Vietnamese Public Administration System," 459.

51. Dang, *Viet-Nam*, 45, 329.

52. Dang, 5.

53. Dang, 143.

54. Debrief no. 15679, box 101, Allan E. Goodman Papers (hereafter GP), Hoover Institution Archives (hereafter HIA), 4. For details on citations and the pseudonyms used when referring to these materials see note 6 in the introduction.

55. Dang, *Viet-Nam*, 180.

56. Catton, *Diem's Final Failure*, 64–65.

57. Quoted in Jumper, "Mandarin Bureaucracy," 52.

58. Tran Ngoc Chau, *The American Syndrome: An Interview with the BBC* (1991), folder 1, box 62, Neil Sheehan Papers, LOC, 10.

59. Quoted in Chau, 58.

60. Tran Van Don, *Our Endless War: Inside Vietnam* (Novato, CA: Presidio, 1978), 25. See also Race, *War Comes to Long An*, chap. 1.

61. Woodside, *Community and Revolution,* 120–22.

62. Catton, *Diem's Final Failure*, 38, 89–90; Miller, *Misalliance*, 231–39.

63. Quoted in Sean Fear, "The Ambiguous Legacy of Ngo Dinh Diem in South Vietnam's Second Republic," *Journal of Vietnamese Studies* 11, no. 1 (2016): 53.

64. Thomas L. Ahern Jr., *CIA and the House of Ngo: Covert Action in South Vietnam, 1954–63* (Washington, DC: Center for the Study of Intelligence, 2000), 32.

65. Miller, *Misalliance*, 200–201.

66. Nguyen Cao Ky, with Marvin J. Wolf, *Buddha's Child: My Fight to Save Vietnam* (New York: St. Martin's, 2002), 45.

67. On implementation see Catton, *Diem's Final Failure*, 129–40.

68. William J. Duiker, *The Communist Road to Power in Vietnam* (Boulder, CO: Westview, 1996), 196; Race, *War Comes to Long An*, 99; Asselin, *Hanoi's Road to the Vietnam War,* 46.

69. Quoted in Asselin, *Hanoi's Road to the Vietnam War*, 51–52.

70. Nguyen, *Hanoi's War*, 52–53.

71. Asselin, *Hanoi's Road to the Vietnam War*, 54.

72. David Hunt, *Vietnam's Southern Revolution: From Peasant Insurrection to Total War* (Amherst: University of Massachusetts Press, 2008), chap. 3; Race, *War Comes to Long An*, chap. 3.

73. Bert Fraleigh, "The Story of America's Counterinsurgency Efforts in Vietnam in the Early 1960s," incorrectly dated January 1966 [1996?], Rufus Phillips Collection, Vietnam Center and Archive, Texas Tech University, Virtual Vietnam Archive (hereafter TTVA), http://www.vietnam.ttu.edu/virtualarchive/items.php?item=23970130040, 2–9, quotes at 3, 9; Debrief no. 3672 (Fraleigh), box 98, GP, HIA, 1–3; Rufus Phillips, *Why Vietnam Matters* (Annapolis, MD: Naval Institute Press, 2008), 108–9.

74. Department of State airgram, subject "Viet Nam Situation," 20 June 1962, folder "Vietnam, general, 6/9/62–6/20/62," box 196, NSF: Countries, JFKL, 2, 3.

75. Although Phillips has published a memoir of his experiences and is relatively well known to historians, Fraleigh has received much less attention. The new sources used in this book allow his role to be explored.

76. Fraleigh, "Story of America's Counterinsurgency Efforts," 9; Debrief no. 3672 (Fraleigh), 3.

77. Phillips, *Why Vietnam Matters*, 104.

78. USAID, *Terminal Report: United States Economic Assistance to South Vietnam, 1954–1975* (Washington, DC, 1976), section "Rural Development & Field Operations," 4–5.

79. William Colby, with James McCargar, *Lost Victory: A Firsthand Account of America's Sixteen-Year Involvement in Vietnam* (Chicago: Contemporary, 1989), 74, 105.

80. Roger Hilsman, "A Strategic Concept for South Vietnam," 2 February 1962, folder "Vietnam strategic concept for South Vietnam 2/2/62," box 3, RHP, JFKL, 1; CIA, Current Intelligence Memorandum, 11 January 1963, folder "Vietnam, general, 1/10/63–1/30/63," box 197, NSF: Countries, JFKL.

81. Jessica Elkind, *Aid under Fire: Nation Building and the Vietnam War* (Lexington: University Press of Kentucky, 2016), chaps. 2, 4.

82. Dang, *Viet-Nam*, 87.

83. Colby, *Lost Victory*, 85, 83.

84. Tran Ngoc Chau, with Ken Fermoyle, *Vietnam Labyrinth: Allies, Enemies, and Why the U.S. Lost the War* (Lubbock: Texas Tech University Press, 2012), 3–169; Thomas L. Ahern Jr., *The CIA and Rural Pacification in South Vietnam* (Washington, DC: Center for the Study of Intelligence, 2001), 116–17.

85. Chau, *American Syndrome*, 13, 15, 51.

86. Stuart E. Methven, *Parapolitics and Pacification*, folder "Special studies—Vietnam [1 of 2]," box 24, NSF, Komer-Leonhart Subject Files (hereafter K-L), LBJL, pt. 4.

87. Chau, *American Syndrome*, 18.

88. Methven, *Parapolitics and Pacification*, 49.

89. Methven, 70; Chau, *Vietnam Labyrinth*, 180–83, 241; Ahern, *CIA and Rural Pacification*, 128–30, 135.

90. Methven, *Parapolitics and Pacification*, 16; Ahern, *CIA and Rural Pacification*, 116.

91. Chau, *Vietnam Labyrinth*, xv.

92. Chau, 237.

93. Ahern, *CIA and Rural Pacification*, 133, 168–69.

94. Don Luce and John Sommer, *Viet Nam: The Unheard Voices* (Ithaca, NY: Cornell University Press, 1969), 3, 44.

95. Elkind, *Aid under Fire*, chap. 3; Luce and Sommer, *Viet Nam*, 18.

96. Luce and Sommer, *Viet Nam*, 11; William A. Nighswonger, *Rural Pacification in Viet Nam: 1962–1965* (Washington, DC: ARPA, 1966), 48–49; George K. Tanham et al., *War without Guns: American Civilians in Rural Vietnam* (New York: Praeger, 1966), 30.

97. Rufus C. Phillips III, interview by Charles Stuart Kennedy, Association for Diplomatic Studies and Training, Foreign Affairs Oral History Project, 19 July 1995, http://international.loc.gov/service/mss/mssmisc/mfdip/2005%20txt%20files/2004phi04.txt (accessed 11 July 2016); Debrief no. 3672 (Fraleigh), 3–6.

98. Phillips, *Why Vietnam Matters*, 130.

99. *USOM Provincial Representatives Guide*, December 1962, Larry Flanagan Collection, TTVA, http://www.vietnam.ttu.edu/virtualarchive/items.php?item=0880215001, 1, 2.

100. *USOM Provincial Representatives Guide*, 3, 1.

101. Fraleigh claimed that he was involved in convincing Wisconsin congressman Clement Zablocki of the value of the Peace Corps, and that Zablocki then sold the concept to President Kennedy. See Fraleigh, "Story of America's Counterinsurgency Efforts," 12. See also Debrief no. 3672 (Fraleigh), 10.

102. He does add that Phillips "fully appreciated the political aim of the [strategic hamlet] program." Colby, *Lost Victory*, 115.

103. *USOM Provincial Representatives Guide*, 3.

104. Debrief no. 3672 (Fraleigh), 25.

105. Johnson to Rostow, memo, 6 September 1961, folder "Vietnam, general, 9/61," box 194, NSF: Countries, JFKL, 1; Johnson to Rostow, memo, 14 October 1961, folder "Vietnam, general, 10/12/61–10/15/61," box 194, NSF: Countries, JFKL, 1.

106. Luce and Sommer, *Viet Nam*, 206.

107. Debrief no. 146612, box 99, GP, HIA, 1.

108. Quoted in Frank Scotton, *Uphill Battle: Reflections on Viet Nam Counterinsurgency* (Lubbock: Texas Tech University Press, 2014), 19.

109. Hilsman and Forrestal to JFK, undated, folder "Vietnam Hilsman trip, 12/62–1/63, basic report," box 3, RHP, JFKL, 5.

110. CIA info report no. -3/520 576, 23 August 1962, folder "Vietnam, 9/28/62–7/27/62," box 3, RHP, JFKL.

111. Forrestal to Bundy, memo, 8 September 1962, folder "Vietnam, general, 9/1/62–9/14/62," box 196, NSF: Countries, JFKL.

112. Lansdale to Diem, 30 January 1961, *Foreign Relations of the United States, 1961–1963* (hereafter *FRUS, 1961–1963*), 30 vols. (Washington, DC: Government Printing Office, 1988–2001), 1:21.

113. Truong Van Toai, with David Chanoff and Doan Van Toai, *A Vietcong Memoir* (San Diego: Harcourt, 1985), 51, 64; Race, *War Comes to Long An*, 172.

114. Methven, *Parapolitics and Pacification*, 10, 52.

115. Dang, *Viet-Nam*, 125–31, 141.

116. Quoted in R. W. Komer, *Organization and Management of the "New Model" Pacification Program, 1966–1969* (RAND document number D-20104-ARPA, 1970), 19.

2. THE JOHNSON ADMINISTRATION AND NATION BUILDING

1. For an account that stresses Johnson's personal agency in escalating the war see Fredrik Logevall, *Choosing War: The Lost Chance for Peace and the Escalation of War in Vietnam* (Berkeley: University of California Press, 2001).

2. Quoted in Frank L. Jones, "Blowtorch: Robert Komer and the Making of Vietnam Pacification Policy," *Parameters* 35 (Autumn 2005): 104.

3. This criticism is made in Harry G. Summers Jr., *American Strategy in Vietnam: A Critical Analysis* (Mineola, NY: Dover, 2007), 104.

4. Memo for the record, 24 November 1963, U.S. Department of State, *FRUS, 1961–1963*, 4:635–37.

5. Robert S. McNamara, with Brian VanDeMark, *In Retrospect: The Tragedy and Lessons of Vietnam* (New York: Vintage, 1995), 102.

6. National Security Action Memorandum (NSAM) 273, 26 November 1963, *FRUS, 1961–1963*, 4:637–40.

7. Memcon, 1 June 1964, *FRUS, 1964–1968*, 1:422–28; telegram, Embassy to State, 29 June 1964, Douglas Pike Collection, TTVA, www.vietnam.ttu.edu/virtualarchive/items.php?item=2120327004.

8. Mike Gravel, ed., *The Pentagon Papers: The Defense Department History of United States Decisionmaking on Vietnam* (Boston: Beacon, 1971), 2:523.

9. Richards to Westmoreland, memo, 30 November 1964, folder "#10: History Backup [II]," box 3, Westmoreland Papers, LBJL.

10. Lien-Hang T. Nguyen, *Hanoi's War: An International History of the War for Peace in Vietnam* (Chapel Hill: University of North Carolina Press, 2012), 65; Pierre Asselin, *Hanoi's Road to the Vietnam War, 1954–1965* (Berkeley: University of California Press, 2013), 148–76; William J. Duiker, *The Communist Road to Power in South Vietnam* (Boulder, CO: Westview, 1996), 245–46.

11. Truong Van Toai, with David Chanoff and Doan Van Toai, *A Vietcong Memoir* (San Diego: Harcourt, 1985), 91.

12. Johnson to Lodge, message, 7 January 1964, U.S. Department of State, *Foreign Relations of the United States, 1964–1968* (hereafter *FRUS, 1964–1968*), 35 vols. (Washington, DC: Government Printing Office, 1992–1999), 1:6–7.

13. National Security Action Memo 314, 10 September 1964, *FRUS, 1964–1968*, 1:758–60.

14. Chester Cooper oral history interview, no. 1, 9 July 1979, LBJL, 9–10; Edward Lansdale oral history, no. 2, 15 September 1981, LBJL, 53.

15. Taylor to State, telegram, 26 February 1965, *FRUS, 1964–1968*, 2:375.

16. Cooper to Bundy, memo, 1 March 1965, *FRUS, 1964–1968*, 2:384–88.

17. *Public Papers of the Presidents of the United States: Lyndon B. Johnson, 1965* (Washington, DC: Government Printing Office, 1966), 1:394–99.

18. Speech draft, 4 March 1965, folder "Vietnam Coordinating Committee, part I, 1965," box 4, Subject Files of the Office of Vietnam Affairs (Vietnam Working Group), 1964–1974, RG 59, National Archives II at College Park, MD (hereafter NARA II), 1.

19. Johnson and Bundy, recording of telephone conversation, 31 May 1965, #7848, LBJL.

20. Johnson and McNamara, recording of telephone conversation, 12 September 1965, #8851, LBJL.

21. Bundy to Johnson, memo, 8 March 1965, *FRUS, 1964–1968*, 2:414–20; Johnson to Lodge, message, 7 January 1964, 6–7.

22. Frank Scotton, *Uphill Battle: Reflections on Viet Nam Counterinsurgency* (Lubbock: Texas Tech University Press, 2014), 148.

23. Bundy to Johnson, telegram, 6 December 1965, *FRUS, 1964–1968*, 3:607–14.

24. Robert Komer oral history interview, no. 2, 18 August 1970, LBJL, 51,

25. Dean Rusk, *As I Saw It* (London: Norton, 1970), 454.

26. Quoted in H. W. Brands, *The Wages of Globalism: Lyndon Johnson and the Limits of American Power* (Oxford: Oxford University Press, 1995), 14.

27. Rufus C. Phillips, *Why Vietnam Matters: An Eyewitness Account of Lessons Not Learned* (Annapolis, MD: Naval Institute Press, 2013), 104, 123–24; William Colby, with James McCargar, *Lost Victory: A Firsthand Account of America's Sixteen-Year Involvement in Vietnam* (Chicago: Contemporary, 1989), 122.

28. Notes of a meeting, 7 December 1965, *FRUS, 1964–1968*, 3:619–22.

29. Chester Cooper, *The Lost Crusade: America in Vietnam* (New York: Dodd, Mead, 1970), 296–97.

30. Johnson and Rusk, recording of telephone conversation, 3 February 1966, #9612, LBJL.

31. Johnson and Manatos, recording of a telephone conversation, 4 February 1966, #9619, LBJL.

32. All quotes in this paragraph from Gravel, *Pentagon Papers*, 2:548–54. On the continued disagreement between agencies see report, "Warrenton meeting on South Viet-Nam, January 8–11, 1966," 13 January 1966, *FRUS, 1964–1968*, 4:58–63.

33. Nguyen Cao Ky, with Martin Wolf, *Buddha's Child: My Fight to Save Vietnam* (New York: St. Martin's, 2002), 35–125; biographic data, "Nguyen Cao Ky," folder "DIA biographic sketches, vol. II 7/65–12/68," box 175, NSF: Country File, Vietnam (hereafter CF), LBJL; Bui Diem, with David Chanoff, *In the Jaws of History* (Bloomington: Indiana University Press, 1987), 158.

34. *Nguyen Van Thieu: President of the Republic of Vietnam* (Saigon, 1969); biographic data, "Nguyen Van Thieu," folder "DIA biographic sketches, vol. VI 7/65–12/68," box 176, NSF, CF, LBJL.

35. Bui Diem, *In the Jaws of History*, 157–58.

36. William Bundy, quoted in George Herring, *America's Longest War: The United States and Vietnam, 1950–1975* (New York: McGraw-Hill, 1996), 137.

37. Bui Diem, *In the Jaws of History*, 157.

38. Ky, *Buddha's Child*, 132–33, 239.

39. Ky, 188–89. On his father-in-law see biographic data, "Nguyen Cao Ky."

40. Gravel, *Pentagon Papers*, 2:548–54.

41. Ky, *Buddha's Child*, 191; Bui Diem, *In the Jaws of History*, 163.

42. NLF statement printed in *Vietnam Courier* (Hanoi), 2 February 1966, 1, 7.

43. Bernard Fall, *Viet-Nam Witness: 1953–66* (New York: Praeger, 1966), 137.

44. Bui Diem, *In the Jaws of History*, 162.

45. On Komer's early life see Frank L. Jones, *Blowtorch: Robert Komer, Vietnam, and American Cold War Strategy* (Annapolis, MD: Naval Institute Press, 2013), chap. 1.

46. Jones, *Blowtorch*, chap. 5; Robert Komer oral history interview, no. 3, 15 November 1971, LBJL, 38.

47. Excerpt from Robert Komer trial testimony in Westmoreland vs. CBS, Larry Berman Collection, TTVA, http://www.vietnam.ttu.edu/virtualarchive/items.php?item= 0251114002, p. 1.

48. Quoted in Merle Miller, *Lyndon: An Oral Biography* (New York: Putnam's Sons, 1980), 465.

49. On "high modernism" see James C. Scott, *Seeing Like a State: How Certain Schemes to Improve the Human Condition Have Failed* (New Haven, CT: Yale University Press, 1999).

50. Such "low modernist" approaches have been discussed in Daniel Immerwahr, *Thinking Small: The United States and the Lure of Community Development* (Cambridge, MA: Harvard University Press, 2015).

51. Report, "Warrenton meeting on South Viet-Nam"; McNamara to Johnson, memo, 30 November 1965, *FRUS, 1964–1968*, 3:591–94.

52. Holbrooke to Komer, memo, 27 February 1967, "Report to the President [8/66]," box 8, Robert W. Komer Files (hereafter RKF), LBJL.

53. Komer to Johnson, memo, 9 May 1966, folder "RWK CHRON FILE May 1966 [2 of 2]," box 6, Robert W. Komer Papers (hereafter RKP), LBJL.

54. Komer oral history interview, no. 2, 25.

55. Komer oral history interview, no. 2, 27.

56. Komer to McNamara, memo, 1 September 1966, folder "McNamara/Vance/ McNaughton," box 5, RKF, LBJL.

57. Komer to Johnson, memo, 9 May 1966.

58. Komer oral history interview, no. 3, 28.

59. Komer oral history interview, no. 3, 32–33. See also Komer oral history interview, no. 2, 26.

60. Komer to Porter, 11 May 1966, letter no. 8, folder "RWK CHRON FILE May 1966 [2 of 2]," box 6, RKP, LBJL.

61. Komer to Johnson, memo, 9 May 1966.

62. Komer to McNamara, memo, 29 September 1966, folder "McNamara/Vance/ McNaughton," box 5, RKF, LBJL; Komer to Johnson, memo, 14 October 1966, folder "RWK CHRON FILE October–December 1966 [3 of 3]," box 6, RKP, LBJL.

63. Komer to Johnson, memo, 14 June 1966, *FRUS, 1964–1968*, 4:419–25.

64. Komer to McNamara, memo, 29 September 1966.

65. Komer to Johnson, memo, 9 May 1966.

66. Komer to McNamara, memo, 29 September 1966.

67. Johnson and McNamara, recording of telephone conversation, 5 October 1966, #10924, LBJL.

68. Carver to Helms, memo, 7 July 1966, *FRUS, 1964–1968*, 4:486–88. Emphasis in original.

69. Helms to Komer, memo, 18 July 1966, *FRUS, 1964–1968*, 4:505–7.

70. Johnson to Rusk, memo, 1 October 1966, *FRUS, 1964–1968*, 4:680–82.

71. Carver to Helms, memo, 6 October 1966, *FRUS, 1964–1968*, 4:712–16, at footnote 6.

72. Carver to Helms, memo, 28 September 1966, *FRUS, 1964–1968*, 4:668–72.

73. Komer to McNamara, memo, 29 September 1966.

74. Komer to Johnson, memo, 28 February 1967, folder "Supplement to Komer report [3/67]," box 8, RKF, LBJL.

75. Komer to McNamara, memo, 29 September 1966.

76. Komer, memo for the record, 2 November 1966, folder "RWK CHRON FILE October–December 1966 [3 of 3]," box 6, RKP, LBJL.

77. Holbrooke to Komer, memo, 27 February 1967, "Report to the President [8/66]," box 8, RKF, LBJL.

78. Komer to Johnson, memo, 28 February 1967. Emphasis in original.

79. Johnson and McNamara, recording of telephone conversation, 5 October 1966, #10923, LBJL.

80. Johnson to Lodge, 16 November 1966, *FRUS, 1964–1968*, 4:848–49; Komer to Johnson, memo, 17 November 1966, *FRUS, 1964–1968*, 4:849–50.

81. Komer to Johnson, memo, 17 November 1966.

82. Rostow to Johnson, memo, 26 January 1967, *FRUS, 1964–1968*, 5:62.

83. DePuy to Goodpaster, memo, 18 April 1967, *FRUS, 1964–1968*, 4:320–26.

84. "Pacification and Nation-building in Vietnam," memo, 17 February 1967, folder "Vietnam memos (A). Vol. 66," box 41, NSF: Vietnam, LBJL, 1, 3, 23.

3. SETTING UP CORDS

1. "Pacification Program in Vietnam," briefing, 23 October 1967, folder "Pacification [2 of 18]," box 18, NSF, K-L, LBJL, 4. The map itself was not placed in the archive.

2. Mark Moyar, *Triumph Forsaken: The Vietnam War, 1954–1965* (Cambridge: Cambridge University Press, 2006), 336–40. Jack Shulimson and Charles M. Johnson, *U.S. Marines in Vietnam: The Landing and the Buildup, 1965* (Washington, DC: U.S. Marine Corps, 1978), 204–5.

3. Moyar, *Triumph Forsaken*, 358–59, 393–94.

4. On this period see John M. Carland, *Combat Operations: Stemming the Tide, May 1965–October 1966* (Washington, DC: Center of Military History, 2000).

5. James C. Scott, *The Art of Not Being Governed: An Anarchist History of Upland Southeast Asia* (New Haven, CT: Yale University Press, 2009), 153.

6. Mike Gravel, ed., *The Pentagon Papers: The Defense Department History of United States Decisionmaking on Vietnam* (Boston: Beacon, 1971), 2:515.

7. Quotes from "Concept of Operations," cable, 14 June 1964, Larry Berman Collection, TTVA, 2. See also Gregory Daddis, *Westmoreland's War: Reassessing American Strategy in Vietnam* (Oxford: Oxford University Press, 2014); Jeffrey J. Clarke, *Advice and Support, the Final Years: The U.S. Army in Vietnam* (Washington, DC: Government Printing Office, 1988), 120–24.

8. Thomas L. Ahern Jr., *The CIA and Rural Pacification in South Vietnam* (Washington, DC: Center for the Study of Intelligence, 2001), 195–96.

9. DIA biographic file, Nguyen Duc Thang, December 1967, folder "Vietnam: [DIA biographic sketches, vol. V] 7/65–12/68," box 175, NSF: CF, LBJL; James McAllister, "What Can One Man Do? Nguyen Duc Thang and the Limits of Reform in South Vietnam," *Journal of Vietnamese Studies* 4, no. 2 (2009): 120; Ahern, *CIA and Rural Pacification*, 196.

10. "Assessment of GVN/FWMAF Program for Revolutionary Development," point paper, 31 March 1966, folder "RD reports [2 of 2]," box 22, NSF, K-L, LBJL, 1.

11. William A. Nighswonger, *Rural Pacification in Viet Nam: 1962–1965* (Advanced Research Projects Agency, 1966), 164.

12. Ahern, *CIA and Rural Pacification*, 203.

13. Richard C. Kriegel, "Vietnamese Attitudes and Behavior Related to Management Problems of the RD Program," March 1969, folder "Comments + res. rept. / VN attitudes + behavior related to mgmt. problems," box 12, HQ MACV, CORDS: Plans, Programs and Policies Directorate (hereafter PPP), CORDS Historical Working Group Files (hereafter CORDS History Files), RG 472, NARA II, 40.

14. Cao Van Vien, *The U.S. Adviser* (Washington, DC: Center of Military History, 1980), 142; Don Luce and John Sommer, *Viet Nam: The Unheard Voices* (Ithaca, NY: Cornell University Press, 1969), 152.

15. Luce and Sommer, 41.

16. "Establishment of the National Training Center," undated, folder "National Training Center Questionnaire," box 16, HQ MACV, PPP, CORDS History Files, RG 472, NARA II, 6.

17. Stuart E. Methven, *Parapolitics and Pacification*, folder "Special studies—Vietnam [1 of 2]," box 24, NSF, K-L, LBJL, 53.

18. Methven, *Parapolitics and Pacification*, 24.

19. Tran Ngoc Chau, with Ken Fermoyle, *Vietnam Labyrinth: Allies, Enemies, and Why the U.S. Lost the War* (Lubbock: Texas Tech University Press, 2012), 240–41; Kriegel, "Vietnamese Attitudes and Behavior," 40–41.

20. Chau, *Vietnam Labyrinth*, 235, 236.

21. Chau, 226–47; Colby to Komer, memo, 16 August 1966, folder "RD—cadre," box 22, NSF, K-L, LBJL.

22. Chau, *Vietnam Labyrinth*, 241–47; "Establishment of the National Training Center," 1; Ahern, *CIA and Rural Pacification*, 196.

23. Colby to Komer, memo, 16 August 1966; Chau, *Vietnam Labyrinth*, 241–47.

24. Nighswonger, *Rural Pacification*, 48–49; George K. Tanham et al., *War without Guns: American Civilians in Rural Vietnam* (New York: Praeger, 1966), 30.

25. Bert Fraleigh, "The Real Story of America's Counterinsurgency Efforts in Vietnam in the Early 1960s," incorrectly dated January 1966 [1996?], Rufus Phillips Collection, TTVA, 28.

26. "Paper and Song Lyrics—the Greatest Years of the Pig: 1962–1964 in the Rural Areas of South Vietnam," undated, Rufus Phillips Collection, TTVA.

27. Debrief no. 21666, box 100, GP, HIA, 10.

28. Rufus C. Phillips, *Why Vietnam Matters: An Eyewitness Account of Lessons Not Learned* (Annapolis, MD: Naval Institute Press, 2013), 133.

29. CFAA newsletter #10, July 1972, folder "CFAA Newsletters, 1971–72," box 45, HQ MACV, PPP, CORDS History Files, RG 472, NARA II, 1.

30. Debrief no. 15681, box 97, GP, HIA, 2.

31. Quoted in Ahern, *CIA and Rural Pacification*, 154.

32. Debrief no. 126712, box 99, GP, HIA, 2.

33. Michael E. Peterson, *The Combined Action Platoons: The U.S. Marines' Other War in Vietnam* (New York: Praeger, 1989), 23.

34. For the quote see Jonathan D. Caverley, "The Myth of Military Myopia: Democracy, Small Wars, and Vietnam," *International Security* 34, no. 3 (2007): 152. See also John A. Nagl, *Learning to Eat Soup with a Knife: Counterinsurgency Lessons from Vietnam and Malaya* (Chicago: University of Chicago Press, 2005), 156–58; Andrew F. Krepinevich Jr., *The Army and Vietnam* (Baltimore: Johns Hopkins University Press, 1986), 174–77; William R. Corson, *The Betrayal* (New York: Ace, 1968), 174–98; Lewis Sorley, *Westmoreland: The General Who Lost Vietnam* (New York: Harcourt, 2011), chap. 11; Max Boot, *The Savage Wars of Peace: Small Wars and the Rise of American Power* (New York: Basic Books, 2002), 286–317.

35. Corson, *Betrayal*, 15, 154–55, 171.

36. Quoted in Mark Moyar, *Phoenix and the Birds of Prey: Counterinsurgency and Counterterrorism in Vietnam* (London: Bison Books, 2007), 45.

37. Corson, *Betrayal*, 172.

38. MACV Dir 10–12, 28 May 1967, "Vietnam 1C (1). Revolutionary Development program. 2 of 2," box 59, NSF, CF, LBJL.

39. Thomas W. Scoville, *Reorganizing for Pacification Support* (Washington, DC: U.S. Army Center for Military History, 1982), 58–59, 65–67; "Pacification Program in Vietnam," briefing, 23 October 1967, 2.

40. Scoville, *Reorganizing*, 66.

41. MACV Dir 10–12, 28 May 1967, 3; Scoville, *Reorganizing*, 67–68.

42. MACV Dir 10–12, 28 May 1967, 4.

43. "Pacification Program in Vietnam," briefing, 23 October 1967, 3. The number of PSAs exceeded the number of actual provinces in the country—forty-four—because three autonomous cities also had PSAs.

44. "Pacification Program in Vietnam," 4; MACV Dir 10–12, 28 May 1967, 4–5; Scoville, *Reorganizing*, 70.

45. Robert Komer oral history interview, no. 2, 18 August 1970, LBJL, 44.

46. "MACV commanders conference, 13 May 1967," memo for the record, 21 May 1967, 2–3; "Opening remarks by Ambassador Ellsworth Bunker at Mission Council meeting, Monday, May 1, 1967, Saigon," undated paper, folder "Vietnam memos (A). Vol. 70 [1 of 2]," box 43, NSF, CF, LBJL.

47. R. W. Komer, *Organization and Management of the "New Model" Pacification Program, 1966–1969* (RAND document number D-20104-ARPA, 1970), 54. See also Sorley, *Westmoreland.*

48. Comments on Kriegel Report, 25 October 1969, folder "Comments + res. rept. / VN attitudes + behavior related to mgmt. problems," PPP, CORDS History Files, RG 472, NARA II.

49. Frank Scotton, *Uphill Battle: Reflections on Viet Nam Counterinsurgency* (Lubbock: Texas Tech University Press, 2014), 188.

50. "MACV commanders conference, 13 May 1967," memo for the record, 21 May 1967, 5.

51. Quoted in Lewis Sorley, ed., *Vietnam Chronicles: The Abrams Tapes, 1968–1972* (Lubbock: Texas Tech University Press, 2004), 100. Emphasis in original.

52. Fraleigh, "Real Story of America's Counterinsurgency Efforts," 7.

53. Komer oral history, no. 2, 47.

54. U.S. Department of the Army, *A Program for the Pacification and Long-Term Development of South Vietnam* (1966), 42.

55. On the unprecedented nature of the mission see U.S. Agency for International Development, *Terminal Report: United States Economic Assistance to South Vietnam, 1954–1975*, "Rural Development," 1.

56. Charles Mohr, "U.S. Opens Study of Aid in Vietnam," *New York Times*, 5 September 1966, 3.

57. Komer, *"New Model,"* 17.

58. Department of the Army, *Program for the Pacification*, 52, 55, 6, 13.

59. "Report on Leverage," undated [summer 1967], folder "Leverage," box 13, NSF, K-L, LBJL, 8, 9, 11.

60. "More for our Effort: U.S. Leverage in Vietnam," report, 7 August 1967, folder "Leverage," box 13, NSF, K-L, LBJL, 3.

61. Komer to Westmoreland and Bunker, memo, 30 January 1968, folder "#28: History File [II]," box 15, Westmoreland Papers, LBJL.

62. Komer to Senior Advisor I CTZ, memo, 30 January 1968, folder "#28: History File [II]," box 15, Westmoreland Papers, LBJL, 1. The memo was distributed to all four DepCORDS.

63. Komer to Senior Advisor I CTZ, memo, 30 January 1968, 2.

64. Komer to Senior Advisor I CTZ, memo, 30 January 1968, 2; Komer for Westmoreland and Bunker, memo, 30 January 1968.

65. Westmoreland to Sharp, telegram, 17 September 1967, MAC #8807 folder "Eyes Only Message File 1 Jul–33 Sep 1967: TO [3 of 3]," box 37, Westmoreland Papers, LBJL.

66. Komer, *"New Model,"* 75.

67. W. W. Rostow, *The Stages of Economic Growth: A Non-Communist Manifesto* (Cambridge: Cambridge University Press, 1960).

68. Komer, *"New Model,"* 66, 72; "Project Takeoff, Volume II: Assessment of Pacification," report, 11 August 1967, U.S. Marine Corps History Division, Vietnam War Documents Collection, TTVA, www.vietnam.ttu.edu/virtualarchive/items.php?item=1201065024, III-1, VI-1.

69. The quote is from "Project Takeoff" report, 11 August 1967, VI-3.

70. "Project Takeoff" report, V-2–V-3.

71. Samuel P. Huntington, "Political Stability and Security in South Vietnam," December 1967, folder "Vietnam 1C (2). Revolutionary Development program. 1 of 3," box 59, NSF, CF, LBJL, iii, 8–10. Emphasis in original.

72. "Goals of Project Takeoff for CY 67," briefing, 27 August 1967, folder "#21: History File. [II]," box 13, Westmoreland Papers, LBJL, 2.

73. "Briefing on Project Takeoff," undated [summer 1967], U.S. Marine Corps History Division, Vietnam War Documents Collection, TTVA, www.vietnam.ttu.edu/virtualarchive/items.php?item=1201065024.

74. Vann to Ellsberg, 19 August 1967, folder "Ellsberg, Daniel. 1967–1969," box 27, Neil Sheehan Papers, LOC, 3.

75. Corson, *Betrayal*, 213. Emphasis in original.

76. Chan Khong Cao Ngoc Phuong, *Learning True Love: How I Learned and Practiced Social Change in Vietnam* (Berkeley, CA: Parallax, 1993), 89, 13–14.

77. On the struggle movement see Robert J. Topmiller, *The Lotus Unleashed: The Buddhist Peace Movement in South Vietnam, 1964–1966* (Lexington: University Press of Kentucky, 2002).

78. Bui Diem, with David Chanoff, *In the Jaws of History* (Bloomington: Indiana University Press, 1987), 166–67.

79. "Goals of Project Takeoff," briefing, 27 August 1967. In the original document "TAKEOFF" is capitalized.

80. Komer, *"New Model,"* 65.

81. Vann to Ellsberg, 19 August 1967, 3.

82. Bui Diem, *In the Jaws of History*, 190.

83. Debrief no. 8664, box 94, GP, HIA, 3 (lobbyist); Debrief no. 206612, box 101, GP, HIA, 9, 10 (diplomat); and Debrief no. 7666, box 99, GP, HIA, 8 (con-man).

84. Debrief no. 166612, box 98, GP, HIA, 14–15; and Debrief no. 30663, box 99, GP, HIA, 1–2.

85. Debrief no. 2667, box 100, GP, HIA, 8.

86. Debrief no. 4668, box 101, GP, HIA, 18.

87. Wagonhurst to all PSAs, undated memo, folder "End of tour report," box 102, CORDS History Files, NARA II, 4. Emphasis in original.

88. Braddock to Eagle, attachment to letter, 21 October 1970, folder "POL 7: Visits, trip reports, 1970," box 9, Subject Files of the Office of Vietnam Affairs (Vietnam Working Group), RG 59, NARA II.

89. Debrief no. 23666, box 94, GP, HIA, 8–9.

90. Wagonhurst to all PSAs, 6–7.

91. Debrief no. 3681, box 97, GP, HIA, 16; Debrief no. 2667, box 100, GP, HIA, 2.

92. Task force minutes, program "CDD," September 1971, folder "Heilman minutes of task force meetings / Taken from Chamber's safe, folder I," box 80, CORDS History Files, RG 472, NARA II, 8.

93. Task force minutes, program "CORDS/PP&P and Mr. John Vann," 11 October 1971, folder "Heilman minutes of task force meetings / Taken from Chamber's safe, folder I," box 80, CORDS History Files, RG 472, NARA II, 19.

94. Vien, *U.S. Adviser*, 148, 149.

95. Debrief no. 30663, 8.

96. Debrief no. 8664, 2–3.

97. Debrief no. 8664, 5; Debrief no. 4668, 19–20; and Debrief no. 7666, 14.

98. Debrief no. 15679, box 101, GP, HIA, 1, 4, 13, 17–18.

99. Debrief no. 15679, 11; Luce and Sommer, *Viet Nam*, 18.

100. Debrief no. 15679, 11, 12, 14.

101. Debrief no. 56712, box 101, GP, HIA, 1, 4.

102. Vien, *U.S. Adviser*, 155, 156.

103. Debrief no. 15679, 7, 5, 11.

104. Vien, *U.S. Adviser*, 146.

105. Vien, 10, 12.

106. Debrief no. 146612, box 99, GP, HIA, 9–10; Nguyen Cao Ky, with Marvin J. Wolf, *Buddha's Child: My Fight to Save South Vietnam* (New York: St. Martin's, 2002), 139, 177, 197.

107. Vann to Ellsberg, 19 August 1967, 4.

108. Warner to Montague, 27 December 1967, folder "Pacification [12 of 18]," box 19, NSF, K-L, LBJL, 1, 2.

109. "Resolution Adopted during the Regular Conference of the An Thai Party Committee," 16 March 1967, *Vietnam Documents and Research Notes Series*, no. 2, 13. "An Thai" was a nom de guerre of the Ninety-Fifth Regiment of the NVA Fifth Army Division.

110. Letter to Comrade Hoai Nam, June 1967, *Vietnam Documents and Research Notes Series*, no. 12, 3–4.

111. On the problem of being separated from the population see "Irregular Conference of Chau Thanh District Supply Council," 7 January 1967, *Vietnam Documents and Research Notes Series*, no. 4.

112. Huss to McManaway, memo, 22 September 1967, folder "RD planning [1 of 2]," box 22, NSF, K-L, LBJL.

113. Huss to McManaway, memo, 22 September 1967, 2.

114. "President Thieu's explanation of his gradualistic approach to governmental reforms and the problems confronting him," intel cable, 14 January 1968, folder "Vietnam 1E (1). Post Inaugural Political Activity. 1 of 3," box 61 2 of 2, NSF, CF, LBJL, 1, 4, 6.

115. "Proceedings of the 28 December Cabinet meeting," intel cable, 2 January 1968, folder "Vietnam 1E (2). Post Inaugural Political Activity. 1 of 2," box 61 2 of 2, NSF, CF, LBJL, 7.

116. Locke to Rusk, telegram, 10 January 1968, folder "Vietnam 1E (2). Post Inaugural Political Activity. 2 of 2," box 61 2 of 2, NSF, CF, LBJL.

117. DePuy, memo for the record, 17 January 1968, *FRUS, 1964–1968*, 6:37–40.

118. DePuy, memo for the record, 17 January 1968.

119. Bunker to Johnson, telegram, 24 January 1968, folder "Vietnam 8B (2) [A]. Bunker's Wkly. Rpt. to the President," box 105, NSF, CF, LBJL, 2; Helms to multiple, memo, 17 January 1968, folder "Vietnam 1C (3)—B2. Revolutionary Development program," box 60, NSF, CF, LBJL; Westmoreland, memo for the record, 9 January 1968, folder "#28: History File," box 15, Westmoreland Papers, LBJL.

4. THE "OPPORTUNITY"

1. George L. MacGarrigle, *Taking the Offensive: October 1966 to October 1967* (Washington, DC: Center of Military History, 1998), 3–30, 431–45.

2. Lien-Hang T. Nguyen, *Hanoi's War: An International History of the War for Peace in Vietnam* (Chapel Hill: University of North Carolina Press, 2012), 87–109.

3. Bunker to Johnson, telegram, 30 October 1968, Saigon #41523, folder "Vietnam 8B (3) [B]. Bunker's Wkly. Rpt. to the President," box 105, NSF, CF, LBJL, 4.

4. Lewis Sorley, *A Better War: The Unexamined Victories and Final Tragedy of America's Last Years in Vietnam* (New York: Harcourt, 1999); William Colby and Peter Forbath, *Honourable Men: My Life in the CIA* (London: Hutchinson, 1978); William Colby, with James McCargar, *Lost Victory: A Firsthand Account of America's Sixteen-Year Involvement in Vietnam* (Chicago: Contemporary, 1989); Robert W. Komer, *Bureaucracy at War: U.S. Performance in the Vietnam Conflict* (Boulder, CO: Westview, 1986).

5. Bunker to Johnson, telegram, 16 January 1969, Saigon #894, folder "8-B. Bunker's weekly report to the president," box 75, NSC Files: Vietnam Subject Files, Richard Nixon Presidential Library, Yorba Linda, CA (hereafter NPL), 2.

6. David W. P. Elliott, *The Vietnamese War: Revolution and Social Change in the Mekong Delta, 1930–1975* (London: Sharpe, 2003), 2:1037.

7. Quoted in Ronald H. Spector, *After Tet: The Bloodiest Year in Vietnam* (New York: Macmillan, 1993), 163.

8. "Appeal by the Front of National, Democratic and Peace Alliance in Central Viet-Nam," *Vietnam Documents and Research Notes Series*, no. 22, 4.

9. Bui Diem, with David Chanoff, *In the Jaws of History* (Bloomington: Indiana University Press, 1999), 185, 196.

10. Nguyen Thi Thu-Lam, *Fallen Leaves: Memoirs of a Vietnamese Woman from 1940 to 1975* (New Haven, CT: Yale University Press, 1989), 169.

11. Bunker to Rusk, telegram, 9 April 1968, Saigon #24361, folder "Vietnam 1EE (4). Post Tet Political Activity," box 63, NSF, CF, LBJL, 2.

12. James C. Scott, *The Art of Not Being Governed: An Anarchist History of Upland Southeast Asia* (New Haven, CT: Yale University Press, 2009), 153.

13. Mission Council action memo, 5 September 1968, folder "Vietnam 8D. Mission Council action memos [1 of 2]," box 106, NSF, CF, LBJL.

14. Lewis Sorley, ed., *Vietnam Chronicles: The Abrams Tapes, 1968–1972* (Lubbock: Texas Tech University Press, 2004), 52.

15. Bunker to Rusk, telegram, 9 April 1968, 5.

16. Bunker to Rusk, telegram, 9 April 1968, 20–21, 45–47.

17. Bunker to Johnson, telegram, 16 May 1968, Saigon #27497, folder "Vietnam 8B (3) [A]. Bunker's Wkly. Rpt. to the President," box 105, NSF, CF, LBJL, 1.

18. Bernard Weinraub, "U.S. Admits Blows to Pacification," *New York Times*, 25 February 1968, 1, 30.

19. Bunker to Rostow, cable, 27 February 1968, box 60, folder "Vietnam 1C (3)—B2. Revolutionary Development program," NSF, CF, LBJL.

20. On the memo's authorship see John Prados, *Lost Crusader: The Secret Wars of CIA Director William Colby* (Oxford: Oxford University Press, 2003), 199.

21. Helms to Katzenbach et al., memo with attachment, 2 February 1968, folder "Vietnam 1EE (1). Post Tet Political Activity. 3 of 4," box 62, 1 of 2, NSF, CF, LBJL.

22. Thomas Ahern, *CIA and the Generals: Covert Support to Military Government in South Vietnam* (Washington, DC: Center for the Study of Intelligence, 1998), 74.

23. R. W. Komer, *Organization and Management of the "New Model" Pacification Program, 1966–1969* (RAND document number D-20104-ARPA, 1970), 84.

24. Komer, *"New Model,"* 85.

25. "Refugee and Social Welfare Program in Vietnam," paper dated "Feb '70?," folder "Misc reports (historical)," box 29, HQ MACV, Office of Civil Operations and Revolutionary Development Support, PPP, CORDS History Files, RG 472, NARA II, 5.

26. Louis A. Wiesner, *Victims and Survivors: Displaced Persons and Other War Victims in Viet-Nam, 1954–1975* (New York: Greenwood, 1988), 163–64.

27. "Project Recovery," memo for the record, 28 February 1968, folder "#17: History Backup [I]," box 6, Westmoreland Papers, LBJL.

28. "Project Recovery," memo for the record, 16 February 1968, folder "#17: History Backup [I]," box 6, Westmoreland Papers, LBJL, 2.

29. Gene Robert, "Saigon Pressing Aid to Refugees," *New York Times*, 25 April 1968, 2.

30. Komer, *"New Model,"* 83.

31. Westmoreland to Sharp et al., telegram, 3 February 1968, folder "Pacification [13 of 18]," box 19, NSF, K-L, LBJL; "Refugee and Social Welfare Program in Vietnam," paper dated "Feb '70?," 5.

32. See the budget data in HQ MACV, CORDS, Community Development Directorate (hereafter CDD), General Records, 1967–1972, boxes 3–5, RG 472, NARA II.

33. Elliott, *Vietnamese War*, 2:1036.

34. Nguyen Cao Ky, with Martin J. Wolf, *Buddha's Child: My Fight to Save Vietnam* (New York: St. Martin's, 2002), 273.

35. Tran Van Don, *Our Endless War: Inside Vietnam* (Novato, CA: Presidio, 1978), 176.

36. Ky, *Buddha's Child*, 139, 197.

37. Bunker to Johnson, telegram, 19 October 1968, Saigon #40697, folder "Vietnam 8B (3) [B]. Bunker's Wkly. Rpt. to the President," box 105, NSF, CF, LBJL, 2.

38. Lansdale to Bunker, memo, 30 January 1968, folder "Vietnam 8E (1). Lansdale memos to Rostow [2 of 2]," box 107, NSF, CF, LBJL, 1.

39. Bunker to Rusk, telegram, 1 February 1968, Saigon #17361, folder "Vietnam 1E (2). Post Inaugural Political Activity. 1 of 2," box 61, 2 of 2, NSF, CF, LBJL.

40. Bunker to Rusk and Johnson, telegram, 9 February 1968, Saigon #18699, folder "Vietnam 1EE (1). Post Tet Political Activity. 2 of 4," box 62 1 of 2, NSF, CF, LBJL.

41. Bunker to Johnson, telegram, 15 February 1968, folder "Vietnam 8B (2) [B]. Bunker's Wkly. Rpt. to the President," box 105, NSF, CF, LBJL, 2.

42. Vann to Holbrooke, 4 April 1968, folder "Barnes, Thomas J.," box 25, Neil Sheehan Papers, LOC, 2.

43. Ellsberg and Vann, telcon transcript, 18 July 1968, "Ellsberg, Daniel. Telephone conversations, 1968," box 27, Neil Sheehan Papers, LOC, 8.

44. Bui Diem, "My Recollections of the Tet Offensive," in *The Tet Offensive*, ed. Marc Jason Gilbert and William Head (Westport, CT: Praeger, 1996), 131.

45. Bunker to Johnson, telegram, 15 February 1968, 8.

46. Johnson to Bunker, telegram, 3 February 1968, no number, folder "Vietnam 1EE (1). Post Tet Political Activity. 3 of 4," box 62, 1 of 2, NSF, CF, LBJL, 2.

47. Bunker to Johnson and Rusk, telegram, 9 February 1968, Saigon #18583, folder "Vietnam 1EE (1). Post Tet Political Activity. 2 of 4," box 62, 1 of 2, NSF, CF, LBJL.

48. Bunker to Rusk, telegram, 18 March 1968, Saigon #22386, folder "Vietnam 1EE (3). Post Tet Political Activity. 3 of 3," box 62, 2 of 2, NSF, CF, LBJL.

49. Bunker to Johnson, telegram, 2 May 1968, Saigon #26229, folder "Vietnam 8B (3) [A]. Bunker's Wkly. Rpt. to the President," box 105, NSF, CF, LBJL, 1.

50. "Threat of Nguyen Duc Thang to Resign as Chief of Staff to the Committee for the Relief of the People," intel cable, 9 February 1968, folder "Vietnam 1EE (1). Post Tet Political Activity. 2 of 4," box 62, 1 of 2, NSF, CF, LBJL; "Vice President Ky's Reasons for

Resigning as Task Force Chairman," intel cable, 22 February 1968, folder "Vietnam 1EE (2). Post Tet Political Activity. 4 of 4," box 62, 2 of 2, NSF, CF, LBJL.

51. "Threat of Nguyen Duc Thang to Resign," intel cable, 9 February 1968, 2.

52. Don, *Our Endless War*, 176–77; Ky, *Buddha's Child*, 237.

53. Bui Diem, *In the Jaws of History*, 186.

54. DIA biographic file, "Lieutenant General Le Nguyen Khanh," September 1968, folder "Vietnam: [DIA biographic sketches, vol. VI]. 7/65–12/68," box 176, NSF, CF, LBJL; Bunker to Rusk, telegram, 3 June 1968, Saigon #28958, folder "Vietnam 1EE (6). Post Tet Political Activity. 2 of 2," box 63, NSF, CF, LBJL.

55. "III Corps Commander General Khang's Comments on Possibility of Future Viet Cong Attacks and the Problems Relating to Viet Cong Tet Offensive," intel cable, 19 February 1968, folder "Vietnam 1EE (1). Post Tet Political Activity. 1 of 4," box 62, 1 of 2, NSF, CF, LBJL, 3.

56. Bunker to Rusk, telegram, 5 March 1968, Saigon #21218, folder "Vietnam 1EE (2). Post Tet Political Activity. 2 of 4," box 62, 2 of 2, NSF, CF, LBJL.

57. Tom Buckley, "One Reform Is Achieved," *New York Times*, 17 March 1968, 3; Komer, *"New Model,"* 84.

58. Bunker to Rusk, telegram, 5 March 1968, Saigon #21218, quote at p. 2.

59. Gene Roberts, "Thieu Discharges 7 Province Chiefs," *New York Times*, 12 March 1968, 1.

60. Bunker to Johnson, telegram, 16 January 1969, Saigon #894, p. 21; Bunker to Johnson, telegram, 12 September 1968, Saigon #37663, folder "Vietnam 8B (3) [B]. Bunker's Wkly. Rpt. to the President," box 105, NSF, CF, LBJL, 2–3.

61. Bernard Weinraub, "American Aides Are Hopeful on Recovery in the Mekong Delta," *New York Times*, 7 September 1968, 12.

62. Bunker to Johnson, telegram, 12 September 1968, Saigon #37663.

63. Bunker to Johnson, telegram, 12 September 1968; Mission Council action memo, 16 February 1968, folder "Vietnam 8D. Mission Council action memos [1 of 2]," box 106, NSF, CF, LBJL, 1.

64. Bunker to Rusk, telegram, 24 April 1968, Saigon #25561, folder "Vietnam 1EE (4). Post Tet Political Activity," box 63, NSF, CF, LBJL, 1, 2.

65. Ky, Lansdale, and Berger, memcon, 26 April 1968, folder "Vietnam 1EE (4). Post Tet Political Activity," box 63, NSF, CF, LBJL, 3.

66. "The New Cabinet of South Vietnam," intel memo, 29 May 1968, folder "Vietnam 1EE (5). Post Tet Political Activity," box 63, NSF, CF, LBJL, 2; Bunker to Rusk, telegram, 6 April 1968, Saigon #24147, folder "Vietnam 1EE (4). Post Tet Political Activity," box 63, NSF, CF, LBJL, 2; Bunker to Rusk, telegram, 18 March 1968, Saigon #22386, p. 3.

67. Bunker to Johnson, telegram, 29 May 1968, Saigon #28566, folder "Vietnam 8B (3) [A]. Bunker's Wkly. Rpt. to the President," box 105, NSF, CF, LBJL, 2.

68. Biographic data, "Tran Thien Khiem," folder "Vietnam: [DIA biographic sketches, vol. VI]. 7/65–12/68," box 176, NSF, CF, LBJL.

69. "The New Cabinet of South Vietnam," intel memo, 29 May 1968, folder "Vietnam 1EE (5). Post Tet Political Activity," box 63, NSF, CF, LBJL, 2; Bunker to Rusk, telegram, 6 April 1968, Saigon #24147, folder "Vietnam 1EE (4). Post Tet Political Activity," box 63, NSF, CF, LBJL, 2; Bunker to Rusk, telegram, 18 March 1968, Saigon #22386, p. 3.

70. Ky, Lansdale, and Berger, memcon, 26 April 1968; Bunker to Rusk, telegram, 3 June 1968, Saigon #28958.

71. Bunker to Rusk, telegram, 3 June 1968, Saigon #28958.

72. Rostow to Johnson, telegram, 13 June 1968, CAP #81287, p. 5 of attachment.

73. Bunker to Johnson, telegram, 19 October 1968, Saigon #40697, p. 3; DIA biographic file, "Lieutenant General Le Nguyen Khanh," September 1968.

74. Gene Roberts, "Saigon Explosion Kills 7 Officials; Mayor Wounded," *New York Times*, 3 June 1968, 1; Ky, *Buddha's Child*, 270.

75. Bernard Weinraub, "Ousters in Saigon a Setback for Ky," *New York Times*, 9 June 1968, 3.

76. Bernard Weinraub, "The Politics: A Firmer Base for Thieu," *New York Times*, 9 June 1968, E3.

77. Bunker to Rusk, telegram, 27 September 1968, Saigon #38867, folder "Vietnam 1EE (8). Post Tet Political Activity. 1 of 2," box 64, NSF, CF, LBJL, 1.

78. Bunker to Johnson, telegram, 8 June 1968, Saigon #29472, folder "Vietnam 8B (3) [A]. Bunker's Wkly. Rpt. to the President," box 105, NSF, CF, LBJL, 4.

79. Komer, *"New Model,"* 84.

80. Rostow to Johnson, telegram, 13 June 1968, CAP # 81287, p. 7 of attachment.

81. DIA biographic file, August 1968, folder "Vietnam: [DIA biographic sketches, vol. VI]. 7/65–12/68," box 176, NSF, CF, LBJL.

82. Bui Diem, *In the Jaws of History*, 262.

83. Komer, *"New Model,"* 83.

84. Bunker to Rusk, telegram, 18 March 1968, Saigon #22386, 6, 10.

85. *Victory in Vietnam: The Official History of the People's Army of Vietnam, 1954–1975*, trans. Merle L. Pribbenow (Lawrence: University Press of Kansas, 2002), 237–38.

86. Bunker to Johnson, telegram, 4 September 1968, Saigon #37046, folder "Vietnam 8B (3) [B]. Bunker's Wkly. Rpt. to the President," box 105, NSF, CF, LBJL, 7.

87. Mission Council action memo, 5 September 1968, folder "Vietnam 8D. Mission Council action memos [1 of 2]," box 106, NSF, CF, LBJL.

88. "Briefing: Pacification in Vietnam," 9 June 1969, folder "Orient and brief files, '67," box 2, HQ MACV, CORDS, PPP, General Records, RG 472, NARA II, p. 3.

89. Sorley, *Abrams Tapes*, 52.

90. Colby, *Lost Victory*, 253. See also a transcript of parts of the conference in Sorley, *Abrams Tapes*, 49–52.

91. Bunker to Rusk, telegram, 6 April 1968, Saigon #24147.

92. Komer, *"New Model,"* 88.

93. "Briefing: Pacification in Vietnam," 9 June 1969, 4.

94. Charles Mohr, "Saigon Curtails Aid to Landlords," *New York Times*, 21 November 1968, 14.

95. Komer, *"New Model,"* 86.

96. Vann to Weyand, 29 January 1969, folder "Weyand, Fred C.," box 30, Sheehan Papers, LOC, 2, 3.

97. Bunker to Rusk, telegram, 27 September 1968, Saigon #38867, p. 3.

5. THE NIXON ADMINISTRATION AND NATION BUILDING

1. Sir Robert Thompson, *Peace Is Not at Hand* (London: Chatto & Windus, 1974), 1.

2. Daniel Ellsberg, *Secrets: A Memoir of Vietnam and the Pentagon Papers* (New York: Viking, 2002), 227.

3. Kissinger to Nixon, memo, 19 March 1970, folder "Vietnamization Vol II. Jan '70–Jun '70 [2 of 2]," box 91, NSC Files, Vietnam Subject Files (hereafter VSF), NPL.

4. Jeffrey Kimball, for instance, writes that pacification was not relevant to Nixon's strategy because it was unlikely to alter the strategic balance or provide leverage at the negotiating table. See Jeffrey Kimball, *Nixon's Vietnam War* (Lawrence: University Press of Kansas, 1998), 74.

5. *Victory in Vietnam: The Official History of the People's Army of Vietnam, 1954–1975*, trans. Merle L. Pribbenow (Lawrence: University Press of Kansas, 2002), 238.

6. Lewis Sorley, *A Better War: The Unexamined Victories and Final Tragedy of America's Last Years in Vietnam* (New York: Harcourt, 1999), 217.

7. Henry A. Kissinger, "The Viet Nam Negotiations," *Foreign Affairs*, January 1969, 214, 215, 212.

8. Kissinger, "Viet Nam Negotiations," 218.

9. H. R. Haldeman, *The Haldeman Diaries: Inside the Nixon White House* (New York: Berkley Books, 1995), 84–85, 216.

10. Nixon, Richard M., *RN: The Memoirs of Richard Nixon* (New York: Grosset & Dunlap, 1978), 393–411.

11. Nixon to Kissinger, memo, 1 February 1969, folder "8-F—Reappraisal of Vietnam commitment. Vol. I," box 64, NSC Files: VSF, NPL; Laird to Kissinger, memo, 11 February 1969, box 64, NSC Files, VSF, NPL.

12. Thieu, Laird, et al., memcon, 8 March 1969, folder "Vietnam: Secretary Laird's trip to South Vietnam, March 5–12," box 70, NSC Files, VSF, NPL.

13. Laird to Nixon, memo, 13 March 1969, folder "Vietnam: Secretary Laird's trip to South Vietnam, March 5–12," box 70, NSC Files, VSF, NPL.

14. Kissinger to Nixon, memo, 7 July 1969, U.S. Department of State, *Foreign Relations of the United States, 1969–1976* (hereafter *FRUS, 1969–1976*), 55 vols. (Washington, DC: Government Printing Office, 2003–2014), 6:283–88.

15. Henry Kissinger, *Diplomacy* (New York: Simon & Schuster, 1994), 684.

16. Kissinger to Nixon, memo, 20 July 1970, folder "Vietnamization Vol II. Jan '70–Jun '70 [1 of 2]," box 91, NSC Files, VSF, NPL.

17. Nixon, *RN*, 404–5.

18. Kissinger to Nixon, memo, 19 March 1970; Kissinger to Nixon, memo, in *FRUS, 1969–1976*, 6:475–76.

19. Lake to Kissinger, memo, 7 September 1970, box 1047, folder "Tony Lake Chron, Sept 1969–Jan 1970," NSC Files, Staff Files—Lake Chron, NPL; Lake and Morris to Kissinger, memo, 21 October 1969, folder "Tony Lake Chrn, Jun 1/9—May 1970 [1 of 6]," box 1047, NSC Files, Staff Files—Lake Chron, NPL; Kissinger to Nixon, memo, 10 September 1969, folder "Discussion on Vietnam in the Cabinet room, 9:30AM, Sept 12, 1969," NSC Files, VSF, NPL; Kissinger to Nixon, memo, 16 April 1970, *FRUS, 1969–1976*, 6:824–26.

20. Lake and Morris to Kissinger, memo, 21 October 1969.

21. Kissinger to Nixon, memo, 20 July 1970.

22. Kissinger to Nixon, memo, 20 March 1970, in *FRUS*, 7:478–80.

23. Kissinger to Nixon, memo, 16 November 1970, in *FRUS*, 7:168–72.

24. Haldeman, *Diaries*, 434.

25. Kissinger, "Viet Nam Negotiations," 211.

26. Moor to Haig, memo, 30 January 1969, folder "1-B—Revolutionary Development program," box 62, NSC Files, VSF, NPL.

27. Kissinger to Colby, 21 February 1969, folder "Vietnam Vol. I: Thru 3/19/69," box 136, NSC Files, Vietnam Country Files (hereafter VCF), NPL.

28. Minutes of NSC meeting, 25 January 1969, *FRUS, 1969–1976*, 6:26.

29. Kissinger to Nixon, memo, 9 May 1969, folder "Vietnam Vol. IV: 4/24/69–5/18/69 [1 of 3]," box 137, NSC Files, VCF, NPL. Emphasis added.

30. Minutes of the SRG, 17 January 1972, *FRUS, 1969–1976*, 7:1032–42.

31. National Security Study Memorandum (hereafter NSSM) 21, 13 February 1969, folder "NSSM 1: Situation in Vietnam," box H-124, NSC Institutional Files, Study Memorandums, National Security Study Memorandums, NPL.

32. Kissinger to Nixon, memo, 13 February 1969, folder "NSSM 22," box H-136, NSC Institutional Files: Study Memorandums, National Security Study Memorandums, NPL.

33. Kissinger to Nixon, undated memo [September 1969], folder "Vietnam Vol. X : Sept 1969 [1 of 2]," box 139, NSC Files, VCF, NPL.

34. John P. Leacacos, "Kissinger's Apparat," *Foreign Policy* 5 (Winter 1971/72): 6.

35. Leacacos, 6; Roger Morris, *Uncertain Greatness: Henry Kissinger and American Foreign Policy* (New York: Quartet, 1977), 165; Marvin Kalb and Bernard Kalb, *Kissinger* (Boston: Little, Brown, 1974), 159.

36. Kissinger to Nixon, undated memo [September 1969]. On Lynn's authorship of this memo see Lynn to Kissinger, memo, 30 August 1969, folder "Vietnam Vol. X : Sept 1969 [1 of 2]," box 139, NSC Files, VCF, NPL.

37. Ellsberg, *Secrets*, 231–45.

38. Ellsberg, 246–49.

39. Lynn to Kissinger, memo, 25 August 1969, folder "VSSG meeting 10–24–69, Mtg 0751," box H-001, NSC Institutional Files, Committee Files, Vietnam Special Studies Group Meetings, NPL.

40. NSDM 23, 16 September 1969, folder "NSDM 23," box H-211, NSC Institutional Files, Study Memorandums, National Security Study Memorandums, NPL.

41. Minutes of NSC meeting, 25 January 1969.

42. Kissinger, "Viet Nam Negotiations," 214; Minutes of the SRG, 15 January 1971, *FRUS, 1969–1976*, 7:260–74.

43. Helms to Komer, memo, 18 July 1966, *FRUS, 1964–1968*, 4:505–7.

44. Sneider to Kissinger, memo, 26 April 1969, folder "Vietnam Vol. IV: 4/24/69–5/18/69 [2 of 3]," box 137, NSC Files, VCF, NPL. Lake's memo is attached. Emphasis in original.

45. SNIE, 16 January 1969, in *FRUS, 1969–1976*, 6:1–2.

46. Kissinger to Nixon, memo, 19 March 1970.

47. "A framework for analyzing the countryside," undated report [November 1969], folder "VSSG meeting 11–19–69, Mtg 00752 (N)," box H-001, NSC Institutional Files, Committee Files, Vietnam Special Studies Group Meetings, NPL, 2.

48. "Framework for analyzing the countryside," 2.

49. "Framework for analyzing the countryside," 5–8.

50. "Framework for analyzing the countryside," 3–4.

51. VSSG minutes, 19 November 1969, folder "VSSG meeting 11–19–69, Mtg 00752 (N)," box H-001, NSC Institutional Files, Committee Files, Vietnam Special Studies Group Meetings, NPL, 3–4.

52. "The situation in the countryside," undated report [late 1969], folder "VSSG meeting 1–14–70, Mtg 00754 (N)," box H-001, NSC Institutional Files, Committee Files, Vietnam Special Studies Group Meetings, NPL, 18.

53. "Situation in the countryside," 20–21.

54. Kissinger to Nixon, undated memo [January 1970], folder "VSSG meeting 1–14–70, Mtg 00754 (N)," box H-001, NSC Institutional Files, Committee Files, Vietnam Special Studies Group Meetings, NPL, 2–3.

55. Lynn and Samson, report, 28 February 1970, folder "Tony Lake Chrn, Aug 1969–June 1970 [2 of 2]," box 1047, NSC Files, Staff Files—Lake Chron, NPL.

56. Robert L. Sansom, *The Economics of Insurgency in the Mekong Delta of Vietnam* (Cambridge, MA: MIT Press, 1970).

57. "Situation in the countryside," 37, 40.

58. Henry A. Kissinger, *White House Years* (Boston: Little, Brown, 1979), 435.

59. Memcon, 1 December 1969, *FRUS, 1969–1976*, 6:499–505.

60. Kissinger to Nixon, memo, 22 January 1970, *FRUS, 1969–1976*, 6:537–40, at footnote 1.

61. Haldeman, *Diaries*, 287.

62. Odeen to Kissinger, memo, 25 February 1972, folder "Vietnam: Nov–Dec 1972 [3 of 3]," box 158, NSC Files, VCF, NPL.

63. Odeen to Kissinger, memo, 15 May 1972, folder "Vietnam: May–Sep '73 [2 of 3]," box 164, NSC Files, VCF, NPL.

6. CORDS AND THE VILLAGE SYSTEM

1. "Two Girls Killed by Explosion at Saigon Girls' School," *New York Times*, 31 January 1969, 3; "5 Enemy Rockets Wound 7 at Hue," *New York Times*, 1 February 1969, 12; "U.S. Troops Repel an Assault by 500," *New York Times*, 2 February 1969, 3.

2. "Opening Statement by Ambassador W. E. Colby," undated document, folder "Opening statements / Amb. Colby," box 15, HQ MACV, Office of Civil Operations and Revolutionary Development Support, PPP, CORDS History Files, RG 472, NARA II, 2.

3. William Colby and Peter Forbarth, *Honourable Men: My Life in the CIA* (London: Hutchinson, 1978), 159–62, quote at 162.

4. Speech at the National War College, transcript, 10 November 1972, William Colby Collection, TTVA, www.vietnam.ttu.edu/virtualarchive/items.php?item=0440225001, p. 2.

5. Quoted in Thomas L. Ahern Jr., *The CIA and Rural Pacification in South Vietnam* (Washington, DC: Center for the Study of Intelligence, 2001), 239.

6. Quoted in Zalin Grant, *Facing the Phoenix: The CIA and the Political Defeat of the United States in Vietnam* (New York: Norton, 1991), 291.

7. Colby and Forbarth, *Honourable Men*, 262.

8. "Status of Pacification—June 1969," memo for the record, 4 June 1969, folder "Misc reports, memos, etc: Jan–Sept, 1969," box 3, HQ MACV, Office of Civil Operations and Revolutionary Development Support, PPP, General Records, RG 472, NARA II, 7.

9. Edward Miller, *Misalliance: Ngo Dinh Diem, the United States, and the Fate of South Vietnam* (Cambridge, MA: Harvard University Press, 2013), 231–39; Philip E. Catton, *Diem's Final Failure: Prelude to America's War in Vietnam* (Lawrence: University Press of Kansas, 2003), 89–90.

10. Speech at the National War College, transcript, 10 November 1972, 4.

11. Colby and Forbarth, *Honourable Men*, 262.

12. Vann to all PSAs, attachment to letter, 1 April 1968, folder "Vietnam assignments: Region III pacification reports [1/2]," box 44, Sheehan Papers, LOC, 3.

13. Alvin Shuster, "Colby, U.S. Pacification Chief for Vietnam, Gives Up Duties and Returns Home," *New York Times*, 1 July 1971, 34.

14. Colby quoted in John Prados, *Lost Crusader: The Secret Wars of CIA Director William Colby* (Oxford: Oxford University Press, 2003), 203; Montague to Quang, attachment to letter, 22 April 1969, folder "CPDC / CC advisory, '69," box 4, PPP General Records, RG 472, NARA II, 4.

15. *Plan for Pacification and Development, 1970*, in folder "P+D plan w/ errata added / Maj E. J. Crampton," box 27, CORDS History Files, RG 472, NARA II, 2.

16. *The Vietnamese Village: Handbook for Advisors*, 1971 ed., Douglas Pike Collection, TTVA, 1.

17. Jeffrey Race, *War Comes to Long An: Revolutionary Conflict in a Vietnamese Province* (Berkeley: University of California Press, 2012), 179–80.

18. "Opening Statement by Ambassador W. E. Colby," 6.

19. Simon Head, "Britain's Vietnam Hardhat," *New Statesman*, 6 October 1972, 460.

20. Robert Thompson, *No Exit from Vietnam* (London: Chatto & Windus, 1969), 147.

21. Robert Thompson, *Make for the Hills: Memories of Far Eastern Wars* (London: Leo Cooper, 1989), 150.

22. Thompson, *Make for the Hills*, 92.

23. Thompson, *No Exit from Vietnam*, 147.

24. Thompson, *No Exit from Vietnam*, 147.

25. Thompson hence anticipated, and invalidated, the arguments later put forth by Harry Summers in his famous critique of U.S. strategy in the Vietnam War. Summers

assailed U.S. leaders for having a strategy that was purely defensive and deprived the United States of the ability to gain the initiative in the conflict. But he neglected that it was nation building that made up the "offensive" component of U.S. strategy—the only possible exit strategy for the United States was to oversee the emergence of a self-sufficient GVN behind a defensive military shield. See Harry G. Summers Jr., *American Strategy in Vietnam: A Critical Analysis* (Mineola, NY: Dover, 2007).

26. For a broader look at the French influence over what is increasingly recognized as a transatlantic counterinsurgency discourse in the 1960s see Elie Tenenbaum, "French Exception or Western Variation? A Historical Look at the French Irregular Way of War," *Journal of Strategic Studies* 40, no. 4 (2017): 554–76. It is also worth noting that the existence of this shared transatlantic discourse complicates any simplistic stereotype of Europeans as world-weary and wise and Americans as hopelessly naïve about the possibilities of counterinsurgency and nation building, a trope that continues to be repeated today. The more telling divide was between the military and civilians.

27. Bernard B. Fall, "The Theory and Practice of Insurgency and Counterinsurgency," *Naval War College Review* 17, no. 8 (1965): 28, 30, 34, 36.

28. Roger Trinquier, *Modern Warfare: A French View of Counterinsurgency*, trans. Daniel Lee (1962; London: Pall Mall, 1964), 4, 5, 30.

29. Trinquier, *Modern Warfare*, 72; Fall, "Theory and Practice of Insurgency and Counterinsurgency," 36.

30. Trinquier, *Modern Warfare*, 30.

31. PPD to Jacobson, memo, 7 January 1969, folder "Misc reports, memos, etc: Jan–Sept, 1969," box 3, PPP General Records, RG 472, NARA II.

32. "The Village Self-Development Program, 1969–1972," booklet, 22 June 1972, folder "VSDP," box 41, CORDS History Files, RG 472, NARA II, 3; Vann to all PSAs, memo, 1 April 1968, 1–2.

33. *Guidelines: Pacification Campaign, 1969*, 15 December 1968, in folder "1-B—Revolutionary Development program," box 62, NSC Files, VSF, NPL, 1.

34. Speech at the National War College, transcript, 10 November 1972, 19.

35. Thompson, *No Exit from Vietnam*, 129.

36. McManaway to Johnstone, undated memo [June 1969], folder "Misc reports, memos, etc: Jan–Sept, 1969," box 3, PPP General Records, RG 472, NARA II. Emphasis in original.

37. Thompson, *Make for the Hills*, 128.

38. Vann to all PSAs, attachment to letter, 1 April 1968, 1.

39. *Vietnamese Village: Handbook for Advisors*, 81.

40. Vann to all PSAs, attachment to letter, 1 April 1968, 2.

41. Louis A. Wiesner, *Victims and Survivors: Displaced Persons and Other War Victims in Viet-Nam, 1954–1975* (Westport, CT: Greenwood, 1988), 184, 216.

42. Westmoreland, "The refugee problem," 4 January 1968, folder "#28: History File," box 15, Westmoreland Papers, LBJL.

43. Forrester to McManaway, memo, 11 December 1970, folder "Pacif. study, Oct–Dec '70," box 10, HQ MACV, CORDS, PPP, General Records, RG 472, NARA II; Wiesner, *Victims and Survivors*, 210.

44. "Vietnamization of CORDS," undated briefing [1971], folder "The VN of MAC-CORDS," box 32, CORDS History Files, RG 472, NARA II.

45. Abrams and Colby to all DepCORDS, memo, 27 June 1971, folder "Project Concern / Opns in Tuyen Duc prov," box 37, CORDS History Files, RG 472, NARA II, 1, 3. Emphasis in original.

46. Douglas C. Dacy, *Foreign Aid, War, and Economic Development: South Vietnam, 1955–1975* (Cambridge: Cambridge University Press, 1986), 237.

47. Roy Reed, "Officer Tells Humphrey of Vietnam Corruption," *New York Times*, 31 October 1967, 3.

48. McPherson to Johnson, memo, 13 June 1967, *FRUS, 1964–1968*, 5:493.

49. Jacobson, memo for the record, 12 April 1970, folder "Memos + messages / Mr Jacobson / Visits," box 14, CORDS History Files, RG 472, NARA II, 2.

50. Fox Butterfield, "Village Cadres Now Aid Thieu Party," *New York Times*, 12 June 1973, 3.

51. For an account by a journalist who reported on this story from South Vietnam see Grant, *Facing the Phoenix*.

52. "Status of Pacification—June 1969," memo for the record, 4 June 1969, 3.

53. Debrief no. 15679, box 101, GP, HIA, 21.

54. *Guidelines: Pacification Campaign, 1969*, 1.

55. Colby to all DepCORDS, attachment to letter, 21 February 1969, folder "1-B— Revolutionary Development program," box 62, NSC Files, VSF, NPL, 2.

56. "Presidential review visit—II CTZ," document, 2 February 1969, folder "Status / Pacif," box 11, CORDS History Files, RG 472, NARA II, 1.

57. Nguyen Tien Hung and Jerrold L. Schecter, *The Palace File* (New York: Harper & Row, 1986), 12.

58. Nghiem Dang, *Viet-Nam: Politics and Public Administration* (Honolulu: East-West, 1966), 72.

59. Berger to State, telegram, 29 October 1970, folder "P+D plan, folder II," box 27, RG 472, NARA II, 8.

60. *Plan for Pacification and Development: 1970*, in folder "P+D plan w/ errata added / Maj E. J. Crampton," box 27, CORDS History Files, RG 472, NARA II, 1.

61. *Community Defense and Local Development Plan: 1971*, folder "CD + LD plan / 1971," box 37, CORDS History Files, RG 472, NARA II, 1.

62. William Colby, with James McCargar, *Lost Victory: A Firsthand Account of America's Sixteen-Year Involvement in Vietnam* (Chicago: Contemporary, 1989), 256.

63. Cao Van Vien, *The U.S. Adviser* (Washington, DC: Center of Military History, 1980), 142.

64. "Pacification in Vietnam," GVN briefing, June 1969, folder "Orient and brief files, '67," box 2, PPP General Records, RG 472, NARA II, 3–4.

65. Jacobson, memo for the record, 12 April 1970, 2–4; Khiem, Colby, Jacobson, memcon, 27 May 1970, folder "Memos + messages / Mr Jacobson / Visits," box 14, CORDS History Files, RG 472, NARA II, 4.

66. Frank Scotton, *Uphill Battle: Reflections on Viet Nam Counterinsurgency* (Lubbock: Texas Tech University Press, 2014), 263.

67. Hung and Schecter, *Palace File*, 12.

68. Bui Diem, with David Chanoff, *In the Jaws of History* (Bloomington: Indiana University Press, 1987), 262.

69. Quoted in Hung and Schecter, *Palace File*, 33.

70. R. W. Komer, *Organization and Management of the "New Model" Pacification Program, 1966–1969* (RAND document number D-20104-ARPA, 1970), 88.

71. Colby, *Lost Victory*, 256; Lewis Sorley, ed., *Vietnam Chronicles: The Abrams Tapes, 1968–1972* (Lubbock: Texas Tech University Press, 2004), 163–64.

72. Vann, "Thoughts on GVN/VC Control," memo, 2 April 1969, folder "Colby, William," box 25, Sheehan Papers, LOC, 1.

73. Komer, *"New Model,"* 87.

74. McManaway to Jacobson, memo, 20 June 1969, folder "Economic warfare files— local government," box 17, HQ MACV, CORDS, CDD, General Records, RG 472, NARA II, 3

75. Colby to Jacobson, memo, 2 August 1969, folder "1602–09: Village self development," box 11, CDD, General Records, RG 472, NARA II, 1.

76. Bunker to Rogers, memo, 22 February 1969, folder "1-B—Revolutionary Development program," box 62, NSC Files, VSF, NPL, 3.

77. Thomas C. Thayer, ed. *A Systems Analysis View of the Vietnam War, 1965–1972* (Washington, DC: OASD(SA)RP Southeast Asia Intelligence Division, 1975), 9:133; Colby, *Lost Victory*, 259.

78. Colby, *Lost Victory*, 259.

79. Bunker to Rogers, memo, 22 February 1969, 3.

80. Thayer, *Systems Analysis View*, 10:120.

81. Thayer, 11:251.

82. "Analysis of Task Force Recommendation No. 2," undated document [late 1971], folder "The future of CORDS," box 35, CORDS History Files, RG 472, NARA II, 3

83. "Village Security," PSG report, 19 September 1969, folder "M/I liaison reports, Jan–Apr '70," box 14, PPP General Records, RG 472, NARA II, 3, 5.

84. Vann, "Thoughts on GVN/VC Control."

85. Colby to Jacobson, memo, 3 October 1969, folder "M/I liaison reports, Jan–Apr '70," box 14, PPP General Records, RG 472, NARA II.

86. Abrams to CINCPAC, memo, 18 January 1969, folder "1-C–Land reform," box 62, NSC Files, VSF, NPL, 1.

87. Craig to DepCORDS [Vann], first attachment to note, 7 February 1970, folder "Ellsberg, Daniel. 1970–1975," box 27, Sheehan Papers, LOC, 1.

88. Colby to Bunker, memo, 7 July 1970, folder "Mr Jacobson / Misc files / A C of S / Folder II," box 20, CORDS History Files, RG 472, NARA II, 1.

7. IMPLEMENTING THE VILLAGE SYSTEM

1. Allan E. Goodman, "South Vietnam and the New Security," *Asian Survey* 12, no. 2 (1972): 121, 122.

2. Robert Thompson, *Make for the Hills: Memories of Far Eastern Wars* (London: Leo Cooper, 1989), 165, 166.

3. William Colby and Peter Forbath, *Honourable Men: My Life in the CIA* (London: Hutchinson, 1978), 285.

4. John Vann, "Statement Prepared for the Senate Foreign Relations Committee," undated document, folder "Opening statements / Amb. Colby," box 15, HQ MACV, Office of Civil Operations and Revolutionary Development Support, PPP, CORDS History Files, RG 472, NARA II, 2, 3.

5. Cao Van Vien, *The U.S. Adviser* (Washington, DC: Center of Military History, 1980), 153.

6. The National Archives (hereafter TNA), Public Records Office (hereafter PRO) FCO 15/1084 Foreign Office and Foreign and Commonwealth Office, South East Asia Department, Registered Files (D and FA Series), 20 May 1969, Coombe to Jones, 3.

7. TNA, PRO FCO 15/1673, January 3, 1972, Brash to Douglas-Home, 5, 10 [original unpaginated].

8. TNA, PRO FCO 15/1673, January 18, 1972, Gordon to Brash.

9. Lewis Sorley, *A Better War: The Unexamined Victories and Final Tragedy of America's Last Years in Vietnam* (New York: Harcourt, 1999), 217.

10. Goodman, "South Vietnam and the New Security," 122.

11. Debrief no. 16612, box 98, GP, HIA, 1.

12. Bert Fraleigh, "The Real Story of America's Counterinsurgency Efforts in Vietnam in the Early 1960s," incorrectly dated January 1966 [1996?], Rufus Phillips Collection, TTVA, 34.

13. Debrief no. 6683, box 97, GP, HIA, 2; Vietnam Area Studies OCO Training Center, n.d., John Donnell Collection, TTVA.

14. Megellas to Abrams, memo, 19 May 1970, folder "End of tour / J. Megellas," box 23, CORDS History Files, RG 472, NARA II, 36

15. Debrief no. 86711, box 99, GP, HIA, 1–2; Debrief no. 30663, box 99, GP, HIA, 7; Debrief no. 25672, box 99, GP, HIA, 14–15.

16. Debrief no. 206612, box 101, GP, HIA, 1–5, quote at 1.

17. Jacobson to Colby, memo, January 29, 1971, folder "Mr Jacobson / Misc files / A C of S / Folder III," box 36, CORDS History Files, RG 472, NARA II.

18. Debrief no. 23666, box 94, GP, HIA, 1–2.

19. Debrief no. 21666, pp. 20–22. On Nguyen Duc Thang's relationship with the Americans see James McAllister, "What Can One Man Do? Nguyen Duc Thang and the Limits of Reform in South Vietnam," *Journal of Vietnamese Studies* 4, no. 2 (Summer 2009): 117–53.

20. Tran Van Don, *Our Endless War: Inside Vietnam* (Novato, CA: Presidio, 1978), 152.

21. Barnes to all PSAs, message, 7 October 1971, folder "Barnes, Thomas J.," box 25, Sheehan Papers, LOC, 2.

22. Vien, *U.S. Adviser*, 155.

23. Debrief no. 18694, box 99, GP, HIA, 10.

24. Debrief no. 16683, box 99, GP, HIA, 3.

25. Debrief no. 6683, p. 7.

26. Debrief no. 26683B, pp. 2, 12.

27. Debrief no. 206612, p. 1.

28. Evaluation of the Province Senior Advisor Training Program, n.d., box 8, folder "PER Vietnam Training Center, 1970," Subject Files of the Office of Vietnam Affairs (Vietnam Working Group), 1964–1974, RG 59, NARA II, 1.

29. Marks to Johnson, attachment to memo, 4 January 1966, box 80, WHCF, Subject File Ex CO 312, LBJL. The inclusion of this document on the training curriculum is noted in Vietnam Area Studies OCO Training Center, n.d.

30. Debrief no. 126712, p. 2.

31. Debrief no. 16612, p. 16.

32. Debrief no. 25672, p. 23.

33. Debrief no. 6683, p. 9.

34. Turner to Vann, attachment to memo, 26 February 1971, folder "End of tour / Reports," box 57, CORDS History Files, RG 472, NARA II, unpaginated.

35. Debrief no. 4696, p. 2.

36. Clark to HQ, memo, 18 December 1970, folder "End of tour report," box 101, CORDS History Files, RG 472, NARA II, 13.

37. Debrief no. 25687 (Lansdale), box 100, GP, HIA, 1–4.

38. Vien, *U.S. Adviser*, 155.

39. *The Vietnamese Village: Handbook for Advisors*, 1971 ed., Douglas Pike Collection, TTVA, 2.

40. Attachment to Letter, Montague to Quang, 22 April 1969, folder "CPDC / CC advisory, '69," box 4, HQ MACV, CORDS, PPP General Records, RG 472, NARA II, 4.

41. *Vietnamese Village: Handbook for Advisors*, 4.

42. Debrief no. 7666, box 99, GP, HIA, 24.

43. Vann to Nesmith, 20 March 1970, folder "Vietnam assignments: Region IV correspondence," box 45, Sheehan Papers, LOC, 2.

44. Robert Thompson, *No Exit from Vietnam* (London: Chatto & Windus, 1969), 147.

45. Attachment to MACCORDS Notice, No. 69–409, 7 April 1969, folder "Village self development: April–May, 1969," box 11, CDD, General Records, RG 472, NARA II, 3.

46. Decree #198, 24 December 1966, subsection "Village/hamlet," folder "'The Blue Book' / Laws and directives," box 14, CORDS History Files, RG 472, NARA II.

47. Thomas C. Thayer, ed., *A Systems Analysis View of the Vietnam War, 1965–1972*, vol. 10, *Pacification and Civil Affairs* (Washington, DC: OASD(SA)RP Southeast Asia Intelligence Division, 1975), 121.

48. "Opening Statement by Ambassador W. E. Colby," undated document, 6; "Status of villages and hamlets," table, January 1972, folder "#6 Local administration," box 63, CORDS History Files, RG 472, NARA II.

49. Decree #45, undated [1 April 1969], subsection "Village/hamlet," folder "'The Blue Book' / Laws and directives," box 14, CORDS History Files, RG 472, NARA II.

50. *Concept and Organization of the National Training Center Vung Tau*, in folder "National Training Center Questionnaire," box 16, CORDS History Files, RG 472, NARA II, 1.

51. "Opening Statement by Ambassador W. E. Colby," undated document, 1.

52. *Concept and Organization of the National Training Center Vung Tau*, 94–98.

53. Memo for record, 10 February 1970, folder "Pacif. study, Jan–Sept '70," box 10, PPP Records, RG 472, NARA II, 1; memo, Craig to Jacobson, 13 October 1971, folder "Talking papers / Mr Jacobson," box 35, CORDS History Files, RG 472, NARA II.

54. Memo for record, 10 March 1969, folder "Effect of the inf co intens.pacif program / Goals 1970 P+D plan," box 9, CORDS History Files, RG 472, NARA II.

55. Brown to CDD director, memo, 23 May 1969, folder "Village self development: April–May, 1969," box 11, CDD, General Records, RG 472, NARA II, 3.

56. "Status of Pacification—June 1969," memo for the record, 4 June 1969, folder "Misc reports, memos, etc: Jan–Sept, 1969," box 3, PPP Records, RG 472 NARA II, 3.

57. Message #93, 2 June 1969, subsection "Village/hamlet," folder "'The Blue Book' / Laws and directives," box 14, CORDS History Files, RG 472, NARA II.

58. William Colby, with James McCargar, *Lost Victory: A Firsthand Account of America's Sixteen-Year Involvement in Vietnam* (Chicago: Contemporary Books, 1989), 265.

59. Debrief no. 15681, box 97, GP, HIA, 31.

60. Debrief no. 15681, box 97, GP, HIA, 32; Debrief no. 6683, p. 4.

61. *Vietnamese Village: Handbook for Advisors*, 86, 87.

62. Former district senior adviser stationed in Phu Yen Province, interview with the author, Austin, Texas, 5 May 2015.

63. Debrief no. 126712, box 99, GP, HIA, 7–8.

64. Debrief no. 24681, box 100, GP, HIA, 47.

65. Evaluation report, "Pay and allowances for province and district chiefs," 19 August 1968, folder "PSG studies / Book II, folder II," box 5, CORDS History Files, RG 472, NARA II.

66. Debrief no. 166612, p. 10.

67. PSG report, "Report on the 3/69-A training course," 1 May 1969, folder "PSG studies / 1969 / Book I, folder I," box 8, CORDS History Files, RG 472, NARA II, 13–14.

68. Debrief no. 15679, box 101, GP, HIA, 15, 16.

69. *Vietnamese Village: Handbook for Advisors*, 42.

70. Burgess to HQ, memo, 5 February 1973, folder "End of tour report / Col R. L. Burgess," box 88, CORDS History Files, RG 472, NARA II.

71. Pacification Research Report, 4/CD/12/72, 28 August 1972, folder "Chau Doc prov," box 116, HQ MACV, CORDS, PPP, CORDS History Files, RG 472.

72. Pacification Research Report, 4/BL/12/72, 30 August 1972, folder "Bac Lieu prov," box 116, HQ MACV, CORDS, PPP, CORDS History Files, RG 472.

73. Elliott to Kosters, memo, 3 February 1970, folder "Civil affairs advisory files—village self development [2 of 4]," box 23, CDD: General Records, RG 472, NARA II.

74. "Year End Assessment of 1971 CD&LD Program for Public Administration Division," undated report, folder "Assessment," box 33, CORDS History Files, RG 472, NARA II, 2.

75. Debrief no. 25687, box 100, GP, HIA, 1–4.

76. "Binh Dinh Province," report, 12 June 1971, folder "Study / Binh Dinh," box 32, CORDS History Files, RG 472, NARA II, 26.

77. Clark to HQ, memo, 18 December 1970, folder "End of tour report," box 101, CORDS History Files, RG 472, NARA II, 13.

78. Task force minutes, program "CDD," September 1971, 3; "CORDS Internal Spring Review of CDD Program for FY 71–74," memo for record, folder "Project review files, '70," box 13, PPP Records, RG 472, NARA II, 2.

79. Berger to State, telegram, 24 December 1970, folder "Election of prov chiefs and mayors," box 17, CORDS History Files, RG 472, NARA II.

80. *Vietnamese Village: Handbook for Advisors*, 4.

81. "Status of Pacification—June 1969," memo for the record, 4 June 1969, 3.

82. Lewis Sorley, ed., *Vietnam Chronicles: The Abrams Tapes, 1968–1972* (Lubbock: Texas Tech University Press, 2004), 50, 51; William Colby oral history interview no. 2, 1 March 1982, LBJL, 9.

83. Speech at the National War College, transcript, 10 November 1972, William Colby Collection, TTVA, www.vietnam.ttu.edu/virtualarchive/items.php?item=0440225001, pp. 19–20.

84. Thompson, *Make for the Hills*, 98.

85. Roger Trinquier, *Modern Warfare: A French View of Counterinsurgency*, trans. Daniel Lee (1962; London: Pall Mall, 1964), 30.

86. Thayer, *Systems Analysis View*, 175–76.

87. Thayer, 213.

88. Colby, *Lost Victory*, 232–38; Colby and Forbath, *Honourable Men*, 168.

89. Document, "Security," undated, folder "Opening statements / Amb. Colby," box 15, CORDS History Files, RG 472, NARA II, 16.

90. Law #3, folder "CORDS programs / TSD," box 18, CORDS History Files, RG 472, NARA II.

91. OSD study, *South Vietnam's Internal Security Capabilities*, May 1969, folder "NSSM 19 [3 of 3]," box H-135, NSC Institutional Files, Study Memorandums, NPL, p. B-22; Ngo Quang Truong, *Territorial Forces* (Washington, DC: U.S. Center of Military History, 1981), 70.

92. Berger to State, telegram, 29 October 1970, folder "P+D plan, folder II," box 27, RG 472, NARA II, 7.

93. Truong, *Territorial Forces*, 69.

94. Dong Van Khuyen, *The RVNAF* (Washington, DC: U.S. Center of Military History, undated), 22.

95. Khuyen, *RVNAF*, 128.

96. Quoted in David Elliott, *The Vietnamese War: Revolution and Social Change in the Mekong Delta, 1930–1975* (London: M. E. Sharpe, 2003), 2:1092. Elliott inserts the word "[commander]" after "Seventh Division," but it appears from the original quote that the cadre is referring to the division, not its commander.

97. *Plan for Pacification and Development: 1970* in folder "P+D plan w/ errata added / Maj E. J. Crampton," box 27, CORDS History Files, RG 472, NARA II, p. I-1–2.

98. Nick Turse, *Kill Anything That Moves: The Real American War in Vietnam* (New York: Metropolitan, 2013), 205–8.

99. Julian J. Ewell and Ira A. Hunt Jr., *Sharpening the Combat Edge: The Use of Analysis to Reinforce Military Judgment* (Washington, DC: Department of the Army, 1995), 83.

100. Ellsberg to Rowen et al., attachment to memo, 9 April 1969, folder "Ellsberg, Daniel. 1967–1969," box 27, Sheehan Papers, LOC, 9; Vann to Ellsberg, 25 June 1969, folder "Ellsberg, Daniel. 1967–1969," box 27, Sheehan Papers, LOC, 3.

101. Sorley, *Abrams Tapes*, 471

102. Vann to Nesmith, 20 March 1970, 1.

103. Truong, *Territorial Forces*, 85–87.

104. Task force minutes, program "Territorial Security," 6 September 1971, folder "Heilman minutes of task force meetings / Taken from Chamber's safe, folder I," box 80, CORDS History Files, RG 472, NARA II, 4–5.

105. OSD study, *South Vietnam's Internal Security Capabilities*, May 1969, p. B-2; Truong, *Territorial Forces*, 45.

106. "Report of Investigation, Los Thuan Village Action, 18 May 1970," memo for record, 21 July 1970, folder "Visits + inspections, folder I, '70," box 13, PPP Records, RG 472, NARA II, 3.

107. Sorley, *Abrams Tapes*, 292.

108. Task force minutes, topic "J-2/Security Intelligence Briefing," 14 October 1971, 2.

109. Elliott, *Vietnamese War*, 2:1302.

110. Pacification research report, subject "Corruption," 30 August 1972, folder "Bac Lieu prov," box 116, CORDS History Files, RG 472, NARA II, 2.

111. Task force minutes, program "Territorial Security," 6 September 1971, 7.

112. Truong, *Territorial Forces*, 104.

113. Holdridge to Kissinger, memo, 2 September 1970, folder "Vietnam: 1 September, 1970 [2 of 2]," box 149, NSC Files, VCF, NPL, p. A-3.

114. Thayer, *Systems Analysis View*, 7:216.

115. Memo for the record, 18 February 1970, folder "Memos," box 24, CORDS History Files, RG 472, NARA II, 2.

116. Sorley, *Abrams Tapes*, 292.

117. *Concept and Organization of the National Training Center Vung Tau*, 102–3.

118. Truong, *Territorial Forces*, 104–6.

119. PSDF report, 8 September 1971, "CDLD / Fact sheets / Semi-annual review / MR IV, folder II," box 71, CORDS History Files, RG 472, NARA II.

120. Pacification Research Report, 4/AG/10/72, 21 July 1972, folder "An Giang, 1970–73," box 116, HQ MACV, CORDS, PPP, CORDS History Files, RG 472.

121. Pacification Research Report, 4/BX/13/72, 21 July 1972, folder "Ba Xuyen, 1972–73," HQ MACV, CORDS, PPP, CORDS History Files, RG 472, NARA II.

122. Truong, *Territorial Forces*, 106.

123. Truong, 70; PSDF report, 8 September 1971.

124. Alexis de Tocqueville, *Democracy in America* (1835; New York: Anchor, 1955), 118.

125. "The Village Self Development Program," undated document, folder "Civil affairs advisory files—village self development [4 of 4]," box 23, CDD, General Records, RG 472, NARA II, 1, 2.

126. "Village Self Development Program," 2

127. Speech at the National War College, transcript, 10 November 1972, 4.

128. Attachment to memo for the record, 31 August 1968, Annex VI, folder "Self help," box 3, CDD, General Records, RG 472, NARA II, 1.

129. "Village Self Development Program," 4.

130. "The Village Self Development Program, 1969–1972," booklet, 17 June 1972, folder "VSDP," box 41, CORDS History Files, RG 472, NARA II, 10.

131. "Village Self Development Program, 1969–1972," 14.

132. "Village Self Development Program," undated document, "Civil affairs advisory files—village self development [4 of 4]," box 23, CDD, General Records, RG 472, NARA II. Emphasis added.

133. "Analysis of the Village Self Development (VSD) Program," PSG report, 19 May 1970, folder "PSG studies 1970 / Book I, Folder III," box 16, CORDS History Files, RG 472, NARA II, 4.

134. *Vietnamese Village: Handbook for Advisors*, 48.

135. *Vietnamese Village: Handbook for Advisors*, 8, 9.

136. Pacification Attitude Analysis System, preliminary survey #3, December 1969, folder "PAAS surveys," box 7, CORDS History Files, RG 472, NARA II, 14, 15.

137. Pacification Attitude Analysis System report, September 1970, US Marine Corps History Division, Vietnam War Documents Collection, TTVA, www.vietnam.ttu.edu/virtualarchive/items.php?item=1201065079, pp. 36, 37.

138. Pacification Research Report, II-LD-1/71, 8–17 January 1971, folder "Lam Dong prov, 1971," box 103, HQ MACV, CORDS, PPP, CORDS History Files, RG 472.

139. Pacification Research Report, I-QNG-10-7-70, 10 July 1970, folder "Quang Ngai prov, 1970," box 105, HQ MACV, CORDS, PPP, CORDS History Files.

140. Crocker to Firfer, memo, 21 May 1970, folder "Effect of the inf co intens.pacif program / Goals 1970 P+D plan," box 9, CORDS History Files, RG 472, NARA II, 1.

141. "Analysis of the Village Self Development (VSD) Program," PSG report, 19 May 1970, 12.

142. Phong and Myer, memcon, 10 November 1970, folder "Civil affairs advisory files—village self development [1 of 4]," box 23, CDD, General Records, RG 472, NARA II.

143. End of tour report, John H, Hayes, section "Community Development Directorate," folder "End of tour / Reports," box 57, CORDS History Files, RG 472, NARA II.

144. Johnstone to Jacobson, memo, 5 July 1969, folder "Effect of the inf co intens.pacif program / Goals 1970 P+D plan," box 9, CORDS History Files, RG 472, NARA II, 1.

145. "Analysis of the Village Self Development (VSD) Program," PSG report, 19 May 1970, 15.

146. Roy L. Prosterman, "Land-to-the-Tiller in South Vietnam: The Tables Turn," *Asian Survey* 10, no. 8 (1970): 751–64.

147. *New York Times*, April 9, 1970, 40.

148. For the situation in I and II Corps see Toyryla to DEPCORDS, memo, 21 July 1971, and Strasser to ACofS CORDS, memo, 26 July 1971, both in folder "CDLD / Elections/ Circulars," box 37, CORDS History Files, RG 472, NARA II.

149. Report, "Land Ownership and Tenancy among Village and Hamlet Officials in the Delta," March 1970, folder "Study / Land ownership and tenancy / Delta," box 23, CORDS History Files, RG 472, NARA II.

150. Eliot to Kissinger, telegram, 20 January 1972, folder "Vietnam: Jan–Feb 1972 [1 of 3]," box 158, NSC Files, VCF, NPL.

151. MacDonald Salter, "The Broadening Base of Land Reform in South Vietnam," *Asian Survey* 10, no. 8 (1970): 724–37.

152. "Land Reform in the Republic of Viet-Nam," press release, 3 July 1974, Douglas Pike Collection, TTVA. The document also claims that no farmer who received an LTTT title had "been forced off his land." This was certainly untrue. Given the fact the document also misstates the number of acres in a hectare, we can reasonably question how familiar its author was with the program.

153. Wilson to Forrester, memo, 23 July 1971, folder "CDLD / Elections / Circulars," box 37, CORDS History Files, RG 472, NARA II.

154. To Melville, memo, 19 July 1971, folder "CDLD / Elections / Circulars," box 37, CORDS History Files, RG 472, NARA II, 2.

155. *Vietnamese Village: Handbook for Advisors,* 32; Douglas C. Dacy, *Foreign Aid, War, and Economic Development: South Vietnam, 1955–1975* (Cambridge: Cambridge University Press, 1986), 233.

156. Farwell to director, attachment to memo, 26 September 1969, folder "GVN village / Taxation," box 12, CORDS History Files, RG 472, NARA II, 1.

157. Colby to Jacobson, attachment to flag note, 20 July 1969, folder "Economic warfare files—local government," box 17, CDD, General Records, RG 472, NARA II.

158. "Year-end Assessment of 1971 CD&LD Program for Public Administration Division," undated document, folder "Assessment," box 33, CORDS History Files, RG 472, NARA II, 3.

159. "Report of financial viability of Vietnamese villages," document, 28 August 1969, 4.

160. Wilson to Forrester, memo, 23 July 1971; Prosterman, "Land-to-the-Tiller in South Vietnam."

161. Thorsen to Farwell, memo, 11 June 1971, folder "LRIP / Local tax program," box 37, CORDS History Files, RG 472, NARA II.

162. "Status report on the LRIP," document, folder "CDLD / LRIP," box 62, CORDS History Files, RG 472, NARA II.

163. *Four-Year Community Defense and Local Development Plan,* folder "CD+LD plan / 1972–75," box 39, CORDS History Files, RG 472, NARA II, p. II-B-1.

164. Douglas Blaufarb, *The Counterinsurgency Era: U.S. Doctrine and Performance, 1950 to the Present* (New York: Free Press, 1977), 277.

CONCLUSION

1. Turner to Vann, attachment to memo, 26 February 1971, folder "End of tour / Reports," box 57, CORDS History Files, RG 472, NARA II, unpaginated.

2. Task force minutes, topic "J-2/Security Intelligence Briefing," 14 October 1971, folder "Heilman minutes of task force meetings / Taken from Chamber's safe, folder II," box 80, CORDS History Files, RG 472, NARA II, 21.

3. Untitled news copy, November 1972, Douglas Pike Collection, TTVA, www.vietnam.ttu.edu/virtualarchive/items.php?item=2151007002.

4. James McAllister, "What Can One Man Do? Nguyen Duc Thang and the Limits of Reform in South Vietnam," *Journal of Vietnamese Studies* 4, no. 2 (2009): 117–53.

5. Marilyn B. Young, *The Vietnam Wars: 1945–1990* (New York: HarperCollins, 1991); Michael E. Latham, *The Right Kind of Revolution: Modernization, Development, and U.S. Foreign Policy from the Cold War to the Present* (Ithaca, NY: Cornell University Press, 2011), 142; David Ekbladh, *The Great American Mission: Modernization and the Construction of an American World Order* (Princeton, NJ: Princeton University Press, 2011); David C. Engerman, Nils Gilman, Mark H. Haefele, and Michael E. Latham, eds., *Staging Growth: Modernization, Development, and the Global Cold War* (Amherst: University of Massachusetts Press, 2003).

6. Viet Thanh Nguyen, *The Sympathizer* (New York: Grove, 2015), 4.

7. William Colby, with James McCargar, *Lost Victory: A Firsthand Account of America's Sixteen-Year Involvement in Vietnam* (Chicago: Contemporary, 1989).

8. Sherard Cowper-Coles, *Cables from Kabul: The Inside Story of the West's Afghanistan Campaign* (London: HarperPress, 2012), 144.

9. For critiques of population-centric counterinsurgency see Gian P. Gentile, *Wrong Turn: America's Deadly Embrace of Counterinsurgency* (New York: New Press, 2013);

Douglas Porch, *Counterinsurgency: Exposing the Myths of the New Way of War* (Cambridge: Cambridge University Press, 2013). Its foundational text was the now-superseded *U.S. Army / Marine Corps Counterinsurgency Field Manual* (Chicago: University of Chicago Press, 2006).

10. Gian P. Gentile, "A Strategy of Tactics: Population-Centric COIN and the Army," *Parameters* (Autumn 2009): 5–17; Harry G. Summers Jr., *American Strategy in Vietnam: A Critical Analysis* (Mineola, NY: Dover, 2007), 56.

11. Hannah Arendt, *The Human Condition* (Chicago: University of Chicago Press, 1958), 191.

Bibliography

ARCHIVAL COLLECTIONS

Gerald R. Ford Library, Ann Arbor, MI.
  White House Photographic Office Collection.
Hoover Institution, Palo Alto, CA.
  Goodman, Allan E. Papers.
John F. Kennedy Library, Boston.
  Hilsman, Roger. Papers.
  National Security Files.
    Countries.
Library of Congress, Washington, DC.
  Sheehan, Neil. Papers.
Lyndon Baines Johnson Library, Austin, TX.
  National Security Files.
  Country File, Vietnam.
  Komer, Robert W. Files.
  Komer-Leonhart Subject Files.
  Memos to the President.
  Komer, Robert W. Papers.
  Recordings and Transcripts of Conversations and Meetings.
  Westmoreland, William C. Papers.
  White House Office Photo Collection.
National Archives (UK), Kew, Richmond, Surrey.
  Foreign Office and Foreign and Commonwealth Office.
National Archives II, College Park, MD.
  Record Group 59. Subject Files of the Office of Vietnam Affairs (Vietnam Working
    Group), 1964–1974.
  Record Group 111. Photographs of American Military Activities.
  Record Group 172. General Photograph File of the U.S. Marine Corps.
  Record Group 306. Miscellaneous Vietnam Photographs.
  Record Group 342. Color Photographs of U.S. Air Force Activities, Facilities and
    Personnel, Domestic and Foreign.
  Record Group 428. General Black and White Photographic File of the Department
    of the Navy.
  Record Group 472.
    HQ MACV, Office of Civil Operations and Revolutionary Development
      Support, Community Development Directorate, General Records.
    HQ MACV, Office of Civil Operations and Revolutionary Development Support,
      Plans, Policy and Program Directorate, CORDS Historical Working Group Files.
    HQ MACV, Office of Civil Operations and Revolutionary Development
      Support, Plans, Policy and Program Directorate, General Records.
Richard Nixon Presidential Library and Museum, Yorba Linda, CA.
  National Security Council Files.
    Staff Files—Lake Chron.

Vietnam Country Files.
Vietnam Subject Files.
National Security Council Institutional Files.
Committee Files, Vietnam Special Studies Group Meetings.
Study Memorandums, National Security Study Memorandums.
Vietnam Center and Archive, Texas Tech University, Lubbock.
Berman, Larry. Collection.
Colby, William. Collection.
Flanagan, Larry. Collection.
Phillips, Rufus. Collection.
Pike, Douglas. Collection.
Shaw, John M. Collection.
U.S. Marine Corps History Division. Vietnam War Documents Collection.
Vietnam Document and Research Notes Series: Translation and Analysis of Significant Viet Cong / North Vietnamese Documents. Bethesda, MD: University Publications of America, 1991.

ORAL HISTORIES

Association for Diplomatic Studies and Training, Foreign Affairs Oral History Project.
Rufus C. Phillips. Interview (19 July 1995).
Lyndon Baines Johnson Library, Austin, TX.
Colby, William. Oral history interview no. 2 (1 March 1982).
Cooper, Chester. Oral history interview no. 1 (9 July 1979).
Komer, Robert. Oral history interview no. 2 (18 August 1970) and oral history interview no. 3 (15 November 1971).
Lansdale, Edward. Oral history interview no. 2 (15 September 1981).
Lathram, L. Wade. Oral history interview no. 1 (21 March 1985).

PUBLISHED PRIMARY SOURCES

Chau, Tran Ngoc, with Ken Fermoyle. *Vietnam Labyrinth: Allies, Enemies, and Why the U.S. Lost the War.* Lubbock: Texas Tech University Press, 2012.
Chinh, Truong. *Primer for Revolt: The Communist Takeover in Viet-Nam.* New York: Praeger, 1963.
Clifford, Clark M. "A Viet Nam Reappraisal." *Foreign Affairs* 47, no. 4 (July 1969): 601–22.
Colby, William, and Peter Forbath. *Honourable Men: My Life in the CIA.* London: Hutchinson, 1978.
Colby, William, with James McCargar. *Lost Victory: A Firsthand Account of America's Sixteen-Year Involvement in Vietnam.* Chicago: Contemporary, 1989.
Cooper, Chester L. *The Lost Crusade: America in Vietnam.* New York: Dodd Mead, 1970.
Cooper, Chester L., Judith E. Corson, Laurence J. Legere, David E. Lockwood, and Donald M. Weller. *The American Experience with Pacification in Vietnam.* 3 vols. Arlington, VA: Institute for Defense Analyses, 1972.
Corson, William R. *The Betrayal.* New York: Ace, 1968.
Dang, Nghiem. *Viet-Nam: Politics and Public Administration.* Honolulu: East-West, 1966.
Diem, Bui, with David Chanoff. *In the Jaws of History.* Bloomington: Indiana University Press, 1987.
Don, Tran Van. *Our Endless War: Inside Vietnam.* Novato, CA: Presidio, 1978.
Elliott, Duong Van Mai. *The Sacred Willow: Four Generations of Life in a Vietnamese Family.* Oxford: Oxford University Press, 1999.

Ellsberg, Daniel. *Secrets: A Memoir of Vietnam and the Pentagon Papers*. New York: Viking, 2002.

Ewell, Julian J., and Ira A. Hunt Jr. *Sharpening the Combat Edge: The Use of Analysis to Reinforce Military Judgment*. Washington, DC: Department of the Army, 1995.

Fall, Bernard. "The Theory and Practice of Insurgency and Counterinsurgency." *Naval War College Review* 17, no. 8 (1965): 46–57.

———. *The Viet Minh Regime: Government and Administration in the Democratic Republic of Vietnam*. New York: Institute of Pacific Relations, 1956.

———. *Viet-Nam Witness: 1953–66*. New York: Praeger, 1966.

Fox, Guy H., and Charles A. Joiner. "Perceptions of the Vietnamese Public Administration System." *Administrative Science Quarterly* 8, no. 4 (1964): 443–81.

Goodman, Allan E. "South Vietnam and the New Security." *Asian Survey* 12, no. 2 (1972): 121–37.

Grant, Zalin. *Facing the Phoenix: The CIA and the Political Defeat of the United States in Vietnam*. New York: Norton, 1991.

Gravel, Mike, ed. *The Pentagon Papers: The Defense Department History of United States Decisionmaking on Vietnam*. 4 vols. Boston: Beacon, 1971.

Haldeman, H. R. *The Haldeman Diaries: Inside the Nixon White House*. New York: Berkley Books, 1995.

Jumper, Roy. "Mandarin Bureaucracy and Politics in South Viet Nam." *Pacific Affairs* 30, no. 1 (1957): 47–58.

Khuyen, Dong Van. *The RVNAF*. Washington, DC: U.S. Center of Military History, n.d.

Kissinger, Henry A. "The Viet Nam Negotiations." *Foreign Affairs*, January 1969, 211–34.

———. *White House Years*. Boston: Little, Brown, 1979.

Komer, Robert W. *Bureaucracy at War: U.S. Performance in the Vietnam Conflict*. Boulder, CO: Westview, 1986.

———. *Organization and Management of the "New Model" Pacification Program, 1966–1969*. RAND document number D-20104-ARPA, 1970.

Ky, Nguyen Cao, with Martin J. Wolf. *Buddha's Child: My Fight to Save Vietnam*. New York: St. Martin's, 2002.

Leacacos, John P. "Kissinger's Apparat." *Foreign Policy* 5 (Winter 1971/72): 3–27.

Luce, Don, and John Sommer. *Viet Nam: The Unheard Voices*. Ithaca, NY: Cornell University Press, 1969.

McNamara, Robert S. *In Retrospect: The Tragedy and Lessons of Vietnam*. New York: Vintage, 1995.

Methven, Stuart. *Laughter in the Shadows: A CIA Memoir*. Annapolis, MD: Naval Institute Press, 2014.

Metzner, Edward P. *More Than a Soldier's War: Pacification in Vietnam*. College Station: Texas A&M University Press, 1995.

Nighswonger, William A. *Rural Pacification in Viet Nam: 1962–1965*. Advanced Research Projects Agency, 1966.

Nixon, Richard M. *RN: The Memoirs of Richard Nixon*. New York: Grosset & Dunlap, 1978.

Phillips, Rufus C. *Why Vietnam Matters: An Eyewitness Account of Lessons Not Learned*. Annapolis, MD: Naval Institute Press, 2013.

Phuong, Chan Khong Cao Ngoc. *Learning True Love: How I Learned and Practiced Social Change in Vietnam*. Berkeley, CA: Parallax, 1993.

Pribbenow, Merle L., trans. *Victory in Vietnam: The Official History of the People's Army of Vietnam, 1954–1975*. Lawrence: University Press of Kansas, 2002.

Prosterman, Roy L. "Land-to-the-Tiller in South Vietnam: The Tables Turn." *Asian Survey* 10, no. 8 (1970): 751–64.

Public Papers of the Presidents of the United States: Lyndon B. Johnson, 1963–1968. Washington, DC: Government Printing Office, 1964–1969.

Rostow, W. W. *The Stages of Economic Growth: A Non-Communist Manifesto.* Cambridge: Cambridge University Press, 1960.

Rusk, Dean. *As I Saw It.* New York: Norton, 1970.

Salter, MacDonald. "The Broadening Base of Land Reform in South Vietnam." *Asian Survey* 10, no. 8 (1970): 724–37.

Sansom, Robert L. *The Economics of Insurgency in the Mekong Delta of Vietnam.* Cambridge, MA: MIT Press, 1970.

Scotton, Frank. *Uphill Battle: Reflections on Viet Nam Counterinsurgency.* Lubbock: Texas Tech University Press, 2014.

Sorley, Lewis, ed. *Vietnam Chronicles: The Abrams Tapes, 1968–1972.* Lubbock: Texas Tech University Press, 2004.

Tanham, George K., with W. Robert Warne, Earl J. Young, and William A. Nighswonger. *War without Guns: American Civilians in Rural Vietnam.* New York: Praeger, 1966.

Thayer, Thomas C., ed. *A Systems Analysis View of the Vietnam War, 1965–1972.* 12 vols. Washington, DC: OASD(SA)RP Southeast Asia Intelligence Division, 1975.

Thompson, Robert. *Make for the Hills: Memories of Far Eastern Wars.* London: Leo Cooper, 1989.

———. *No Exit from Vietnam.* London: Chatto & Windus, 1969.

———. *Peace Is Not at Hand.* London: Chatto & Windus, 1974.

Thu-Lam, Nguyen Thi. *Fallen Leaves: Memoirs of a Vietnamese Woman from 1940 to 1975.* New Haven, CT: Yale University Press, 1989.

Toai, Truong Van, with David Chanoff and Doan Van Toai. *A Vietcong Memoir.* San Diego: Harcourt, 1985.

Trinquier, Roger. *Modern Warfare: A French View of Counterinsurgency.* Translated by Daniel Lee. 1962; London: Pall Mall, 1964.

Truong, Ngo Quang. *Territorial Forces.* Washington, DC: U.S. Center of Military History, 1981.

Tuyet Mai, Nguyen Thi. *The Rubber Tree: Memoir of a Vietnamese Woman Who Was an Anti-French Guerrilla, a Publisher and a Peace Activist.* Jefferson, NC: McFarland, 1994.

U.S. Agency for International Development. *Terminal Report: United States Economic Assistance to South Vietnam, 1954–1975.* Washington, DC: AID, 1976.

U.S. Department of State. *Foreign Relations of the United States, 1961–1963.* 30 vols. Washington, DC: Government Printing Office, 1988–2001.

———. *Foreign Relations of the United States, 1964–1968.* 35 vols. Washington, DC: Government Printing Office, 1992–1999.

———. *Foreign Relations of the United States, 1969–1976.* 55 vols. Washington, DC: Government Printing Office, 2003–2014.

U.S. Department of the Army. *A Program for the Pacification and Long-Term Development of South Vietnam.* 1966.

Vien, Cao Van. *The U.S. Adviser.* Washington, DC: Center of Military History, 1980.

SECONDARY SOURCES

Ahern, Thomas L., Jr. *The CIA and Rural Pacification in South Vietnam.* Washington, DC: Center for the Study of Intelligence, 2001.

——. *CIA and the Generals: Covert Support to Military Government in South Vietnam*. Washington, DC: Center for the Study of Intelligence, 1998.

Anderson, Benedict. *Imagined Communities: Reflections on the Origins and Spread of Nationalism*. New York: Verso, 1982.

Anderson, David. *Trapped by Success: The Eisenhower Administration and Vietnam*. New York: Columbia University Press, 1991.

Arendt, Hannah. *The Human Condition*. Chicago: University of Chicago Press, 1958.

Asselin, Pierre. *Hanoi's Road to the Vietnam War, 1954–1965*. Berkeley: University of California Press, 2013.

Atwood, Mark Lawrence. "Too Late or Too Soon? Debating the Withdrawal from Vietnam in the Age of Iraq." *Diplomatic History* 34, no. 4 (2010): 589–600.

Bergerund, Eric M. *Dynamics of Defeat: The Vietnam War in Hau Nghia Province*. Boulder, CO: Westview, 1991.

Berman, Larry. *Lyndon Johnson's War*. New York: Norton, 1989.

——. *No Peace, No Honour: Nixon, Kissinger, and Betrayal in Vietnam*. New York: Free Press, 2001.

——. *Planning a Tragedy: The Americanization of the War in Vietnam*. New York: Norton, 1982.

Biggs, David. *Quagmire: Nation-Building and Nature in the Mekong Delta*. Seattle: University of Washington Press, 2010.

Blaufarb, Douglas. *The Counterinsurgency Era: U.S. Doctrine and Performance, 1950 to the Present*. New York: Free Press, 1977.

Boot, Max. *The Savage Wars of Peace: Small Wars and the Rise of American Power*. New York: Basic Books, 2002.

Brands, H. W. *The Wages of Globalism: Lyndon Johnson and the Limits of American Power*. Oxford: Oxford University Press, 1995.

Brigham, Robert K. *Guerrilla Diplomacy: The NLF's Foreign Relations and the Viet Nam War*. Ithaca, NY: Cornell University Press, 1999.

Brocheux, Pierre. *The Mekong Delta: Ecology, Economy, and Revolution, 1860–1960*. Madison: University of Wisconsin–Madison, 1995.

Carland, John M. *Combat Operations: Stemming the Tide, May 1965–October 1966*. Washington, DC: Center of Military History, 2000.

Carter, James M. *Inventing Vietnam: The United States and State Building, 1954–1968*. Cambridge: Cambridge University Press, 2008.

Catton, Philip E. *Diem's Final Failure: Prelude to America's War in Vietnam*. Lawrence: University Press of Kansas, 2003.

Caverley, Jonathan D. "The Myth of Military Myopia: Democracy, Small Wars, and Vietnam." *International Security* 34, no. 3 (2007): 119–57.

Chapman, Jessica M. *Cauldron of Resistance: Ngo Dinh Diem, the United States, and 1950s Southern Vietnam*. Ithaca, NY: Cornell University Press, 2013.

Clarke, Jeffrey T. *Advice and Support: The Final Years, 1965–1973*. Washington, DC: Government Printing Office, 1998.

Coffey, Ross. "Revisiting CORDS: The Need for Unity of Effort to Secure Victory in Iraq." *Military Review*, June 2008: 8–18.

Collins, James Lawton, Jr. *The Development and Training of the South Vietnamese Army, 1950–1972*. Washington, DC: Department of the Army, 1975.

Cowper-Coles, Sherard. *Cables from Kabul: The Inside Story of the West's Afghanistan Campaign*. London: HarperPress, 2012.

Dacy, Douglas C. *Foreign Aid, War, and Economic Development: South Vietnam, 1955–1975*. Cambridge: Cambridge University Press, 1986.

Daddis, Gregory A. *Westmoreland's War: Reassessing American Strategy in Vietnam.* Oxford: Oxford University Press, 2014.

Deutsch, Karl W., and William J. Foltz, eds. *Nation-Building.* New York: Atherton, 1963.

Dobbins, James, Seth G. Jones, Keith Crane, and Beth Cole DeGrasse. *The Beginner's Guide to Nation-Building.* Santa Monica, CA: RAND, 2007.

Dobbins, James, Seth G. Jones, Keith Crane, Andrew Rathmell, Brett Steele, Richard Teltschik, and Anga Timilsina. *The UN's Role in Nation-Building: From the Congo to Iraq.* Santa Monica, CA: RAND, 2005.

Dobbins, James, John G. McGinn, Keith Crane, Seth G. Jones, Rollie Lal, Andrew Rathmell, Rachel M. Swanger, and Anga R. Timilsina. *America's Role in Nation-Building: From Germany to Iraq.* Santa Monica, CA: RAND, 2003.

Drinnon, Richard. *Facing West: The Metaphysics of Indian-Hating and Empire-Building.* New York: Meridian, 1980.

Duiker, William J. *The Communist Road to Power in Vietnam.* Boulder, CO: Westview, 1996.

———. "Phan Boi Chau: Asian Revolutionary in a Changing World." *Journal of Asian Studies* 31, no. 1 (1971): 77–88.

Ekbladh, David. *The Great American Mission: Modernization and the Construction of an American World Order.* Princeton, NJ: Princeton University Press, 2011.

Elkind, Jessica. *Aid under Fire: Nation Building and the Vietnam War.* Lexington: University Press of Kentucky, 2016.

Elliott, David W. P. *The Vietnamese War: Revolution and Social Change in the Mekong Delta.* 2 vols. London: Sharpe, 2003.

Engerman, David C., Nils Gilman, Mark H. Haefele, and Michael E. Latham, eds. *Staging Growth: Modernization, Development, and the Global Cold War.* Amherst: University of Massachusetts Press, 2003.

Fear, Sean. "The Ambiguous Legacy of Ngo Dinh Diem in South Vietnam's Second Republic." *Journal of Vietnamese Studies* 11, no. 1 (2016): 1–75.

Fearon, James D., and David D. Laitin. "Neotrusteeship and the Problem of Weak States." *International Security* 28, no. 4 (2004): 5–43.

Fukuyama, Francis, ed. *Nation-Building: Beyond Afghanistan and Iraq.* Baltimore: Johns Hopkins University Press, 2006.

Gabriel, Ralph H. "American Experience with Military Government." *American Political Science Review* 37, no. 3 (1943): 630–43.

Gellner, Ernest. *Nations and Nationalism.* Oxford: Blackwell, 1983.

Gentile, Gian P. "A Strategy of Tactics: Population-Centric COIN and the Army." *Parameters* 41 (Autumn 2009): 5–17.

———. *Wrong Turn: America's Deadly Embrace of Counterinsurgency.* New York: New Press, 2013.

Gilbert, Marc Jason, and William Head, eds. *The Tet Offensive.* Westport, CT: Praeger, 1996.

Gilman, Nils. *Mandarins of the Future: Modernization Theory in Cold War America.* Baltimore: Johns Hopkins University Press, 2003.

Goodman, Allan E., and Lawrence M. Franks. "The Dynamics of Migration to Saigon, 1964–1972." *Pacific Affairs* 48, no. 2 (1975): 199–214.

Goscha, Christopher. *Vietnam: A New History.* New York: Basic Books, 2016.

Hatcher, Patrick Lloyd. *The Suicide of an Elite: American Internationalists and Vietnam.* Stanford, CA: Stanford University Press, 1990.

Hellman, John. *Emmanuel Mounier and the New Catholic Left, 1930–1950.* Toronto: University of Toronto Press, 1981.

Herring, George C. *America's Longest War: The United States and Vietnam, 1950–1975.* New York: McGraw-Hill, 1996.

———. "'Peoples Quite Apart': Americans, South Vietnamese, and the War in Vietnam." *Diplomatic History* 14, no. 1 (1990): 1–23.

Hietela, Thomas R. *Manifest Design: Anxious Aggrandizement in Late Jacksonian America.* Ithaca, NY: Cornell University Press, 1985.

Hodgkin, Thomas Lionel. *Vietnam: The Revolutionary Path.* New York: Palgrave, 1981.

Hung, Nguyen Tien, and Jerrold I. Schecter. *The Palace File.* New York: Harper & Row, 1986.

Hunt, David. *Vietnam's Southern Revolution: From Peasant Insurrection to Total War.* Amherst: University of Massachusetts Press, 2008.

Hunt, Richard A. *Pacification: The American Struggle for Vietnam's Hearts and Minds.* Boulder, CO: Westview, 1995.

Immerwahr, Daniel. *Thinking Small: The United States and the Lure of Community Development.* Cambridge, MA: Harvard University Press, 2015.

Isaacs, Arnold R. *Without Honor: Defeat in Vietnam and Cambodia.* Baltimore: Johns Hopkins University Press, 1983.

Johannsen, Robert W. *To the Halls of the Montezumas: The Mexican War in the American Imagination.* Oxford: Oxford University Press, 1985.

Jones, Frank L. "Blowtorch: Robert Komer and the Making of Vietnam Pacification Policy." *Parameters* 35 (Autumn 2005): 103–18.

———. *Blowtorch: Robert Komer, Vietnam, and American Cold War Strategy.* Annapolis, MD: Naval Institute Press, 2013.

Kalb, Marvin, and Bernard Kalb. *Kissinger.* Boston: Little, Brown, 1974.

Khanh, Huynh Kim. *Vietnamese Communism: 1925–1945.* Ithaca, NY: Cornell University Press, 1982.

Kilcullen, David. *The Accidental Guerrilla: Fighting Small Wars in the Midst of a Big One.* London: Hurst, 2009.

Kimball, Jeffrey. *Nixon's Vietnam War.* Lawrence: University Press of Kansas, 1998.

Kissinger, Henry. *Diplomacy.* New York: Simon & Schuster, 1994.

Kramer, Paul A. *The Blood of Government: Race, Empire, the United States, and the Philippines.* Chapel Hill: University of North Carolina Press, 2006.

Krepinevich, Andrew F., Jr. *The Army and Vietnam.* Baltimore: Johns Hopkins University Press, 1986.

Lam, Truong Buu, ed. *Patterns of Vietnamese Response to Foreign Intervention: 1858–1900.* New Haven, CT: Yale Southeast Asia Studies, 1967.

Latham, Michael. *Modernization as Ideology: American Social Science and "Nation Building" in the Kennedy Era.* Chapel Hill: University of North Carolina Press, 2000.

———. *The Right Kind of Revolution: Modernization, Development, and U.S. Foreign Policy from the Cold War to the Present.* Ithaca, NY: Cornell University Press, 2011.

Logevall, Frederick. *Choosing War: The Lost Chance for Peace and the Escalation of the War in Vietnam.* Berkeley: University of California Press, 1999.

———. *Embers of War: The Fall of an Empire and the Making of America's Vietnam.* New York: Random House, 2012.

Long, Austin. *On "Other War": Lessons from Five Decades of RAND Counterinsurgency Research.* Santa Monica, CA: RAND, 2002.

Long, Ngo Vinh. *Before the Revolution: The Vietnamese Peasants under the French.* Cambridge, MA: MIT Press, 1973.

MacGarrigle, George L. *Taking the Offensive: October 1966 to October 1967.* Washington, DC: Center of Military History, 1998.

Marquis, Jefferson P. "The Other Warriors: American Social Science and Nation Building in Vietnam." *Diplomatic History* 24, no. 1 (2000): 79–105.

Marr, David G. *Vietnamese Tradition on Trial, 1920–1925*. Berkeley: University of California Press, 1971.

McAllister, James. "What Can One Man Do? Nguyen Duc Thang and the Limits of Reform in South Vietnam." *Journal of Vietnamese Studies* 4, no. 2 (2009): 117–53.

Miller, Edward. *Misalliance: Ngo Dinh Diem, the United States, and the Fate of South Vietnam*. Cambridge, MA: Harvard University Press, 2013.

Miller, Merle. *Lyndon: An Oral Biography*. New York: Putnam's Sons, 1980.

Miller, Paul D. *Armed State-Building: Confronting State Failure, 1898–2012*. Ithaca, NY: Cornell University Press, 2013.

Morris, Roger. *Uncertain Greatness: Henry Kissinger and American Foreign Policy*. New York: Quartet, 1977.

Moyar, Mark. *Phoenix and the Birds of Prey: Counterinsurgency and Counterterrorism in Vietnam*. London: Bison Books, 2007.

———. *Triumph Forsaken: The Vietnam War, 1954–1965*. Cambridge: Cambridge University Press, 2006.

Nagl, John A. *Learning to Eat Soup with a Knife: Counterinsurgency Lessons from Vietnam and Malaya*. Chicago: University of Chicago Press, 2005.

Nguyen, Lien-Hang T. *Hanoi's War: An International History of the War for Peace in Vietnam*. Chapel Hill: University of North Carolina Press, 2012.

Nguyen, Viet Thanh. *The Sympathizer*. New York: Grove, 2015.

Ninkovich, Frank. *The Global Republic: America's Inadvertent Rise to World Power*. Chicago: University of Chicago Press, 2014.

O'Ballance, Edgar. *The Indochina War, 1945–54: A Study in Guerilla Warfare*. London: Faber, 1964.

Peterson, Michael E. *The Combined Action Platoons: The U.S. Marines' Other War in Vietnam*. New York: Praeger, 1989.

Pho, Hai B. *Vietnamese Public Management in Transition: South Vietnam Public Administration, 1955–1975*. Lanham, MD: University Press, 1990.

Popkin, Samuel L. *The Rational Peasant: The Political Economy of Rural Society in Vietnam*. Berkeley: University of California Press, 1979.

Porch, Douglas. *Counterinsurgency: Exposing the Myths of the New Way of War*. Cambridge: Cambridge University Press, 2013.

Prados, John. *Lost Crusader: The Secret Wars of CIA Director William Colby*. Oxford: Oxford University Press, 2003.

Preston, Andrew. *The War Council: McGeorge Bundy, the NSC, and Vietnam*. Cambridge, MA: Harvard University Press, 2006.

Race, Jeffrey. *War Comes to Long An: Revolutionary Conflict in a Vietnamese Province*. Berkeley: University of California Press, 2010.

Rear, Michael. *Intervention, Ethnic Conflict and State-Building in Iraq*. New York: Routledge, 2008.

Scott, James C. *The Art of Not Being Governed: An Anarchist History of Upland Southeast Asia*. New Haven, CT: Yale University Press, 2009.

———. *The Moral Economy of the Peasant: Rebellion and Subsistence in Southeast Asia*. New Haven, CT: Yale University Press, 1976.

———. *Seeing Like a State: How Certain Schemes to Improve the Human Condition Have Failed*. New Haven, CT: Yale University Press, 1999.

Scoville, Thomas W. *Reorganizing for Pacification Support*. Washington, DC: U.S. Army Center of Military History, 1982.

Sercombe, Peter, and Ruanni Tupas, eds. *Language, Education and Nation-Building: Assimilation and Shift in Southeast Asia*. Basingstoke, UK: Palgrave, 2014.

Shafer, D. Michael. *Deadly Paradigms: The Failure of U.S. Counterinsurgency Policy*. Princeton, NJ: Princeton University Press, 1988.

Sheehan, Neil. *A Bright Shining Lie*. London: Pimlico, 1988.

Shulimson, Jack, and Charles M. Johnson. *U.S. Marines in Vietnam: The Landing and the Buildup, 1965*. Washington, DC: U.S. Marine Corps, 1978.

Sorley, Lewis. *A Better War: The Unexamined Victories and Final Tragedy of America's Last Years in Vietnam*. New York: Harcourt, 1999.

———. *Westmoreland: The General Who Lost Vietnam*. New York: Harcourt, 2011.

Spector, Ronald H. *Advice and Support: The Early Years, 1941–1960*. Washington, DC: Center of Military History, 1983.

———. *After Tet: The Bloodiest Year in Vietnam*. New York: Macmillan, 1993.

Stewart, Geoffrey C. "Hearts, Minds and Cong Dan Vu: The Special Commissariat for Civic Action and Nation-Building in Ngo Dinh Diem's South Vietnam, 1955–1957." *Journal of Vietnamese Studies* 6, no. 3 (2011): 44–100.

———. *Vietnam's Lost Revolution: Ngo Dinh Diem's Failure to Build an Independent Nation, 1955–1963*. Cambridge: Cambridge University Press, 2017.

Summers, Harry G., Jr. *American Strategy in Vietnam: A Critical Analysis*. Mineola, NY: Dover, 2007.

Suri, Jeremi. *Liberty's Surest Guardian: Rebuilding Nations after War from the Founders to Obama*. New York: Free Press, 2012.

Tana, Li. *Nguyen Cochinchina: Southern Vietnam in the Seventeenth and Eighteenth Centuries*. Ithaca, NY: Cornell University Press, 1998.

Tenenbaum, Elie. "French Exception or Western Variation? A Historical Look at the French Irregular Way of War." *Journal of Strategic Studies* 40, no. 4 (2017): 554–76.

Tocqueville, Alexis de. *Democracy in America*. 1835; New York: Anchor, 1955.

———. *The Old Regime and the French Revolution*. 1856; Mineola, NY: Dover, 2010.

Topmiller, Robert J. *The Lotus Unleashed: The Buddhist Peace Movement in South Vietnam, 1964–1966*. Lexington: University Press of Kentucky, 2002.

Trinquier, Roger. *Modern Warfare: A French View of Counterinsurgency*. New York: Praeger, 1964.

Trullinger, James W. *Village at War: An Account of Conflict in Vietnam*. Stanford, CA: Stanford University Press, 1994.

Turley, William S. "Urban Transformation in South Vietnam." *Pacific Affairs* 49, no. 4 (1976/77): 607–24.

Turse, Nick. *Kill Anything That Moves: The Real American War in Vietnam*. New York: Metropolitan, 2013.

United States Army. *The U.S. Army / Marine Corps Counterinsurgency Field Manual*. Chicago: University of Chicago Press, 2006.

Weeks, Philip. *Farewell, My Nation: The American Indian and the United States, 1820–1890*. Arlington Heights, IL: Harlan Davidson, 1990.

Wiesner, Louis A. *Victims and Survivors: Displaced Persons and Other War Victims in Viet-Nam, 1954–1975*. Westport, CT: Greenwood, 1988.

Woodside, Alexander. *Community and Revolution in Modern Vietnam*. Boston: Houghton Mifflin, 1976.

———. *Vietnam and the Chinese Model: A Comparative Study of Vietnamese and Chinese Government in the First Half of the Nineteenth Century*. Cambridge, MA: Harvard University Press, 1971.

Young, Marilyn B. *The Vietnam Wars: 1945–1990*. New York: HarperCollins, 1991.

Index

Page numbers followed by letters *f* and *t* refer to figures and tables, respectively.

Revolutionary Development (RD) program, 70–73, 75, 78, 82, 83, 91; Communist offensives of 1968 and, 97; Thompson on, 134
Revolutionary Development Support division, of MACV, 76
RF. *See* Regional Forces
Rogers, William, 116
Rostow, Walt, 14, 38; theory of economic takeoff, 82
rural areas, of South Vietnam, 3; Accelerated Pacification Campaign and, 112–13; alienation of population in, U.S. military operations and, 134, 137, 169–70; American presence in, 4, 39; Americans' inability to comprehend and influence, 47, 154–56, 176, 177; battle for control and allegiance of, 3; Communist offensives of 1968 and, 99, 102, 111; Communist presence in, 25–27, 41–42, 45, 51, 76, 99, 111, 130, 132–33, 137; CORDS training on, 154–55; corruption and impact on, 161; Diem regime's policies in, 35; distrust of GVN in, 40, 42, 150, 151, 163, 182; Easter Offensive of March 1972 and, 127; in final years of war, 150; French colonial regime and, 22–23; vs. governing class, 21; GVN's inability to establish ties with, 12, 13, 16, 22, 32, 33–34, 45–47, 66, 68, 135–36, 157–58, 171, 184, 186–87; involving in nation building, 131–33, 137; politico-religious groups in, 28, 31; ties with GVN, U.S. efforts to strengthen, 38, 49, 175–76; and Viet Minh's success, 135–36; VSSG assessment of, 124–26. *See also* village(s)
rural areas, of Vietnam: support for Communist movement in, 11, 15, 16, 25–27, 37, 40, 66; Viet Minh administration of, 26–27. *See also* rural areas, of South Vietnam
Rusk, Dean, 53, 54, 63

Saigon: artillery strikes on, 129; Communist offensives of 1968 and, 95, 97, 98f; CORDS personnel in, 4; fall of, 1–2; GVN personnel concentrated in, 22; Iron Triangle around, 94
Sansom, Robert, 125
scholar-gentry, and Vietnam's tradition of governance, 20, 21
Scott, James C., 68
Scott, Winfield, 6
Scotton, Frank, 13, 53, 78, 143
security: vs. control, 124; focus on, Nixon administration and, 115; in Komer's vision of nation building, 61–62; superficial calm of 1969–72, 5, 149–50, 187, 188; and village system, 139

self-defense, village system and, 137, 164–75
self-development, village system and, 137, 175–80
self-government, in village system, 137, 156–64
Smith, Wayne, 121
Sommer, John, 43, 70
Sorley, Lewis, 77, 150
South Vietnam: Cold War politics and, 3; creation of, 29; national identity associated with, absence of, 10, 14–16, 31, 133; undercover Communist cadres in, 28–29; as weak state, 2–3. *See also* Government of Vietnam (GVN); nation building, in South Vietnam; rural areas, of South Vietnam
Spanish-American War of 1898, 6
state building, vs. nation building, 11
State Department. *See* U.S. State Department
State of Vietnam (SVN), 29, 30
Strategic Hamlet Program, 35, 45, 47, 139
Summers, Harry, 190, 214n25
SVN. *See* State of Vietnam

Tana, Li, 20
tax collection, village, 182–83
Taylor, Maxwell, 38, 77
tenant farmers, 22, 34; French colonial regime and, 22; Land to the Tiller (LTTT) initiative and, 181
Tennessee Valley Authority (TVA) on the Mekong, idea of, 52–53
territorial forces, GVN, 164–75; casualties of, 169; control over, 170–71; draft avoidance and membership in, 173–74; infiltration by Communist sympathizers, 171, 172, 175; reluctance to engage enemy, 171–73, 175; training courses for officers in, 173
Tet Offensive of 1968, 103; CORDS's effectiveness after, 4; and People's Self-Defense Force (PSDF), origins of, 166; refugees from, 101; U.S. calculations in response to, 104, 105
Thang. *See* Nguyen Duc Thang
Thich Tri Quang, 84
Thieu. *See* Nguyen Van Thieu
Third World, disintegration of European empires in, 9–10
Thompson, Sir Robert, 134–35; critique of nation-building efforts, 137–38; on government control, 135, 136; influence on Komer, 61; Kissinger and, 126; after Nixon's election, 114; on security in early 1970s, 149; on self-defense program, 166; at Vietnam Training Center (VTC), 152; on village administrative structure, 158

CPSIA information can be obtained
at www.ICGtesting.com
Printed in the USA
LVHW092021260719
625490LV00004B/73/P